Mystic Memoirs

Volume I

Beyond Belief Experiences

EDITED AND WITH AN INTRODUCTION BY

T.L. Woodliff and Ruth Souther

CRYSTAL HEART IMPRINTS LLC
Springfield IL

ALSO EDITED BY T.L. WOODLIFF AND DR. RUTH SOUTHER

The Chaos of Covid: True Stories of Surviving, and Sometimes Thriving, During the Pandemic
Published by Crystal Heart Imprints

ALSO BY DR. RUTH SOUTHER

Fiction

Immortal Journey Series

Death of Innocence

Surrender of Ego

Rise of Rebellion

Non-Fiction

The Heart of Tarot

The Elemental Priestess

Purple Reign: How I Reclaimed My Power

ALSO BY T.L. WOODLIFF

Fiction

Glass Cauldron Series

Grimoires of the Galerè

Familiars of the Galerè P1

Shaman & Warrior

Familiars of the Galerè

Non-Fiction

Break Through Your Barriers

Myth Magic ~ Carya

Assess Your Writing From The Inside Out

INTRODUCTION

"You had to be there. I just can't explain it. It was… impossible!"

Picture this: You learn that someone has experienced something unique—a rare and improbable, if not seemingly impossible, occurrence. Eager to learn more, you buy the book and dive into the story, hoping to be caught up in the journey and *know it*. You are already cheering them on and want the world to accept that such improbable things actually *do* happen in this world.

And then you read the explanation, *you had to be there.* Or it might go something like, *it was the most magical, awesome experience and nothing like I'd ever felt before!*

Ugh.

But I get it. Trying to describe the indescribable is *hard*. It also requires thick skin, as each rewrite is met with the annoying feedback, *but what does that mean?* by we editors.

These authors rose to that challenge.

For several, they needed to break their experience down into small segments, analyzing each moment. If you're struggling to adequately describe such moments, we strongly advise using this powerful technique. It's one method we've uncovered that shifts the 'impossible to describe" into the living, raw emotions and powerful settings we readers crave. In the first half, the book is filled with logic-defying experiences and all the confusion that goes along with redefining what life on this planet actually includes: voices screaming over thunderous hurricanes; shadows warping into solid shapes; segments of time that simply vanish.

The second half of the book focuses on events that held a spiritual component—an awakening. These authors allow us to understand the words *wonder* and *awe* as we become immersed in the experience alongside them.

What a ride!

One author shares an experience that reshaped her worldview. Though grounded in concrete understandings, we include it here as the break between the two styles to show the power of putting your experience into a new reality—the written word, and in this case, a poem.

In these stories, some authors share how their worldview understanding was challenged, while others provide great insights into how only a slight distance from everyday norms may bring us all greater clarity.

While most of the stories are short and easy to read in one sitting, a few of them go on a deeper journey, providing the reader with insights into the aftereffects that such strange occurrences may bring. One story describes a death/resuscitation event from the author's childhood. However, it had a powerful impact later on in life and, while difficult to read, leaves the reader grateful to know such people are out there doing important work.

Our latest anthology truly has us standing at the edge of perception. As we begin to focus on Volume II, we keep coming back to the lessons learned here, with these authors, and are humbled by the bravery of everyone to stand up and tell the tale.

TABLE OF CONTENTS

PART ONE

POEM

*Dedicated To Everyone Who Has
Experienced The Inexplicable*

At the Crossroads

Mark Anthony Wyatt

The event that changed my life occurred back in the autumn of 2013, in the early hours of the morning, at an ancient crossroads about a mile from the historic town of Stratton, in Cornwall, and very close to two significant locations: The first being Stamford Hill, the site of the 1643 English civil war battle, and the second, the Government Communications Headquarters (GCHQ) top secret facility run by the security agencies of the British and American governments, located on the nearby cliffs at Morwenstow.

Crossroads have long been acknowledged as special places where practitioners of magic can enhance natural powers to aid their spell work. They are said to hold some diabolical significance, too, as in the story of the blues musician Robert Johnson, who allegedly sold his soul to the devil at a crossroads in return for his extraordinary talent with the guitar. Historically, criminals were hung at crossroads, and those who had committed suicide were buried there due to a commonly held superstition that the ghosts of these people would be confused by the different routes available at a crossroads and, therefore, unable to find their way back to their village to haunt anyone.

Interestingly, I would find out later, via local Cornish witnesses who relayed to me their own weird experiences as I was researching my *Spirit of Cornwall* books, that the crossroads where I had my strange experience was in the middle of an area of ongoing high strangeness, a paranormal crosshairs of sorts. To give you a couple of examples of the kind of paranormal activity that I soon became aware of in that area, the small country village of Poughill, located just below that crossroads, has many ghostly associations. Witnesses came forward to report seeing English civil war soldiers hiding in hedgerows and terrified galloping horses that ran through a brick wall like it wasn't even there. I also heard from a senior employee of the huge GCHQ government base that he and some colleagues had seen a black triangle UFO hovering directly over the high-security base. I believe that whatever it was that I encountered in the early hours of the morning at that remote crossroads may have also been taking an interest in that high-tech base, as it was only a short distance away.

So, you may be wondering what strange event happened that night and what exactly I encountered? Well, the evening had begun ordinarily enough. I had dropped Dexter, my eldest son, off at his friend's place on the edge of Stratton village, just past the battlefield site on the hill. Dexter plays bass and guitar, and he'd gone up there to rehearse with his bandmates. As he was removing his bass and amp from the car, he said, "I'll ring you later, Dad, to let you know when to come and pick me up." I recall asking him to not make it too late as I had to be up early in the morning to go to work, and Dexter responded, "Alright, Dad, it won't be too late. I'll ring you at about ten-thirty." I remember him walking away, laden with his equipment, toward a partially opened garage door that was emitting the sound of loud power chords and just the faintest whiff of a sweet-smelling illegal substance.

Since there was no proper public transportation in rural areas of Cornwall, I preferred to transport my children to and from their friends' houses, as they often lived in out-of-the-way country areas. At least that way, I could sleep untroubled by worries of their safety, walking home alone on dark, remote country lanes in the small hours.

The Bude area, where we lived, is bordered by the sea to the north and primarily agricultural land with small villages inland for many miles around. Bude is about fifty minutes from Barnstaple, the nearest town to its north, and is ninety minutes from Exeter, the closest city to the south. The country roads that connect Bude to the outlying areas are generally much darker than their urban counterparts; there is minimal street lighting in the Cornish countryside. To back that up, I will reference a study by a London university that found the North Cornwall area (where Bude is located) is amongst the darkest in the whole of the U.K., with minimal light pollution. With that in mind, I'll continue with my story.

Later that night, I was back at home in Flexbury, a district of Bude that is very close to the sea, sitting alone in our front room, dividing my attention between the TV and a book about Admiral Horatio Nelson. As expected, at around ten-thirty, Dexter rang my mobile phone. He said, "Alright Dad, come and get me, please."

I replied, "Yes, no worries, Dex, I'll be up there in about ten minutes." After ending the call, I put my phone on the coffee table alongside me; just to be clear, the phone was not on silent mode; I wouldn't have even known how to do that in 2013.

My phone then immediately began to ring again. It felt like I had only just put the phone down a split second earlier.

It was Dexter again, and he sounded very annoyed. "Where the hell have you been, Dad?"

His cross words took me by surprise and, to be honest, angered me. I said something like, "Bloody hell, Dex, give me a chance; I've only just put the phone down from your call!"

There was a short pause at his end. He then replied, "Dad, that was two and a half hours ago."

I checked my watch, and he was right; it was now just before one o'clock in the morning. I had seemingly just lost two and a half hours! Confused, with my mind in turmoil, I apologized to Dexter, telling him I would get him as soon as possible.

I remember feeling awful that I had made him wait so long, thinking how awkward it must have been for him to sit outside his mate's place for so long waiting for me to arrive. Grabbing my car keys from the drawer unit in our hallway, I opened the front door, then walked briskly out into the street. Victoria Road was slumbering under the light of a waxing moon. In the near distance, I could hear the sound of waves crashing around the rocks under Maer Cliff. If I had still been drowsy after being so abruptly awakened from a deep sleep, the chilly night air would have immediately roused me.

Hurriedly walking down the road in the direction of Crooklets Beach, I rounded the corner into Summerleaze Avenue, where my Suzuki Vitara jeep was parked, right outside my friend Dick's bicycle shop. Living in the north Cornish countryside, at that time, we were rather spoilt, as there were so few policemen working in the area to pull us over for speeding, which was fortunate that night as I drove my car like a Finnish rally driver going through a Swedish forest. My exhaust had recently blown, so I probably woke up everyone in the neighborhood, too.

Now, please bear in mind when you are reading this, and I know it's hard to picture the scene if you've not driven on any of our smaller British country roads, that I was driving on roads only a few feet wider than my car. If you are native to Britain, as I am, this is perfectly normal; it's no big deal to us, but I know from experience that some foreigners do struggle with it.

As I approached the quiet, rural crossroads that would alter my life's course, I slowed right down in the unlikely event that there might be another vehicle in the vicinity. A right turn was required, but naturally, being as I was in Britain, I had to look to the left first. It was, as expected, clear. Then I looked over to my right, and that's when I saw it. Standing in the middle of the road was an owl, but this was no ordinary owl; this owl stood taller than my Suzuki's three-and-a-half-feet-high bonnet (or hood if you're an American). I would estimate the owl's body to have been somewhere around two-and-a-half feet across at its widest point, its shape resembling an obese little man. Weirdly, as is common with many other paranormal experiences, the abnormality of the owl's unnatural scale didn't strike me at first glance; it's odd how that is so often the case.

I decided to wait a moment to see if the massive owl would fly away, allowing me to make the necessary right turn and get on with my journey. The owl was staring me down with its mesmerizing dark eyes, but oddly, I got the feeling that it wasn't an owl at all but some strange dwarf-like tubby man masquerading as an owl. He gave the impression of being a pompous policeman who was deciding what he was going to do with me. At that time, I had a strong intuition that I had disturbed some strange activity and that he may have been concealing something not meant for human eyes. Enhanced by the moonlight, there seemed to be a kind of light, blurry haze all around him; a few feet to his rear, I could only just see the murky outline of the field hedge.

As I pushed the button on my car's door to lower the side window, I remember shouting at the gigantic owl, "Hey, you, get out of the ******* road!" I felt a bit daft talking to an owl as if it would understand my English and good old-fashioned Anglo-Saxon swear words. In any case, my angry words failed to produce the desired result, so I decided to drive very slowly toward the massive creature, thinking that if I gently pushed it out of the way with the bumper, it might be a bit less arrogant and fly away. But as I drew closer, it just continued to stare me down, like a bully in a school playground.

When the bumper was about two feet from touching the owl's body, it just suddenly took off, oddly flying toward me rather than away, as one would expect with a wild creature. As it passed by, close enough for me to touch its outspread right wing, it gave me one last contemptuous stare with its mesmerizing dark eyes. Perhaps it had understood my swear words after all. The resultant down draught from its enormous flapping wings was so powerful that it rocked my car from side to side.

A bit shaken from the odd encounter, I continued on toward the house where I had dropped Dexter off much earlier that night. When I arrived, there was Dexter, sitting on his amp and looking a bit disgruntled, his bass leaning at an angle against a little stone wall, a rollie poised in his right hand. Sulkily, he got up, stubbed his rollie out on the wall, and then started to load his equipment into the back of the jeep. Having done that, he got into the front passenger seat.

I apologized to him again for the delay and told him that I must have fallen asleep in the armchair, but by then I already strongly suspected that the real reason for my delay may not have been quite so simple. Something else must have happened, but what?

As we drove away, turning left to go back past the battlefield site, now on my right side, leading up toward the crossroads again, I asked Dexter how his rehearsal had gone. Having got over his earlier exasperation with me, he replied happily enough, saying that they had a gig at *The Carriers* pub in Bude on Saturday night.

As I approached the crossroads, I cautiously studied the area ahead to see if the huge owl may have returned, but fortunately, there was no sign of it. I decided to tell Dexter about what I had just seen there, only ten to fifteen minutes earlier. After carefully relaying the incident, Dex slowly looked around at me like I was crazy, then said, "Owls aren't *that* big, Dad."

A few days later, as I continued to ponder the strangeness of the encounter, I sought the advice of my friend Derek, who shares my fascination with unusual occurrences. Derek listened carefully to my story, then looked at me just a little bit too long and echoed

Dexter's words, "Owls aren't *that* big, Mark." I could sense a pattern emerging.

Quickly perusing his bookcase, Derek found a copy of *The Observer Book of British Birds* and we went through it together, looking for something that resembled what I'd seen. We also investigated various migrant birds, as sometimes birds are blown off course into areas where they are not native. Other than the more normal-sized owls, I couldn't see any birds resembling the colossal owl I had witnessed that night. In further research, we found that some people had reported seeing undocumented owl species in Britain, and apparently, some of these were called *Big Hoots*, which was precisely the reaction I received in the coming weeks when I relayed my strange experience to more people—some of them thought it hilarious.

Defeated, I eventually gave up both telling the story and looking for a rational explanation.

This is where we leave the ornithology behind us, and we return for a second helping of high strangeness. A few years later, while staying in Illinois, I was revisiting some rough notes that I'd made in the aftermath of my weird owl experience, as I wanted to accurately recall any further details, with a view to including the experience in my next book, *The Spirit of Cornwall: A Haunted Legacy*.

I'd been writing at my host's kitchen table for several hours straight, intensely focused. I was mentally exhausted and ready for a much-needed break. Grabbing a beer from the fridge, I went over to the sofa, picked up the remote control, and put *YouTube* on to the TV, trawling through innumerable videos that came up automatically on my host's TV—mostly about gardening, camper vans, and tiny houses; her obsessions at the time. My eyes were suddenly drawn toward a paranormal-themed video thumbnail that was incongruously included with the others.

This unexpected video thumbnail pulled me in like metal filings to a magnet. It showed the archetypal alien—you know the one, yes, *that* one—the one with the big almond-shaped eyes, alongside an owl. The eyes of both creatures seemed to be communicating directly with me. The synchronicity of finding that particular video at just that moment (given that I had literally just closed my laptop, satisfied that I had completed the chapter on my strange owl experience) was astounding. What were the odds? I felt compelled to watch that video; I felt powerless to resist.

It was a video podcast called *Expanded Perspectives*, produced and hosted by two Texas lads, Cam and Kyle. After some initial mundane chat, the narrative soon turned to the strange connection between owls and aliens. They now had my full attention. One of the hosts was relating a story they had received from one of their listeners in Texas. Here's his story transcribed from my notes:

"I was alone in my car, driving down a dark country road at night. I spotted a giant owl. It was about five feet high and stood at the side of the road in front of me. I slowed right down, unwound my window, and had a good look at it. It didn't fly away. I got a very weird vibe from the owl. It was as if the owl was angry with me and wanted me to leave. I drove off feeling confused and scared."

This witness instinctively knew there was something very odd about his large owl sighting; it just hadn't felt right, so he later decided to visit a hypnotist. He was hoping to recover any possible repressed memories. In his altered state, the hypnotist asked the witness to fully describe the owl, beginning at its head and working downwards. Later in the session, there was a long pause and the hypnotist asked him what he was looking at now. After another long pause, the witness nervously responded, "The owl is wearing red boots!"

Hearing this account, I was absolutely flabbergasted. The Texas witness and I were on separate continents when we had our experiences, and yet the details—including the descriptions of the countryside—were astoundingly similar, with the exception of the red boots, of course.

The researcher and writer, Mike Clelland, has been studying peoples' weird large owl experiences, synchronicities, and the nature of consciousness for almost ten years now; his own odd owl encounters sparked his initial interest.

When I had my strange experience at the crossroads in 2013, I knew nothing about Mike Clelland or the suggested connection between owls and aliens. It was only after my strange experience—when I started looking online to see if anyone else had experienced something similar—that I began to see Mike Clelland's name regularly cropping up. His first book on the subject, published in 2015, around two years after my experience, titled *The Messengers: Owls, Synchronicity, and the UFO Abductee*, was a deep study of the phenomenon.

The popular theory in ufology is that some unknown intelligences may be communicating with us telepathically, using screen images to mask their true appearances. As an example of this, I recall Mike Clelland discussing a case where someone had been confronted by a huge owl. This particular witness heard the mantra: *Owl, owl, owl, owl, owl* repeated over and over again in his head as he observed the strange bird.

Now, was that the witness's brain trying to make sense of what he was looking at? Or, as I just suggested, was the thing he was looking at sending him that suggestion telepathically?

Another important aspect of Mike Clelland's research has been the missing time element of peoples' large owl encounters. Witnesses have often reported losing time *during/after* their huge owl encounters, which also ties into the older fairy lore, where missing time also plays an integral part in some of the stories.

You will have noted my emphasis on the words *during* and *after*. This is because I feel my experience was slightly different from all the other cases I've heard about, as I may have lost time *before* meeting the huge owl at the crossroads.

I remain confident that I didn't just fall asleep. Dexter rang me several times throughout that missing time period, desperately trying to get hold of me, and I'm sure that any one of those calls would have woken me up had I only been asleep. The fact that my own possible missing time occurred before the event and not during/after the event (which is so at odds with every other witness account I've ever read) is the bigger puzzle to me. I still can't get my head around it. It makes no sense.

Research suggests there is often a transformative, portent element to these huge owl sightings: the encounters precipitate remarkable changes or upheaval in the experiencers' lives. I had no idea of this research when my encounter happened. But in retrospect, I believe that encounter was a transformative moment for me as well.

In 2013, I was living a quiet, unassuming life as a self-employed landscape gardener in rural Cornwall. In the years since, my life has changed beyond measure and in ways my former self could not have even dreamed. The world suddenly seemed to open up for me in unimaginable ways. Looking back now, I believe that the owl encounter was the spark that ignited my latent ambitions.

Within a few months, I had begun to take my writing more seriously and was well on my way to becoming an author. My first book, *Wyatt's Weird World*, published in early 2016, opened many doors, leading to guest appearances on various radio and podcast shows in the UK, Canada, and the US. The amazing new people I have met along the way have enriched my life, allowing me access to new opportunities.

***

As I conclude this piece, now a full ten years after that initial weird event, I've written two more books and have a few in the works. Additionally, I am fortunate to write, produce, and present *The Cuckoo Town Podcast*, which focuses on the paranormal, the arts, and literature. I'm also occasionally invited to deliver presentations at conferences, and one of my more recent contacts has asked me to work with him on some fascinating documentaries next year. Life continues to present wondrous opportunities.

Perhaps my experience that night *was* a cosmic nudge onto a divergent path, one that is now more creatively aligned with the passions in my life.

****

MARK ANTHONY WYATT

Born on the Ides of March 1960, Mark's earliest infancy was spent on the site of a derelict, haunted 400-year-old gunpowder works, concealed on the wooded banks of the Tillingbourne, amidst the verdant rolling Surrey Hills of south-east England.

Mark is the author of three books, 'Wyatt's Weird World' (published 2016, revised 2021), 'The Spirit of Cornwall: A Haunted Legacy' Volumes 1 and 2, (2019), and is a contributing author to a 2023 essay collection, edited by the renowned folklorist, Joshua Cutchin, 'Wee Folk on the Big Screen,' published by 'Educated Dragon Publishing.' The essays in the latter book explore how traditional folklore infuses multiple genres of contemporary cinema. His contribution, 'The Magic, Myth, and Mystery of Twin Peaks,' took a deep dive into how the ancient folklore of the forest, going back beyond the Romans and Greeks, heavily influenced the early 1990s TV series, and its accompanying film, 'Twin Peaks,' created by David Lynch and Mark Frost.

Mark's currently completing a book he started many years ago; it's perhaps best described as a part-serious, part-zany biography about the years he spent living in Cornwall (in the UK) working as a gardener on the north coast, to be titled 'Surf 'n' Turf!' He's also putting together a follow-up to 'Wyatt's Weird World,' 'Wyatt's Weird American World.'

When he isn't reading, writing, or researching, Mark enjoys restoring old properties, walking, traveling, listening to paranormal and cultural podcasts, playing guitar, and listening to music. He has given lectures on various paranormal and cultural topics at locations as far-reaching as Nashville in the U.S.A., and High

Wycombe in the U.K. If anyone out there is interested in hearing Mark talk about any of his weird or cultural research, he can be contacted via e-mail at markawyatt1960@zoho.com

The Shadow Man

MERIAH OSTERHOUT

An unwelcome presence haunted the halls of my childhood home. His massive figure towered over me as he crept out of the darkness. Glowing red eyes hovered within his pitch-black form when he stared me down. While the sight of him could not be ignored, he slithered through the halls in complete silence.

I was powerless and alone in my encounters with this menacing shadow man. He prowled through my home with unwavering confidence, as if he'd been doing this for years or even decades before we arrived. This horrible apparition fixated on me, the youngest, and it felt like a personal attack.

I didn't understand what he was, a simple ghost? Or something worse? It seemed odd that he wore a classic bowler hat and a long black trench coat—human traits coupled with inhuman, and seemingly demonic intentions.

The more I tried to ignore this awful form, the more he appeared. The first time he visited my room is etched in my memory—as if to say, "There is no hiding from me, there is no safe place."

I awoke unexpectedly from a deep sleep. To a small child, the quiet stillness of the night was nothing short of unbearable. As I lay there, I wished I could hear my mom talking on the phone or my big brothers causing trouble in the next room.

I looked up, staring at my night light. The familiar pattern of half-moons and stars dancing around and around was a temporary relief. As I adjusted to face the other side of the room, I began to make out the outline of a large man wearing a hat, standing deathly still at the far end of my bed. His enormous, all-black figure hovered over me.

I panicked.

An involuntary whimper escaped from my throat. My eyes began to water as a feeling of helplessness washed over me. I squeezed my eyes shut and screamed as loud as possible.

In one fell swoop, I grabbed my comforter, tossed it over my head, and pressed myself against the opposite corner of my bed. I continued to scream and sob until my mom barreled through the door.

This time was just like every other. The shadow was gone, and Mom saw nothing. She chalked it up to "another bad dream." I was yet again left feeling dismissed, confused and completely alone.

A perfectly executed plan; the predator was isolating his prey.

When I first started to see the shadow, it was just a dark outline of a man throughout the house, usually the basement. I'd catch a glimpse of a black shape moving out of the corner of my eye. I'd whip my head around to find nothing dark anywhere in sight. Not a person or thing around that could have explained what I saw.

From those small, yet unsettling moments, his role in my life gradually intensified. Each encounter was more fearful than the last until (in one form or another) the whole family was affected by his awful presence.

I was four years old when my mom bought the house in 1999. I was not just the youngest, but the only girl. My brothers, David and Paul, are five and six years older.

Our mom had her hands full. A single mother of three with a house to support, she worked constantly as a nurse at Wilson Hospital in Johnson City, NY. She was always on the move. If she wasn't cleaning, she was cooking. If she wasn't taking us kids to school or daycare, she would be running errands. And if she wasn't doing any of those things, she (rightfully) attempted to catch some shut-eye.

My older brothers were often burdened with watching me after school and on weekends. It only took a couple of short years to learn to get creative, sometimes scrappy, and think on my feet when it came to those two. When left alone, the boys couldn't resist causing trouble. I, on the other hand, observed and learned to plan a safety strategy if things went south, which they did now and again.

We grew up in the '90s and early 2000s. Back then, to be reckless and carefree was trendy. This inspired David and Paul to take their ideas of "fun" to the next level, and I was usually along for the ride. Whether we liked it or not, like when they rode down the roof above our front porch with a skateboard into the bushes below. The last time this happened ended with a hard fall on the concrete sidewalk and a broken arm.

Or when we all went sledding down the steepest part of the local cemetery, which had a direct drop onto Floral Ave in Johnson City—I held on for dear life, zooming down the twisting path. I'd keep my eyes pinned on the spot I needed to roll off the sled, to avoid landing directly in front of oncoming traffic at full speed.

I'll never forget watching them blow up matchbox cars behind the shed in our backyard. Who needs eyebrows anyway?

Even back then, not every kid had the freedom we had growing up. I imagine most people were horrified by the amount of space we were given. Since our mom was doing the mom and dad part completely alone, in my eyes, she did the best she could.

I knew all the drills: stay close to home, memorize your address and phone number, be aware of your surroundings—the list goes on. But at that time, it was not the living I feared. Not when the shadow man was always trying to get my attention.

His unwanted appearances had become more unpredictable as the years passed. He'd show up in the foyer while we all watched TV, just staring. I'd see him walking outside, clearly wanting to make his presence known, but to what end?

Even when he wasn't around, I could always count on David or Paul to remind me of my ghostly foe.

"Remember when Meriah woke us all up in the middle of the night, screaming like a baby?" One of them would mock.

I had no impulse control and could not handle their sly comments—so, I yelled. Often.

"Shut up!" My face lit up with heat.

"You shouldn't lie about things like that."

"I'm not lying! He was there—in my room."

"Nothing was in your room. Just admit you made it up."

"He. Was. Real."

"Why would you lie Meriah-Evil-Maria?" They both giggled.

My full name is Meriah Eva Maria. Unfortunately for me, it's a family name. To be honest, I admired the nickname. I enjoyed the idea that on a certain level, I scared my big brothers. I may have been small, but I was mighty in my own way.

"I'm not lying!" I screeched.

"It was just a bad dream. Don't be such a brat."

The shadow man finally got my brothers' attention on one particularly frightening day. Not in the way I would have liked, but nevertheless, his memory lives on in a story my mom still talks about.

It was an ordinary day at our house. There wasn't a cloud in the sky. A balmy breeze flowed through every open window, beckoning me to go outside. If I wasn't trailing my brothers or 'helping' mom cook and clean, I would've been outside, covered in grass stains and dirt.

As I opened the back door, off to the right was a sturdy, and slightly neglected garage. We didn't have much use for it, other than storing equipment for our pool located at the farthest end. To the left of the yard stood a massive tree, home to all sorts of wildlife. I loved to watch the tree branches swing gently in the wind, just a few feet above our trampoline.

I made my way past the pool, the trampoline and the big tree to the side of the house and into the front yard, which was home to one of my favorite places. The lilac bush that sat in our front yard was only big enough to hold one small person. Directly in the middle of it, the branches formed the most comfortable seat. The flowers' beautiful light and dark purple color, followed by the euphoric scent of the lilacs, can only be described as heavenly.

I'd waste hours in that small tree, plucking the flowers to put in my hair, and using others to make a glorious dirt pie. Mostly, I sat and stared at the world through lilac-covered lenses—that is until something else caught my attention.

Sneaking behind the front porch and into the driveway was the shadow, once again making himself known. Outside, I felt exposed and vulnerable. Though the feeling of weakness engulfed me, I reminded myself that I always felt hidden from the world in my little lilac tree.

I fixed my eyes on the corner of the porch to see if he would come back around. This time, I wouldn't let the shadow catch me off guard.

Although, if he didn't return, I had to wonder, *where is he going?* It felt as if he wanted me to notice him slip behind the side of the house.

Just then, I heard the trampoline springs squeaking in the backyard. A moment later, a terrifying realization hit.

My brothers must be jumping on the trampoline—the shadow man was heading towards the backyard. Oh no!

I jumped down from the bush without thinking twice. I felt a knot form in my throat like I wanted to cry. That feeling of helplessness arose, and it was strong.

What could the shadow man do to my big brothers?

I always felt like his presence carried some sort of darkness with it. A darkness that I would never be able to comprehend. If he had limits to what he was capable of, I wouldn't know.

I ran past the house, on the opposite side of where I saw him, heading straight for our trampoline. Paul started to come into view, then David. They seemed fine at first glance. Still, I couldn't help but fear the worst. I continued to run until I had a full view of the backyard.

This ghost terrified me enough in the past that it forced my instincts to take over. They may not be able to see the shadow, but I could. I felt that my ability to see him was my protection. I feared my family's ignorance could be their downfall.

Why else would I have this ability if not to protect them?

As I rounded the corner and looked past our back porch, I saw nothing in my immediate view. I continued to search, still wary and on edge.

"What are you doing?" David's brows were scrunched as he gawked at the wild look on my face.

"Nothing." I answered quickly.

Reluctantly, I continued to walk toward the other side of the house. I could feel my face was drained of its color. Still, I did my best to remain collected to hide what I was trying to do from my brothers. "What are you guys doing?"

My deflection appeared to work as David looked away and began to jump around on the trampoline again. "Not much. Wanna play popcorn?"

"Sure," I uttered over my shoulder, still inching my way to the opposite side of the house, to the last place I spotted the shadow man just seconds before.

Once I had a full view of the other side, it was clear the ghost was nowhere to be found. The whole driveway appeared normal. I turned back around, and the rest of the yard was still clear. As I walked back to the trampoline, a nagging feeling that I had been tricked plagued me. But everything seemed to be fine.

For now.

Not long after mom made dinner that evening, she retired to her room to sleep. She was most likely preparing to work at an ungodly hour the next morning.

Our mom's room was on the first floor, and the kids were on the second. As I lay on my top bunk, I began to grow weary-eyed watching Nickelodeon. From my room, I could hear a familiar video game. Echoes of cars screeching and crashing into each other came from my brothers' closed door across the hall.

At some point during an episode of Nick-at-Nite, I decided I needed to go downstairs for a glass of water before I fell asleep. I climbed down from my top bunk, walked towards the hall, and poked my head outside the door frame to look at the descending stairs.

It was too dark.

I stood there for a moment and debated whether I should push open my brothers' door for some sense of protection. Then I quickly decided the consequences of that action outweighed the benefits. There was this gut feeling that something wasn't right, but I encouraged myself to shake it off and press on.

At the bottom of the staircase, I could see that the light was on in the foyer area. Unfortunately, it only lit up the bottom half of the staircase. My goal was to get across the hall and through the dark section as quickly as possible.

I knew the shadows were my enemy's favorite place to hide.

I slipped out of the safety of my room and headed toward the stairs when a familiar but uncomfortable feeling began to take over. I didn't know why yet, but it told me to stay alert.

Adrenaline took over as my senses went into overdrive. The hair on my neck stood up, and then chills worked their way down my entire body, even though there was nothing around to explain why I felt this way. I could hear my brother's taunts in my head, "Don't be such a baby, Meriah."

So, I walked slowly and focused my gaze straight ahead.

Moments later, I had to wonder if my eyes were playing tricks on me as I started to make out part of a shadow coming up the stairs.

Twice in one day? It can't be. Why won't you leave me alone?

I froze, then blinked. When it didn't go away, I hoped it was my mom for a split second but still, I couldn't move. My throat felt tight as I stood there, trying to see what shape the shadow made as it moved closer.

It was too large.

This shadow was not my mom, and I could not ignore him. It's not often he walks toward me. I'm used to him staring menacingly or slipping out of my view.

Without looking away, I take a couple of steps back and reach up with one arm to turn on my bedroom light, but it doesn't make a difference. He was still coming this way and moving fast. When the shadow inched closer, I was able to make out his whole body.

To my disbelief, this time, the shadow man was holding a knife at eye level.

I panicked, and yet couldn't help but pause and focus once more to make sure I was really seeing what I thought I saw. Again, I blinked hard and fast a couple of times.

What do I do? I thought, which was followed by another horrible question that crept into my mind: *Is this the shadow man? Or a shadow of a man holding a knife walking up my stairs?*

I screamed as loud as I possibly could. It was a scream that seemed to erupt from the pit of my soul. I turned quickly to open my brother's door, but Paul beat me to it.

I slammed it shut behind me and yelled, "He's got a knife, he's got a knife! A man is coming up the stairs with a knife!"

We all jumped into the furthest bed together, staring at the door. Hot tears made their way down my face, but none of us made a sound. My heart, still beating out of control, was probably the loudest thing in the room as we stared and waited for the door to move.

A split second later, David jumped up, grabbed a BB gun from his closet, and plopped back down on the edge of the bed.

The door still hadn't moved.

Paul looked at David and whispered, "Give me the gun." Surprisingly, he handed it over.

David looked around frantically, but we all remained quiet. He found a butter knife he used as a screwdriver on a nearby shelf, which I guess was better than nothing.

After a few minutes, we looked at each other and silently rose. David got in front of me, Paul grabbed my shoulders and positioned himself behind me as we moved toward the door. Steadily, he turned the doorknob, paused, then slowly opened the door.

"Do you see anything?" I whispered, clutching David's T-shirt.

"Shh."

Another sudden realization dawned on me just then—I knew at my core that this was the shadow man. A ghost that, while menacing, hadn't actually touched or hurt us physically. The incident earlier that day, in my eyes, proved that he was just taunting me.

From my brothers' point of view, this could be a real person—to them, this was war.

We walked in a single-file line down the stairs. We were even brave enough to check the house before entering Mom's room.

They still haven't made fun of me—not yet anyway.

It was a welcoming thought but watching them walk around the house on edge felt surreal. The same way I felt a million times before when no one seemed to notice. David finally broke the silence while we looked in dark corners and behind curtains.

"Maybe your screaming scared him away."

Moments later, we woke Mom to tell her. The four of us looked around together once again. She acted the same way she did the other times I saw him - a bit unfazed, maybe slightly amused but what could she do? No one was there.

None of us said much after that. We all retired to our separate rooms. Out of us all, the boys were probably the most unsettled. For me, well it was just another ghostly encounter.

Though the man in the black hat was a disturbing addition to my childhood, he wasn't the only issue we faced. Not too long after this incident, my family would go through a lot.

Unbeknownst to us, our mom's mental health was slowly deteriorating. She fell victim to an unforgiving and all-consuming disease. Mental illness and addiction forced her to seek help and focus on battling her own inner demons. My brothers and I were forced to live apart. I went to live with my aunt Heather on my dad's side, and they went to live with their father.

That was the end of our family as we knew it.

Because of the sudden shock that my family was no longer and would never be what it once was, I blocked out many of my childhood memories in that house. I forgot about almost everything for a few years and dismissed memories of seeing the ghost. It wasn't important anymore.

Growing up with my aunt, I would hear hushed side conversations:

"...I'm sure she barely remembers anything anyway." My grandma presumed.

"Probably—she was too young, and the school counselor said she was handling everything really well." My Aunt Heather declared.

They had to deal with the consequences too. My Aunt Heather was only 25 years old when I started living with her. Just barely beginning to start a family of her own. The more I heard I was "too young to remember," or "couldn't possibly comprehend what happened," the more I internalized it.

I allowed it to become my reality.

Some memories simply got lost. It's not that I didn't want to reminisce. I just didn't think I should. As a kid, I didn't know much about what I *should* do. We all told ourselves the stories we needed to hear to get through them and continue our lives.

Though my mom and I always remained close, I never went back to live with her. I hadn't seen my brothers for years. Even our extended family on my mom's side disappeared from my life entirely.

Over time, certain things would trigger an old memory. As if I watched a movie play out in my head, and my waking mind would return to a specific moment from those days. At first, it was just flashes, and the more I thought about those flashes, the stronger the memory would become.

Though my ability to see spirits was mostly suppressed, what haunted me afterward were these memories—the good and the bad. At a young age, I made the decision that I'd escape the area as soon as I could, and with it, all the unwanted reminders it gifted me. My time in New York was always limited.

With this in the back of my mind, during my sophomore year of college, the urge to reconnect with my roots while I still had the chance weighed on me heavily. To heal from what I went through, I sought to reclaim relationships that once meant everything.

My cousin Nick and I spent the first few years of our lives as best friends. I hadn't seen or heard from him in 12 years. That changed when I reached out on social media. A couple of short days later, I saw my cousin for the first time.

We talked and talked about the years we missed together. We reminisced about the ones we shared. Nick told me stories about people and places I hadn't thought about since the day they happened. He'd mention a name and a flood of memories would come rushing back like a tidal wave.

"Do you remember my friend Jordan?"

I stared at him wide-eyed. "Oh my gosh, Jordan! I remember when we all used to ride our bikes down to that old park in your neighborhood. I picked up a basketball for the first time with the both of you. How is he?"

Nick's eyes also lit up every time I remembered something we did together.

"Yeah, Jordan's good, although I don't hear from him much. Remember when we were all at the park and there was some creeper staring at us from across the street?"

My stomach tensed from disgust at the thought of that scene. "Not until now, and honestly, I cannot believe we were allowed to go there alone."

"Yeah, but when I told my mom about it, we weren't allowed anymore."

"That's right, we had to stay at your house and play Monopoly." I didn't try to hide the sarcastic scowl that formed on my face.

"I used to love Monopoly." Nick truly did love that dumb board game.

"I never did, I never knew how to play either, I just asked you what I should do every time it was my turn to go." We laughed.

"You used to tell me there were ghosts in your old house." Nick blurted.

I froze, then turned to face him as I replied, "I haven't talked about that in a long time, but there was a ghost in that house."

"Yeah, I know." He looked at me as if he wanted to have this conversation for a long time.

He knows? The thought left me stunned. My brows furrowed, while I stared straight into his eyes. "Are you saying you saw him too?"

"I didn't want to tell you. I didn't want to scare you more."

I said nothing at first, attempting to wrap my mind around the truth that he had apparently known all along - "Wait a minute, you saw the shadow man, too?"

All those years passed, and nobody else saw anything to my knowledge. There were times I questioned myself, I wondered if kids could truly imagine something so undeniably real happening right before their eyes. I hated second-guessing myself and doubting my own mind. What can I trust if I can't trust what's right in front of me?

Nick tried to form the right words to respond. I got the feeling he was still trying to protect me, and I grew a little agitated, but he finally came out with it - "You used to say you saw the clown-looking thing."

It happened again. That one sentence brought back such a vivid memory and once again, it was like I watched a movie replay in my head.

I was sleeping on my top bunk when I awoke suddenly. Through sleepy eyes, I saw something that caught my attention in the back right corner of my room. My vision adjusted to make out a strange shape. Hanging upside down was a skinny being, with long fingers and sharp fingernails. Its face had weird black and red markings, reminding me of a clown.

Hanging there and staring at me, it began cocking its head as if it were studying me. I was forced to wake up, once again, in a state of pure terror. I relied on nothing but my thoughts to calm me down.

It's just a ghost, and it's not real. It's just a ghost, it's not real...

But it wasn't just a ghost, and I knew that. I didn't want to consider the other possibilities. Not just a shadow, or a man, but a demon. A sinister and truly evil creature.

Why was this happening to me?

I flung the blanket over my head and stayed completely still. My heartbeat was so aggressive I could feel it in my throat. I lay there for hours with my eyes squeezed shut, hugging my knees to my chest until sleep took over my panicked state.

I don't remember telling anyone about it, but I must have told Nick - he was my trusted confidant in those days after all.

"Oh, my God." I paused. "Nick. I completely blocked out seeing that thing. And as soon as you said something, it was like I was taken back to that memory so clearly - you saw *that* thing?"

He nodded before responding.

"I spent the night one time. I was in your room on the bottom bunk. I woke up looking at it, hanging in the corner at the end of your bed. I didn't say anything because I knew you were already scared, but when I got home, I told my mom I was never going over to your house ever again. Didn't you notice, I never came back to spend the night?"

He went on to describe the skinny clown demon in detail. I didn't tell him the specifics of the memory, but everything he said matched.

Seeing Nick after so many years was overwhelming enough, but to have so many memories come flooding back by simply being in his presence, including the fact there was a demon-looking spirit in our house right before our family was torn apart - what word means sadness, validation, hope, and confusion all at the same time?

Senior year of college, I got more proof that I wasn't "just dreaming" or "imagining things." My ability to connect with the spirit world had surfaced again.

This time, it wasn't just a shadowy figure I saw out of the corner of my eye (which happened often). It was a full-blown shadow man, once again that manifested, but this time in the kitchen of my tiny apartment. I saw him from head to toe, under a bright white kitchen light. His black shape was undeniable. Looking away from me, he stared past the kitchen into the next room.

Without thought, I screamed. I genuinely thought I had an intruder. I was terrified.

As if I startled him or interrupted something he'd done a million times without me noticing. He then evaporated into thin air just as fast as he appeared.

Then a few years later, as a post-grad, I discovered a close family friend saw a shadow man in a black hat one night while babysitting me. She too vowed she would never step foot in our house again.

The understanding I once ached for did eventually find its way to me. Though, twenty-plus years later, I still wake up every night without explanation. Whether something unseen is there lurking in the dark – Let's just say, I try not to dwell on the possibility.

I can't help but wonder, was the shadow man meant to be a warning that worse things were on their way? Or maybe those lower vibration energies fueled the despair that soon hit my family. Perhaps, these entities were simply attracted to the chaos and hurt silently living and growing within our mom.

Maybe I was meant to draw a simple lesson from all of this: to trust myself. I never needed others to validate what occurred in that house. A whole series of experiences served as concrete proof that I was always able to rely on my intuition. Now, I'm not afraid to question my perceived reality.

What exists beyond the visible light spectrum? What's driving someone's mental illness? Why does this person or place make me feel sick or uneasy?

I've accepted that I can see what others refuse to acknowledge. The things I experienced in that house were just the beginning and they shaped me into who I am today. Because of those memories and the lessons that followed, my world is not black and white - or even just shades of grey. My world is colorful, complex, and interesting.

****

MERIAH OSTERHOUT

Meriah has a variety of passions and interests that have fueled multiple pursuits in her life. She's not afraid to try new things and take a leap of faith. For most of her life, she was raised in Upstate NY. After college, she moved to Texas for a few years but inevitably ended back up north in the beautiful state of Massachusetts.

In her early twenties, her passion for social justice led to a degree in Political Science and Government, where she found a love for writing while working for the college's school newspaper.

Additionally, she's always admired the field of holistic healing and wellness.

Meriah has pursued this knowledge with intensity over the years, which brought about skills relating to herbalism and nutrition, yoga, as well as meditation, mindfulness and so much more. Meriah's own experiences have fueled an unending curiosity for mystery, philosophy, psychology, the paranormal, and the supernatural. This is where her writing comes to life.

In recent years, she's begun writing fiction and in October 2023 she won a contest through Writer's Digest where she competed with at least 120 other entries. Meriah's ultimate goal is that her work can inspire others to be imaginative and creative whenever possible. After all, there is no need for life to be mundane.

Apparitions, Premonitions & Ties that Bind

MICHELLE ANGONE

Ave Maria played in an elevator kind of way. Slow and slightly out of key. Not a vocal to be heard, but I knew the song well enough from Mass. A thickness like snow clouds filled the room, full, heavy gray, white. The room felt like my uncles had held a circle, but no one coughed, and the incense smelled more like church than the boys' bedroom at my grandma's house.

Uuum, wooh, uuum, wooh. My breath came and went just the way the hippies at the park had taught us. *Thump, thump, thump.* The beat of my heart filled my ears.

A long rectangular box appeared before me, shiny white and ornate, as I moved one foot and then the other. Both of my hands clasped the silver rim. I knew it should have been cool beneath my hands, but the metal was warm. My fingers were grown, ladylike. Unlike my mom's long, pretty fingers, mine were pale, soft, and stubby with a delicate little ring encircling my finger. I concentrated on it to try to stop my lady fingers from vibrating.

I sucked in a deep breath as I looked down.

A man in a dark suit, still and cold, lay within the box. Scarred, grayish hands were wrapped in a black rosary. The face held a blueness to it and the same ashiness as his frosted hands. The closed eyes did not look rested or sleeping. They squinted and were noticeably glued shut.

His mouth sealed taut and grimaced and jaw clenched tight, promising never to speak another word. Somewhere in the depths of my soul I knew the face, but I couldn't place it. The age escaped me, being older than my uncles and younger than my granddaddy. His short dark brown hair didn't seem right. It laid unnaturally as if someone had used an entire can of my Nana's hairspray to plaster it in place.

My fingers reached for his arm. Frigid, stiff, solid, and void of life. I jumped as if I had been burned. Turning, I ran from the wretched gray place as the screams escaped my mouth.

"No!" I sat straight up, tears pouring down my face. "No." The box and the lifeless man lingered in my head. "No." I needed it to go away. "No." My heart and my head thumped in unison. My hands covered my ears as I squeezed my eyes shut. "No!" Tears burned my cheeks.

My room filled first with the house and all those strange beings existing within it. It was full to the point of overfilling, suffocating me with their curiosity. They came closer to either watch the show or to comfort me. I didn't know which one and I did not care. If they couldn't wake me from the horrible nightmare, then they need not bother being in my room. The light switched on, just as my fear turned to resentment.

"Here now. What's this about?" my Nana, both sleepy and irritated, stood beside my bed.

I held my breath and tried to control my sobs. I wanted to tell her about my dream, but I couldn't get the words out. I wanted to ask if she could sleep with me or me with her, but instead, I sniffled.

Cranky and in no mood to deal with me again, she said "I have to be up in two hours."

The light on the pink walls began to feel like a hug as I pulled the covers up and grabbed the nearest stuffed animal. My breath slowed. I felt silly and just a little mean for waking her up. "I'm sorry."

"That's better, baby. Get some sleep."

"Can I have the light?"

"Just close your eyes, you'll be fine." The gentleness of her voice held the smallest hint of disappointment. She had to be up before the sun, and I had woken her up by screaming in the night again.

Sometimes I would sneak my light on until my mom came home or my granddaddy went to bed. I could sleep with the light on all night, just fine, if they'd let me. I was told there were outrageous light bills and keeping a light on all night just wasted money. They tried plugging one of those little night lights into the wall outlet. Those creepy things caused shadows to breathe in the air. A few nights of me whimpering over such nonsense made my family realize nightlights were not the solution.

The tiny room with the canopy bed, without a canopy, didn't have room for a bedside table. Stuffed animals filled the room along with cloth dolls in big hoopskirt dresses on the shelves next to the bed. A big dresser with a mirror just tall enough not to reflect me while I slept sat to the right. They tried to be creative with a place to put a little lamp.

When they put a lamp on the shelves, it made the dolls look at me sideways itching to start up a conversation. A lamp on the dresser lit up the mirror. When light reflected into the mirror, the people on the other side were able to look straight at me. I definitely couldn't tolerate the watchers all night long.

A window faced the street on the left side of the bed and the streetlight shone through the lacey curtains. In the winter, the window frosted over, changing the shadows in the room as cars drove by. Every couple of hours headlights danced across my walls.

Another window just off the foot of the bed faced my oak tree and the neighbor's house out back. My grandma put a box fan in the window during the summer to 'pull the heat out,' leaving the curtains wide open. During those nights, I just watched the breeze blow the oak branches across the star-filled sky until sleep took me.

But gazing at those stars didn't help much. Staying up until I fell into an exhausted sleep was all it took for the dreaded dream to come.

On such nights, my poor Nana would get me bathed and tuck my little butt into bed. "Get some sleep now. Tomorrow's another day."

Off to bed she went, and I'd jump from the bed to the switch just as she left. I focused on Big Bird. He hung from the foot of the four-poster bed. His head slumped to the side, his bloated belly and dandling legs centered me. Terrifying but reassuring as I at least knew I was awake and in my bed.

I'd glance to the right, and see the shadow watching me again. Black against the dim night, his form took up most of the doorway, hands to his side, the ever-present hat on his head. I closed my eyes yet could not turn away.

If only I could grab the blankets and pull them over my head, then I would not know if he was there, and the shadows would quit dancing on the walls. If I moved, he would move to the side of the bed, and stand over me. I knew he would be there. I knew the dresser mirror would disappear again.

Make it go away. Please go away. But he would not go, he never did. I peeked up at him, as he watched. I waited as he waited. Every night we kept the silent vigil, waiting for the darkness to ease and the radio buzz from down the hall.

Nana woke up at 4:00 am five days a week. I waited all night for the hallway light to finally turn on as she prepared for work. Only then could I float into sleep, if even just for just a little while.

Those were the lonely nights in my childhood bedroom. Just me, Big Bird, and the Man with the Hat. It didn't happen all the time. In fact, if the kids were there, the man never came. He stayed down the hall in the little alcove by the bathroom where he belonged. Perhaps my loneliness could have summoned him to my room. Maybe my fear of an empty bed sent out such a big signal he couldn't help himself from watching me.

He didn't come to me on the dream nights.

Thankfully, the nights alone in the little room at the top of the stairs only lasted a few months here and there, scattered over my childhood.

The house and the lives of everyone in it lacked consistency in most things but one, my grandparents' bedroom. I heard they once had the downstairs room, but I only ever knew them to have the room next to the bathroom upstairs. The immaculately clean and overly dark room always smelled of lemon pledge and never even had a hint of cigarette smoke.

The door made a terrible pop and creak when it opened because it didn't fit in the frame quite right. They had nice, heavy wood furniture, a bedspread covered with warm-colored silky roses, and a crucifix over the bed from Nana's daddy's casket. She made the bed every morning, even though they'd just crawl back into it every night.

Sometimes when us kids were bold, we would hide in the tiny closet while playing hide and seek. Under the bed had plenty of room for hiding, although I wouldn't. Once I dreamed my grandpa's Gretsch guitar case morphed into a coffin when he opened it, so I never dared scootch under the bed with it. Besides, the room had a heaviness to it that kept your feet from wanting to enter.

Although the house was large, almost every noise made on the second floor could be heard downstairs. If we hopped the stairs or stood on the banister, someone would yell, "Settle down up there."

Everyone who ever spent just one night knew our house was spooky. My granddaddy was certain we had a ghost or two.

Granddaddy used his version of a lady's voice, "Just as plain as anything, I heard it. Lloyd! Lloyd, you hear?" Then he switched to his own Kentucky drawl, "I'd say 'yeah.' Then I remembered no one was home but me. Then, just a bit later, I'd hear the toilet flush and someone walking around up there." He would look around all serious, "Again, no one was home but me."

He'd be talking to one of the adults, one of my uncles or my mom but all the kids would be paying attention. We knew the story had to be true because he didn't crack a smile or start to laugh. Instead, he just shook his head and lit a Winston cigarette.

"Aww Dad, the kids across the street told us about the house when we moved in. Said no one would come inside because of it being haunted and all." My uncle cracked a beer. "I've seen some shit in here."

"Oh, you were probably just drunk. Ain't nothing in this house to be worried about," Nana laughed.

"That's right, there's nothing to be afraid of. That's just my mama checking in on me, that's all. She won't hurt anything. Just wants me to know she's here is all."

Granddaddy's mama passed on back in Kentucky when he was little. We all knew the story. She had gotten some infection after giving birth and never recovered. He said he only had a few memories of her, but he felt her with him his whole life.

I often wondered if his mama really did check in on him. I mean, he had a creepy photo of her in the peach frame right next to their bedroom door. She had a stern look on her face and her eyes kind of followed you around if you looked at her too long.

Old-timey grandmama Fanny Belle created another reason to stay clear of Nana and Granddaddy's bedroom. I didn't need her yelling my name. I had enough issues with all the inhabitants stirring up trouble at night, no one needed to start talking to me during the daylight hours too.

Our house had a revolving door for wayward relatives. Some stayed for a few weeks, some for months, and some for years. Lucky me, I had just always been there. I had been there so long I never remembered being anywhere else. Most of the time we had other people in the house. Thinking back, I can only recall two or three times when I was the only one living at home other than my grandparents. Mostly we lived in a house of chaos filled to the brim with family.

My mom was the baby of the family. She only moved out when she married my dad. It didn't last no time, though. She ended up back home with me before she even got out of her teens.

Mom had rightly claimed the big bedroom as her own being she was quite the staple and all. The big room had a door that connected it to the little room I sometimes had. The canopy bed was in front of the door which made it unable to open. It had two twin-sized beds pushed together to make a king-sized bed.

Sometimes the big bed filled up with women and small children. One of the aunts and her kids from Kentucky, having man troubles, inevitably found themselves sharing that bed. They would stay for however long it took them to straighten things out or move on. Sometimes my cousins' mama found her way back home to us. It made no difference if she was divorced from my uncle or not. Once someone became one of Nana's kids, they were her child forever.

No matter who shared that bed, we snuggled together and kept each other warm and safe at night. I'm not sure if we were being safe from the ghosts or from whatever man did them wrong and it didn't matter. A full bed was the most comfortable place in the world to sleep.

Sometimes my mom was the only woman in the bed with two or more of us little kids. I always tried to sleep closest to my mom, or at least in the middle. Without a mama flanking the sides, you never knew who or what might show up in the night to watch you sleep. Mostly her room was a like base when you played tag. If you were lucky enough to get to bunk in there for a while, you knew nothing was going to bother you while you slept.

I liked it when one of the boys was home. The house became more alive at night with real live people in it. They'd be up all night drinking and having a good time. They made so much commotion the ghosties didn't have time or space to mess around with us. We could just fall asleep listening to everybody laughing at all hours.

I remember waking up and the kitchen would be clean, and someone would make us a good breakfast. They'd let us watch cartoons and play all we wanted as long as we stayed quiet so they could catch a cat nap.

When there was a full house, or the summer heat got to be too much, us kids would have to sleep downstairs. Our house was old, and we had only a window unit until I turned eleven. The adults would nail blankets up to the doorways and shut the door to the upstairs which made the dining room the coolest and most peaceful room in the house. Sometimes they would leave the giant stereo cabinet on and listen to hippie music all night long. And when it got dark, we were safe from all the people hiding in the shadows.

In cooler weather, we were sent to the little TV room off the formal living room. The door never quite shut right and left a gap just the right size for the Old Lady on the Stairs to peek in. It never seemed so bad if there were a lot of us or we could sneak the lamp on all night. Oh, but those nights when there were just a few of us, those were scary.

There were things in the good living room as we called it. They were not people like the Man in the Hat or the Old Lady on the Stairs. No, they made loud noises and whispered and made the mice in the walls nervous. We would huddle together with our heads under the blankets as far from the door as we could get. We could have slept on the long couch but if we did, we'd be far away from each other and be even more afraid.

Thankfully, my uncle was the only one who had to sleep in the tv room by himself. We found out when we were teenagers why he didn't mind the room so much. Turns out you could come and go out the window or bring people in and no one upstairs could hear it.

Our lives made perfect sense, to us. We understood it could confuse outsiders looking in. Sometimes it just got easier to refer to each other as brother and sisters. Especially for Stevie and I who were there together the most for whatever reason. I guess when you are potty trained together, you get to decide how you refer to each other. The trouble was the chaos of it all. We were not always together. Sometimes they were just gone.

One time in the car with my mom and Nana, I had asked where Stevie and Stacy were. We had all been together for half-a-year and one weekend they went to their mom's for a visit that had lasted a bit too long for my liking. The days were darker and the temperatures had started to drop. The holidays were well on the way. I had this sinking suspicion I'd be alone for Santa's visit.

"We dropped them off at the orphanage," they giggled from the front seat.

I burst into tears, but they did not seem to understand why I didn't find it funny. "Well, don't cry, we didn't give them away. They went home to their mom."

I knew I'd be sleeping in the little room again by myself. I cried big ugly tears all the way home.

That night I woke up to giggles and snickering coming from the little room below my bedroom.

"Michelle, come and get us," he whisper-laughed.

"They're home!" I took those steep stairs two at a time and ran into the TV room. More giggles erupted from behind the white chair. I flipped on the light, my heart pounding, "Found you!" but they were not there.

I searched behind the couch, behind the curtains, behind the door, yet no one was there. The giggles continued as I searched the good living room, the dining room, and the kitchen. My heart did not have time to sink as curiosity overwhelmed me. I knew they were not there, but how could it be? Shadows darted, but they were all the wrong size, hiding in spots too small for even Stacy to fit.

"Shelly, come and get us," Stacy's high-pitched voice beckoned.

I lifted the velvety brown chair skirt, "Come out, come out wherever you are."

Snickering from the black iron heat register in the floor.

"The basement!" Our playroom was down in the odd-smelling limestone basement. The play kitchen, doll house, and trucks tried to make the cavelike room cheery, but it didn't help much. It was scary down there, especially when the laundry room light was off.

I switched on the light and peered down the steep wooden steps. "Stevie? Stacy?"

"Down here Michelle," he pleaded.

I braved the stairs one step at a time. "I don't see you," I said looking around our play space.

"Back here," the Stevie-like voice snickered from the dark hollow of the laundry room entrance.

The space behind the furnace had always frightened us. It was a small, musty-smelling place my grandparents used as storage for old things no one had a need for anymore. We didn't dare venture to the back when we played. The room seemed to expand into a much larger room and although we never saw anything, we just knew bad things lived there.

I didn't think it was actually them, but I was tempted to investigate. I wanted to tell them later that I had gone to the scary place in the dead of night. But when I heard the sound of too many children laughing, I ran up both flights of steps and right into my mom's bed. She didn't even notice me until the alarm went off.

"Someone was sneaking ice-cream out of the freezer last night," Granddaddy looked at me while he poured his coffee into his thermos for work.

"Who?" I pictured the giggling kids getting into the freezer after scaring me away.

"You left the basement door open babydoll," he winked at me.

My eyes widened. I had left the door open, that part was true. But I wasn't getting into the freezer in the middle of the night. I hadn't even gone that far into the playroom. I couldn't exactly explain why I was down there and decided to stay silent.

"I won't tell," he ruffled my hair and smiled.

The kids were gone for a long while. It could have been months, or it could have been a year. Our lives were like that. One minute I had an older brother and a little sister and the next I simply didn't. It was for the best, really it was, but man, sometimes the loss caused my belly to rumble and my head to throb for weeks at a time. I seemed to always suffer from headaches and a bad tummy. I either couldn't go to school or the nurse just sent me home.

New dreams started during one of those absences. Maybe the night people needed a break every once in a while. Or maybe the rumblies just left me completely exhausted so sleep could take me now and again.

The dreams were simple. I saw the inside of a church and a closed casket. These were different from the one with the shiny white casket. That dream hurt my soul. No, these dreams would be brief. I would see the inside of St. Mary's and in the center aisle near the altar, a black casket sat with the lid down. It was a quick visit to the funeral of some unknown person.

The morning after, my grandma sat at the table with a sad faraway look in her eyes.

"Are you okay, Nana?"

"No baby, someone back home has died." She took a sip of her tea and shook her head.

"Did someone call?"

She shook her head, "No, but they will."

"How do you know?"

"I just do. I just do."

"Did you dream the funeral too?" Her head shot up and her eyes looked into mine.

"Don't you pay no mind to silly dreams." She reached over and rubbed my back.

"Anyone call yet?" my mom asked, as she sat down at the table. My Nana just shook her head no.

I can't remember who passed at that particular time. I just know later in the day someone called and a few days later we were off to Kentucky for a funeral. After a while, it became such a pattern I no longer thought of it as odd. We would wake up and we all had our way of just knowing. Nana would have the laundry going and the bags packed, sometimes before we even got the call.

The rumbly tummy, headache dreams could be good, too. Sometimes after a shared dream, we'd meet in the kitchen, and everyone would be all smiles. Eggs and bacon would be frying, coffee brewing, tea heating, and Nana singing along to the country station on the radio.

Some nights I saw a cradle or a highchair in my dreams. I would wake up knowing we were going to have a baby in the family somewhere. The best part would be watching us try to figure out who the new mama would be. Every woman who walked into the house got a good look up and down and lots of questions. Most of the time Nana would know with just one look and she would get a straight answer out of whomever it was.

Things did not always end well. One night I could dream of cradles and highchairs and everyone in the house would be giggles and smiles. Sometimes another dream would come, and the cradle tipped over or the highchair crashed to the ground. Sometimes, little ones only stayed in their mama's bellies for a very short time. Sometimes hearts would break and sometimes there was an air of relief. I learned to watch and observe and let my Nana do all the talking. No need for me and my mouth to add to anyone's pain.

The worst of the dreams still came to me when I was all alone. I still saw the man, I still ran, and I still screamed. One morning after a particularly bad night, I decided I needed some answers. My mom was sitting on the couch in the small TV room when I approached her. "Why do we have these dreams?"

She looked up from her book "You just had a nightmare. People have nightmares sometimes."

"Yeah, but what about the dreams we all have? Those aren't nightmares. I don't even wake up from those. I just remember them." I sat down next to her, fearing I'd be dismissed.

Mom closed her book and looked around. "I have ESP." Her tone was matter-of-fact although she lowered her voice.

It was like she was sharing some mysterious secret about the things that went on in our house and our lives and she wasn't supposed to tell. I too looked around and whispered, "What's ESP?"

She rolled her eyes and gave an audible sigh. "A gift. I know things before they happen. I know what someone is going to say before they say it and sometimes what they are thinking." Her eyes widened and a grin crossed her lips, "I even know things back home or about my friends when no one has told me."

"So, we all have ESP?"

"I have ESP. You have an overactive imagination." She reached for her book, but I wasn't about to let the conversation go.

"Do you see ghosts?"

"Spirits. I see my grandmother. We have a bond."

I played with the thought for a moment. I did not have a special bond with any of the people walking around the house in the dead of night. "But what about the other spirits in the house? Do you know them?"

My mom's lips pursed, and she narrowed her eyes. "You need to stop watching scary movies."

"They aren't vampires." I had never considered the idea of the man in the hat being a vampire before. Maybe, but no, vampires were people and not shadows.

"Who said anything about vampires?"

"All the scary movies have vampires. I ain't ever seen one with a ghost, have you?" An argument brewed under the surface and I knew she was getting ready to open her book back up. "The man in the cowboy hat, what about him?"

"Your granddaddy?"

"What? No, the guy by the bathroom." I knew I'd lost my chance.

She shook her head and raised her book up to her face, "This is why I keep taking my books away from you."

We didn't have many books in the house other than Granddaddy's Westerns and the two sets of encyclopedias. Louis L'Amour paperbacks were stacked in the bathroom and the TV room, always at the ready whenever Granddaddy needed one. Even though he had only gotten through the eighth grade, he told me he had read every single volume of both sets of encyclopedias. He had to be one of the smartest people I had ever known to get through all those boring pages.

We had a small collection of Mickey Mouse books that introduced me to Jack and the Beanstalk and Cinderella. They came in the mail once a month until the subscription ran out. One Christmas I got a big blue book full of Mother Goose rhymes. It was filled with really pretty pictures in deep dark colors. I memorized a lot of the rhymes and would go around reciting them to whoever would listen.

Someone gave me a Children's Bible for my First Holy Communion. My granddaddy read the entire thing to us kids. He took the time to do voices and show us the illustrations as he went. Turns out just about everyone in the Bible looked like my uncles and the guitar playing preachers at the park we got to see sometimes. It was a good enough book, but it didn't sound like the Bible readings at church.

My mom had a yoga book with black and white photos of a lady in a leotard bending into different poses. Some of the photos just had her bending her hands into interesting positions which I always tried to mimic. I learned how to bend each one of my fingers all the way back to my wrist. The full-body stretches were a bit more difficult. Bending myself into all those shapes felt as if my legs might pop off like Barbie's when we bent her the wrong way.

The very last photo had a white candle with a tall flame. The point was to just stare at a lit candle and do nothing. Every time I was around a candle I'd try to practice. I'd stare at it until the fire started to dance around and around. Sometimes I'd suck my breath in and watch the flame grow higher and higher until someone asked me what the hell I was doing. It was like watching a candle take on a mind of its own was somehow my fault.

I fell in love with one of her books. It had letters in shining gold engraved into the white cover that felt almost like leather. Even after I could read I had no idea what all those gold letters said. The pages told a story in softly illuminated paintings. A lot of it reminded me of the Bible but the god-man wasn't sandaled hippie Jesus. His skin was a pale blue color, and he played a flute. He didn't run around with a bunch of men. Nope, the beautiful blue man got to have his wife in his book.

Even though it was my favorite book, my mom kept hiding it from me. She acted like the priest was going to get mad at her because I was looking at it. I'd get it out and marvel over the pictures. I couldn't tell if they were drawings or paintings or what. All the images looked like the statues at St. Mary's but in print. Just as soon as

I thought I had the story figured out, the book would be gone again.

"Where'd the book go?"

"I put it up." She waved me out of her face.

"But I was reading it."

"You weren't reading anything."

"You don't know."

"I know you can't read."

"Yes I can!"

"You're eight years old. You can't read all those big foreign words."

"Then what's wrong with looking at the pictures?"

"It's from a cult."

"What's that?"

"People who make you believe what they want you to believe."

"Sounds like church."

"It's not like church, they tell you to bring all your friends and family. They sing and dance, and make you chant."

"What's a chant?"

"Special words you repeat to worship their god."

"Like at church?"

"No, not like church. They are Hare Krishnas. They don't pray to Jesus. They pray to Krishna."

"You can do that?"

"Do what?"

"Pray to someone else?"

"No. They do that in India."

"Then how did you get the book?"

"The Krishnas gave it to me."

"In India?"

"No at the bar."

"Their guys go to the bar?"

"Catholics go to the bar."

"But they don't hand out Bibles."

"Go play!"

"But the kids are gone again."

My mom stared blankly at me, the irritation radiating off of her in waves.

"Can I have the book back?"

"It's in my closet."

I would get to have it and study it until she'd get weird and take it away again. We played the game with the book for years until it got lost and forgotten in the clutter of the closet and our lives.

In the early part of fifth grade, I fell sick with a mysterious illness. As we walked home from school, I complained to my friends about the pain in my arm. I held it as if in a sling close to my body and felt the bones ache. Nothing had happened to me, one minute I was fine and the next my bones hurt. By evening my wrist was bent near my chest and I could hardly move my arm or hand at all. The next morning my leg bones began to ache too.

A day later my leg did not work the way it should. I felt like my Nana said she did after a long week at work. The difference being I was ten years old, and my weeks were not long at all. Most of the time I played Barbies which didn't take any muscle-pulling.

There were doctor visits and lots and lots of tests without any answers. Eventually, my pediatrician gave up and sent me to St. Anthony's Hospital an hour away. I was excited about staying in a hospital. I guess I thought it would be an adventure and I would have lots of fun. Best of all I didn't have to go to school. Maybe I assumed I'd get to spend a lot of time with my mom and Nana, and it would be like a girls' getaway but that did not happen.

When I got to the hospital, they hooked me up to wires and wheeled me from one strange room to another. The nurses stuck white sticky patches to my chest and even my head. Sometimes I was told to stay awake and other times ordered to sleep.

The endless sticks with needles, both to take my blood and check my reflexes, made me feel like Nana's tomato pin cushion. Turns out I had a lot of blood to give, even if I were a slow bleeder, but I didn't even have reflexes.

I thought the doctor liked to hit my leg and arm with his little hammer thing to see if he could trick them into moving. He would look at me and I would look at him and he'd hit me again. I tried to will my knee to kick and my elbow to swing, but they just wouldn't move.

Nana had to go home and get back to work. My mom got sick and couldn't come see me anymore. I was in the pediatric ward with nurses, nuns, and what appeared to be a lot of dying kids. I had never been anywhere without my family before getting left in the hospital.

On the first day I was alone, an ancient sister came to visit me. I just knew I had died. I opened my eyes and there she sat in full habit, all of five hundred years old, with the morning sun rays shining directly on her.

"Good morning, my girl." She closed the black Bible in her hands and smiled. "You looked like you were having a good sleep. I couldn't bring myself to wake you."

"Good morning, Sister. Should I stand or something?" We were taught to stand up and treat the sisters at school with respect when they entered the room. Truth be told, the sisters at school were mean and the ones that still wore full habits gave me the creeps.

"I was told standing is a bit difficult for you right now. Thank you for offering." Her dark eyes twinkled with kindness, unlike the nuns at my school.

"Sister? Am I dead?"

"Oh, sweet heavens, no." She looked around and then down at her long black dress, the giant rosary, Bible in her hand, and laughed. "I guess I do look a bit like something on the other side."

I'm not sure I ever learned her name. I knew she was a nun and a nurse. I had no idea they could even be both. She had worked at the hospital for a very long time. It was her job to acquaint me with the ongoings of the ward. She taught me how to order my meals with the menu. She took me to the shower rooms and told me she would personally take me for my baths. Every appointment I had, which she assured me would be many, would be accompanied by her.

"I am also to keep you up to date on your studies. Mostly we will concentrate on using both of your hands to draw pictures. First thing every morning we will have Scripture and Eucharist and every evening we will have a fun story. How does that sound?" She gave me another of her big toothy smiles.

I did not have the heart to tell her it sounded like kindergarten. I also didn't understand that first thing in the morning meant 6:00 am.

Late on my first night, the night sisters made their rounds to check on all the children in the ward. They strolled down the hall in a cluster, rosaries clanking, heads down, their habits sweeping the floor. One by one they split off and drifted off presumably to each room. The tiny hairs on the back of my neck prickled up and goose bumps covered my entire body when a sister stepped into my room. It felt as if someone had opened a window, the cold chilled me to the bone.

"Hello?" I tried to steady my voice, but it was scratchy and weak anyway. She silently turned and left my room, and I switched on the TV.

Later the night nurse came to take my vitals, "Why are you still awake? It's past one."

"I couldn't sleep after the night sisters came around."

"Night sisters?" She adjusted my pillow.

"Yeah, the whole group of them out in the hall. I almost peed when the one came in here."

The nurse widened her eyes and quickly smiled. "Sweetheart, we do not have night sisters roaming the hallways."

"Can I have the big light on?"

She gave me another wide-eyed look and hit the switch. "You can have the light on all the time if you like."

My real, live, ancient, smiling sister came in every single day as promised. She had no regard of weekend or weekday and read to me straight out of the Bible. She would also give me communion. I had no clue nuns could do either one, but she assured me she could.

She also encouraged me to ask questions. If she saw my nose wrinkle or my mouth twitch she would say, "Do you have an opinion about this?"

At first, I would not dare question or comment, but as I got to know her, it turned out I had a lot to say. I loved that she gave me the chance to talk and I'm positive she loved having someone to whom she could explain the difference between symbolism and face value. She even knew a whole lot about Krishna and told me reading mythology made me smarter.

In the afternoons, she brought me crayons, colored pencils, and paper. I learned to use mind over matter to make my left hand do what my right used to do without thinking. It wasn't long before I could print the alphabet and even scratch out my name in a very rough cursive. She said I saw numbers differently and that made it hard for me to write them with my left hand but I needed to take my time and I would eventually get it. Once I started walking better, she let me go to the playroom to do my lessons.

She and I became strange friends, with me being the broken girl and her being old enough to actually be the bride of Christ. She sat with me after my psychology appointments and let me gripe and groan about the stupid questions. She told me convent stories and I told her about the ghosties in my house, our weird dreams that came true, and even about the ESP.

"Does the man in the hat visit you here?"

"Oh no, he can't leave the house. I don't even think he can leave the upstairs. He just goes from his little spot by the bathroom to my room at the end of the hall. It's a straight shot."

"I suppose the lady of the stairs only lives on the stairs."

"Well, she doesn't live anywhere, she isn't alive. She takes little walks around the dining room sometimes, but she mostly just stands at the bottom of the stairs watching everyone go about their lives."

She gazed deep in my eyes. The look she gave me was like when one of the boys at school got in trouble and the nuns wanted me to tell them everything I knew about it. "Are you afraid of her like the Man in the Hat?"

I giggled, "No, she doesn't creep up on you when you aren't expecting it. She just looks around and gives off this real nice feeling. I think she just loves us. I like her."

"Do you want them to go away?"

"I want the scary ones to leave me alone. It wouldn't be right to make them leave. I mean they were there before me. Besides it isn't their fault I can see them." I shrugged.

"Maybe you can ask them to leave you alone." She let out a happy sigh.

"Can I do that?"

"Of course. It is your house too."

"What about the dreams? The one that makes me scream at night?" This was the question I needed the answer to the most.

"Sometimes a dream is just a dream." She smiled. "Although you already know that. Sometimes dreams can be a premonition of things to come. It sounds like you understand that as well." Her ancient hands, cool, crinkled, and boney took mine in hers. "Perhaps you know the man in the casket, and this is God's way of preparing you for what will come."

"Sister, how do I make it go away? I want it to stop."

"My girl, you haven't had this dream in all the time you've been here. Maybe it comes to you in chaos and all you need is stability."

I laughed at the thought. My life was chaos and I had no control over making it stable. "How does that work?"

"Someday all the choices in your life will be yours. Until then, try not to be afraid of the gifts you have been blessed with. What if you didn't run after you touched him? What if you stayed and made peace with who the man is?"

There was that word again, gift. Why did I have to deal with a gift I didn't want? Why couldn't I just decide it was time for it to go away? "What if I just want it to stop? Do you know how I can turn it off?"

"I think a gift like that is a blessing. Embrace our Lord Jesus and let him take the fear away. You can turn to the Blessed Virgin for comfort." She pulled me in for a tight hug.

I could not imagine seeing Jesus that way. Kumbaya and all that, he did not seem like the type of guy who could protect you in the night. Maybe she was right about his mom. I felt more comfortable with the Holy Mother anyway.

Eventually, my hand uncurled, my leg loosened up, and I got to go home. Those doctors never figured out what happened to me or why it all stopped working. After the stiffness went away, I was simply fine. Maybe a bit weaker in my hand but fine just the same.

Life went back to normal, but everything had changed, including our house. The first floor went through a remodel. Granddaddy and his friend almost knocked the entire front of the house down, but they saved it with a hope and a prayer. They moved the kitchen to part of the dining room, the dining room to the kitchen, added a family room, got rid of the porch, and opened up the stairs just a bit. The poor ghosties had no idea what was going on.

The adults started acting like adults almost all at once. Family visited instead of drifting in and out like they did before. No one showed up in the middle of the night for a six month stay anymore.

Stacy left when she was eight. Her dad and stepmom had a baby girl and she went home to them to be a big sister. My mom gave me my own baby sister later that same year. Stacy never got to come home to us again after the babies came. Eventually, she got tired of it all and packed up and moved to Colorado with her mama.

It worked that way for us. Once another crop of kids popped up, you just pitched in and started raising them. She still spent the night from time to time but our time as sisters had ended. It is a weird feeling to have to treat your little sister like a cousin after so many years together. My teen years left me needing to fill the empty spot she left in my heart any way I could.

Stevie became more transient as we entered our teens. He moved from his grandma's to his dad's, and back home in an erratic pattern that only he understood.

We were almost exactly nine months apart and had spent the majority of our lives together. It seemed like I followed him, a few months behind, from one destructive phase to another. We learned to adapt and adjust to do whatever it was we needed to do. We found ourselves living a bit recklessly, even by our standards. None of it mattered, we were young and invincible.

He took the old TV room as his bedroom and we both took full advantage of that window. There wasn't much to be afraid of in those days. I'd creep down the stairs and hang out with him for hours. Turns out we didn't give two shits about all those ghosties if we were high, so we just stayed that way.

In all honesty, all the kids around us grew up the same way. Fringe behaviors were just part of the culture. The only difference between the two of us and the rest of the delinquent kids in our neighborhood was our legendary big, red haunted house. Soon enough, half the kids on the west end of town were climbing in and out of our window.

We spent late nights engulfed in a cloud of sandalwood, Marlboro Lights, and weed. Although we had been surrounded by music and musicians our entire lives, music became language to us in those days.

"I can't take it," turned into, "Listen to this song."

We could tell everything about each other just by the song of the moment. *"Beth, I hear you calling, but I can't come home right now,"* couldn't be taken at face value. A song like that meant he was getting ready to leave. It was the emotion, not necessarily the sentiment. *"I am the one who can fade the heat. The one they all say just can't be beat,"* that equaled a heaviness that made us both cry.

Stevie got tired, or burned out, or just plain lonely for his mama. One day he decided to leave and be with his real sister. Before he left me behind, he moved my stuff to his room.

He left all the time, but he'd never left the state before. I didn't know what to do without the one person who knew me inside and out. There was no one to step in when my mom and I got into screaming matches; no voice that could say my name in a way that made me take a breath and clear my head enough to think; no brotherly arms to wrap around me when my heart was broken. It didn't matter how hard I looked, no one smiled away the tears of everyday life with me the way Stevie did.

I didn't deal with the loneliness of it all very well. I couldn't handle the things in the good living room peeping in at me while I tried to sleep. I watched the images on the wood walls move from panel to panel all night every night. Distorted screaming faces and terrifying shapes and images made me afraid to blink. With the ceiling light shining down on the bed I contemplated my sanity for months on end.

The light had to be on. There was simply no sleep to be had if it were out. An unknowing lived in the darkness, but in the light images came to life, slithering in the shadows.

The damn dream returned as soon as I accepted the way the walls moved. The clouds. The fucking casket. The man I did not know. Night after excruciating night I sat up screaming until I just gave up on the idea of sleep.

I had zero problems finding misfits willing to escape whatever they had going on in the middle of the night to hang out with me. A little *tap tap* on the window and out I would go. We had a nice little setup as long as we were quiet. A metal patio table, a fence to block the view of the road, and a room to crash in if anyone needed a place to sleep. We'd be out on the patio by midnight, and everyone was gone or asleep by the time that 4:30am alarm went off. If anyone in that house knew, they never said anything about it.

Those couple of years took from me without ever giving back. Life had always been hard but the fast-forward button got pushed while I was busy surviving. The house and all those things in it turned on me. It abandoned me and stole everything I never knew I wanted. My choices, my missteps, my doing. Blessings and misfortune were one and the same, leaving me to figure it out.

She appeared once and only once. Not as a shadow or a hint, but in full vivid real-life color. Right out of the wall with no regard for turned-on lights, pleas, or tears. The black of her gown flapped in the breezeless night as she came to rip away my hopes and dreams.

Her sad eyes were the grey-blue of an angry sea. Her wild honeyed hair flowed without sound in the still night. She floated to me just as the pain ripped me apart. Naïve and stupid, between my pillow-muffled cries I begged for help. She wrapped my anguish in her arms, lowered her head, and drifted back to wherever she came from. Gone away with my heart, she tried to steal my mind as well. She vanished back into the wall. I was left a hollowed out empty shell.

Trauma changed everything I believed myself to be. The silly crushes I thought might be love no longer fit the new me. The friends I just *knew* would last a lifetime did not understand my changed behavior, so I left them behind. Who knows, maybe they left me behind. Our late-night patio parties became part of my history.

The outside world proved to be a whole lot scarier than the big red brick house. Sometimes a girl just needs a minute to catch her breath and readjust. Sometimes the gods played chess with your life, and you need to get a hold of the rule book. And sometimes you need to nail your own window shut and glue yourself back together.

Weird things happen when you withdraw from the outside world. The lens shifts your perspective of reality, slowly and then all at once. You wake up one morning and you have completely reinvented yourself. Well, at least that's what I did. I changed my clothes, my makeup, my attitude, even my way of speaking. Anything before had no place in the after.

Part of the change was a need to finally to figure out the damn house I lived in and why I was so weird. Normal people did not have to manage premonitions or acquired unearthly housemates. It was time to go beyond the other weirdos in my family and see if anyone else had the same problem.

I got a job in the music store at the mall. Many lunch breaks were spent at the bookstore reading through the occult section. The girl at the counter, intrigued by my questions, directed me to Buckland's big blue book. Before long, every kid with a crystal around their neck wandered in to chat with me while browsing the newest tapes.

I soon learned I was far from the only oddball in our little steel town. I may not have found any answers, but I did find the misfits. On random Friday nights, I found myself out at Sinnissippi Park trying to summon spirits on the Indian mounds.

"I demand the powerful warrior of this mound to rise and show himself to me," said by some guy with long stringy hair.

"How do you know it was a warrior?" a doubting-Thomas would ask fifteen minutes after sitting on top of a random mound in the dark.

"Yeah, and how do you know it was a man?" a budding young feminist chimed in.

"I've got a fifth of Jack." The real reason anyone bothered to show up in the first place finally became clear.

Other weekends I could be found around a table watching some idiot dressed in black try to move a pencil with his mind. It never worked. We'd sit and we'd watch. Inevitably someone would slam their fists on the table and the pencil would fly into the air. "Look! It moved!"

One time a group of us mall-working girls sat in a circle of salt on a kitchen floor. "Anyone bother to read a book on this?"

"Nah, some psychic friend of my aunt told me what to do," a somewhat dirty girl reeking of patchouli walked round the outside of the salt line.

"So, what do we do?"

"We call the Guardians of the East." a girl with dyed black hair chimed in.

"Which way is East?" The medicine-bag-wearing girl narrowed her eyes.

Goth girl walked around the circle, "This looks like East."

The rest of us shook our heads in agreement even though no one had a clue what East looked like.

The patchouli smelling girl pointed her finger in the air. "Hail to the Guardians of the watchtowers of the East!" Her cheeks turned a delightful shade of pink and we erupted into a fit of uncontrolled laughter. "What's the rest of it? Damnit!" We roared and passed our ritual bottle of Boone's Farm around and enjoyed the rest of the night.

Shut up in my room on my days off I would drag out my candle magic book and run around grabbing olive oil, herbs, and sewing needles. I'd search the closets for discarded unused candles my Nana had forgotten about and claim them as mine.

The spells and charms in the books bored me to death. Ritual bathing, putting together my makeshift altar, and setting the scene was fun but I felt like it was a game. Reciting the words straight from the book was awkward. Once the stage was set, I'd wing it and adlib words, if I bothered to use any. I would mess around and just see what I could do.

Near the end of my senior year, my best friend and I started dating. I tried to scare him away by letting him experience my house. The joke was on me, he lived in a house with a life of its own too.

My boyfriend's family lived in the oldest house in the entire area. The ballroom in the attic had a thick haze during the day and played a faint tune in your head if you let it. There were cold spots in the basement and the hairs on my arms stood up whenever I walked through one. "It's just Elija Wallace. He and one of your relatives were the original scouts for the area. I bet you didn't know that."

"My family is full of degenerates."

"I like degenerates," he gave a bastardly smile and kissed me.

Stevie made his way home around that time. He and my boyfriend became fast friends. I often found the two of them passed out in the middle of the day. Kevin with his long brown hair, concert t-shirt, and ripped black jeans sprawled out on one couch. Stevie with his immaculately styled nearly black hair and tight rolled designer jeans with a plain black t-shirt curled up on the other couch. I got into this weird habit of racing home between school and work to feed them lunch. I knew if I didn't feed them, they just wouldn't eat.

At night, after I got off work, tucked my sister in, and my grandparents went to bed, we'd start our night. Our only plans centered around either being home or gone when my mom got off work at midnight.

Stevie took his pick of my friends and spent his time rotating through them. There was no judgment from me. He was gorgeous and the silly girls threw themselves at him. He often had two or more girls going at the same time. On more than one occasion I got stuck with two girls who believed themselves to be his girlfriends. I had to navigate the situation making sure neither found out about the other. I became an expert at managing his women for him.

Our summer was filled with adventure, laughs, and love. One night we almost drove off to California with nothing more than two packs of cigarettes and my $120 paycheck. We couldn't go home and collect Stevie's guitar and Kevin's drums at one in the morning. Instead, we accidentally broke into the rod and gun club believing we had discovered it.

Stacy came home to celebrate our grandparents' fortieth anniversary that June. She stayed at her dad's but we went and got her every night after her little sister went to bed. We'd sneak into the park or hang out at the cemetery in the dead of night, chasing Stevie and his friends through the woods. The perfect snapshot of time right before we all became adults.

I ended up pregnant about the same time Stevie's mom was diagnosed with stage-four cancer. He went back to Denver to spend the holidays with his mom.

"It might be my last Christmas with my mom."

"You have to go." My eyes filled but I wouldn't allow the tears to spill.

"I'll be back when the baby comes." He wrapped his arms around me and hugged me tighter than he ever had before. "Don't worry, he's a good guy. You'll be okay." We finally had a normal goodbye.

I had a healthy and happy pregnancy until I was diagnosed with toxemia in the third trimester. I went on bedrest and my family moved Kevin into the house. We all just waited for my son to make his entrance. We burned up the phonelines between Illinois and Colorado keeping track of Nora's growing cancer and my growing belly. I did not understand my life was in just as much danger as my aunt's.

Kevin remembers the birth. I only remember the choice.

I drifted in a fluffy haze of clouds. She was radiant, her voice melodic and tender. "The child will live. You must choose. Be with your son or stay here."

Whoosh. My eyes opened a sliver, "Why isn't he crying?"

Blackness, the clanking of metal, so many voices...

"He's getting some oxygen."

A heavy silence fell over the room as my breathing slowed. Finally, a loud angry cry allowed me to fall into a deep sleep. My healthy nearly ten-pound son was born at 4:20 am, naturally but under emergency conditions, on Stevie's twentieth birthday. Within twenty-four hours, and with the help of a lot of IV fluids, I was awake and moving.

Right on cue with a smile as big as the sun, Stevie walked into my hospital room with flowers in his hands. "Where's my nephew?"

Tears started falling and wouldn't stop until he hugged me. "You know I'm never giving you another birthday gift ever again, right?"

"Fair. I'm happy to share my day with him."

He came home to help his mom settle in with his grandma. He could only stay long enough to get her moved in and see us home with the baby.

"She's never going to see her own grandchildren, you know?" He smiled down at my son in his arms.

"What's mine is yours. Lucky baby gets to have an extra grandma."

My mom and I spent every minute we could with Nora. I let the baby lie next to her on the bed as I remembered snuggling up to her beautiful long black hair in our big bed. The once curvy Latina figure had become emaciated and her flowing locks had all but disappeared. Yet, every day, we packed as much joy as we could into the time we had.

She taught me how to make enchilada sauce from scratch just like her mom. The three of us told each other all the stories. Nora and my mom joked about their wild days and I joined in with my adventures with Stevie and Stacy. We planned my wedding and she advised me on traditions I should include.

When she stopped eating, we brought her peanut butter milkshakes.

"You guys, I haven't been this skinny since high school."

"But where'd your ass go?"

The biggest laugh escaped her frail little body, "Probably the same place as my sex drive."

That time was a retelling of my childhood years, letting me be a knowing participant in the ways of the adults. I understood that my mom and Nora were sisters again and my heart hurt for them.

Nora collapsed outside the church right after the wedding ceremony. Her kids rushed to the hospital while the rest of us continued the wedding celebration. It was her idea and she wouldn't have it any other way. We didn't have time or the need for dreams, it all unfolded right before our eyes. She never left the hospital. She crossed over two weeks later surrounded by her children, her family, and with an ex-husband on either side holding her hands.

Stacy came home, emancipated herself, and brought her Colorado boyfriend with her. She was aunt to my son and for some time we were sisters again. All those years apart slipped away. She was at my side when my husband and I welcomed our second child into the world two short years later.

Kevin and I somehow found ourselves living in one strange house after another. If a rocking chair took on a mind of its own, he would simply remove it. If I cried out in the night, he kissed my forehead and wrapped his arms around me.

Sometimes he would bring me a witchy book the lady at the comic shoppe suggested for me or a cool rock he found walking around his parents' property. He acquired an old Morgan Greer tarot deck one night and he and I taught ourselves how to use it, making up our own spreads.

We bought an old house complete with a little boy who sat on the stairs who and played with the kids' toys in the night. Even if she were fast asleep under our blankets, we pretended the cat made all that noise. We could be in the middle of a lively conversation and one of us would become suddenly quiet because the little ghost kid decided to walk halfway down the steps.

"Oh, you saw that too." He gave me a knowing look and one of those deviant grins.

I loved that house, although it scared the hell out of my kids. I had to remind myself what it was like for me and then try to ward their bedroom.

We lost my Uncle Steve five years after we lost Nora. Lung cancer came for him and it was fast. A misdiagnosed bronchitis at first, followed by the inevitable diagnosis. My mom and Nana watched both him and my small children while his wife worked and I went to school. He watched cartoons with my kids and they told each other silly jokes. The kids got to have a version of my big-brother-uncle, that I had never seen before.

School didn't work out for me, which turned out to be the biggest blessing. I was able to help during the last few months. When he no longer wanted my kids to see him, I was able to keep them away.

Luckily, he got to see both his older kids married. He even had the chance to meet and love Stevie's baby girl. His family and friends surrounded him the last few days. We all got our chance to say our goodbyes and his wife recorded each and every one. His three kids and wife were with him as he left.

The night before the familiar casket awaited me in my dreams. I was up and already waiting when I got the call telling me he was gone. I had the unfortunate job of telling my granddaddy his son had passed.

"It should have been me," he said as the tears began to fall.

Everyone went their own ways after we lost Steve.

We found ourselves in the same place our parents had found themselves after my time at St. Anthony's Hospital. We too had suddenly become adults. Stevie and his little family were in Denver, Stacy and her husband went to Vegas, and Kevin and I moved a couple of hours away to Central Illinois.

Small children take up a lot of time and even when you don't mean to, you drift away from your siblings.

Every dream I ever had about the perfect life became reality. My husband and I were madly in love. My children were my entire world. Circumstances and the inability to afford childcare awarded me the ability to be a stay-at-home mom.

I had time, and yet time kept slipping away from me. I drowned a hundred times in my dreams. No matter how hard I tried, my head kept going under the surface of the water. I stopped sleeping. His gentle breathing in the night gave me something to count and concentrate on.

Water became a beach where my anguish visited me. Perfect and beautiful, it broke me night after night. There was no one to tell or explain it to. A past I had left behind so many years ago tormented first my nights and then my days.

I sent my kids away from me, sometimes merely to another room, and other times back to visit their grandparents for days at a time. They were not permitted to see me slowly cracking. I would not let them see me break. In my head, I was doing all the right things.

When it showed its precious face in full daylight, I tried pretending I was fine. But the tears came one day, and they simply wouldn't leave. My heart ripped itself into shards of glass only to go back together to do it all over again. I was fighting a demon I couldn't bear to win against. I deserved the haunting.

My husband found me crumpled on the floor unable to catch my breath. The sobs breaking free as screams. His jaw clenched, his eyes filled with tears. It was too much. I couldn't take it anymore. He couldn't take it anymore.

We had two entirely different plans of action. I planned the end. An unexplained calmness overtook me. My demon beckoned. I smiled. I cleaned. I waited.

Sitting together on the couch I apologized. We snuggled. The demon nodded. With a great elation, I kissed his cheek, "I love you." The demon led me to the bath. The steam surrounded me like an otherworldly haze. The water burned my skin. I took the instrument in my hand.

BAM! The door kicked open. His face panicked and frenzied.

I slipped the object behind the shampoo bottle. "Are you okay?"

"You're not," his calm voice did not match his face.

"I can take a bath." The demon had gone.

"I can sit with you." He soaped up the poof and began washing my arm, then my back. "We need to talk."

We didn't need to talk. He needed to talk. He needed to threaten me. He needed his wife back. "Make an appointment right now or I will have you locked up."

It's funny to be so close to diving off the edge and be perfectly fine with it. Yet when someone threatens to send you to the nuthouse, the urge to survive suddenly kicks in.

Months. It took months of sitting in Judy's office combing over every bit of abandonment and neglect to start feeling human again.

"I don't understand why it all hit me now. I had everything I ever wanted. Why did it all fall apart when I was happy?"

"You were safe, and you had the time. All these things were going to come up eventually. Anything you push down will find a way to come up. Trust me, I know." I felt like I knew a little too much about her. It helped me trust her enough to be honest, though.

One morning I woke up and I was fine. I climbed out of a black hole, the sun was shining, and my world was perfectly back to normal. It almost felt like a trick. I told him something was different. A few days later we found out I was pregnant again.

"What do you mean you're fine?" she asked during our last session.

"I mean it's over. I was waiting for the light at the end of the tunnel, but instead, a switch turned on and the tunnel doesn't even exist."

"How?"

"I'm pregnant!" I beamed.

"I didn't know you were trying," she frowned.

"It's hard for me to have babies. Trying doesn't mean much." We both laughed.

"It could have been a hormone imbalance. The pregnancy hormones may have…."

"Flipped the switch."

"Just promise me you will always feel things in the moment. Don't push the big things down."

"Don't worry. He'll bring me right back if I slip."

The demon disappeared taking the suicidal depression with her. I didn't look back or wonder what had happened. The demon may have been the worst haunting I had ever dealt with but it certainly wasn't the first. Once the light came back on, it never so much as dimmed again.

We were blessed with a couple of years of utter and complete normalcy. No dreams, no ghosts, no magic, just the mundane everyday bliss of raising our children. I clipped coupons, became a room mom, and made my family my entire world. We made sure to go home and visit as much as we could.

Stevie had divorced, remarried, and moved to Florida. He and his new wife were just a couple of weeks from moving yet again. She enabled his wayward spirit and it unsettled me. He and I shared a few phone calls and I tried to convince him to come home for a visit. Our grandparents needed a new bathroom and with him being between jobs, I knew it was the perfect excuse to get him home. Kevin even offered to pay for his gas. Stevie only laughed and promised he would try.

We had gone back home for a big family cookout. The weekend was uneventful though I simmered an unexplainable anger. No matter that chatter and the laughter I was fidgety and moody. We left in the late afternoon before I had a chance to lose my temper.

I stared out the window as Kevin drove home. Something about the sky and the clouds perplexed me. I convinced myself the clouds were out of place.

"Isn't that weird?"

"What's weird?" He readjusted himself behind the wheel.

"The clouds. They look like the ones over the ocean." I tapped on the glass. "What do you think is causing that?"

He looked up at the blue September sky, back at me, and then to the road.

"Why would ocean clouds be over the corn fields?"

"They're just clouds," he frowned.

"Yeah, but they're just ocean clouds." I started planning a beach vacation. The baby was already sixteen months old, just the right size to enjoy building sandcastles.

Ocean clouds crept into my head. The ocean was calling me. I briefly thought of the demon and how she tormented me in my sleep as we walked on the beach. Although, those ocean clouds were heavy and gray and warned of an impending storm. Fluffy and light clouds scattered across an intense blue late summer sky would not leave my mind.

I put the kids to bed, showered, and settled in to watch something ridiculous and mind-numbing on the TV. After a long weekend of too much family I welcomed the solitude. Of course, the phone had to ring.

"Your mom is on the phone. She sounds like she's upset." He pulled me out of my daydream. We exchanged a *what else is new* look as he passed me the phone.

"Hey. What's up?"

"Baby, I have some really bad news. You need to get Kevin."

"He's already upstairs. What's going on."

"It's Stevie. He's gone," she let out a little sob.

"Gone where? What the hell are you talking about?" My living room began to blur as every hair on my body stood at attention. "Mom?"

"Stacy called. He's dead, baby."

An unearthly noise escaped my mouth. My chest tightened as a sharp jolt of electricity struck my heart. It split in half and shattered into a million shards of glass. I threw the phone across the room and ripped my hair with both hands. Kevin ran to me. My body violently shook as tears burned my cheeks. If I spoke or just pointed at the phone, I don't know. His eyes welled up, a million questions crossing his face.

He talked and I sank deeper and deeper into the couch. A primal need engulfed me. The core of my being screamed into the universe, *"MOTHER!"* I curled into the embrace of no one. My head resting on a chest that was not there, but I felt arms enfold me, a loving cheek on my head. If it were his mama or if it was the one true Mother of us all, I do not know. The depth of my need called out to the Universe and the liminal answered.

A cigarette found its way to my hand as Kevin poured two glasses of whiskey. They didn't know how long he had been gone, maybe a couple of days. By his own hand. He had done it. Big Bird flashed through my mind.

I whimpered, "I want to go home."

The house took on a hue of sepia and a thick haze overtook the air. Hundreds of little bubbles drifted from room to room. My Nana sat folding a basket of clothes, her movement automatic. Granddaddy sat in his chair, his lips quivering, "Why did he do this?"

I dropped to my knees and hugged his neck.

Every tear, every faked smile, every abandoned second of his thirty years flashed through my memories. "I don't know. I don't know."

I called Stacy so many times. I walked a tightrope, carefully balancing between what I wanted and what I was being offered. It wasn't my place to ask anything. For the first time in my life, I had to be just a cousin. My childhood rumblies returned.

"Will the casket be open?"

"We aren't sure yet."

"If it isn't, can I please see him?" I would never be able to accept his death if I couldn't see him.

"They don't know if they can make him presentable." Her voice was tight and I knew she wanted to say more.

I wanted to say more. I wanted to be there with her, but no one had extended an invitation. It was like a punishment for something I was unaware of doing. My grief, no matter how consuming, had to take a backseat to what she was going through. She had lost so much in fifteen years. Her mom, her dad, and her brother were gone. I would not insinuate myself on her. She had a sister, a real sister, and another brother. Who was I?

We went to the funeral home on the day of the visitation. That morning I put on my makeup. I needed to be pretty for Stevie. I chose a dress he would like and fixed my hair just so. For him, because I knew he would do the same for me.

I wrote Stevie a letter. I poured my heart out. I told him everything I may have forgotten to say while he was still here. I told him I was sorry. I told him I understood. I told him I would never be afraid because I knew he waited for me on the other side. I asked him to come when it was my time. I put the letter in an envelope with two silver dollars for the ferryman and a lock of my hair to take a piece of me with him. The funeral director promised to slip the envelope in with him for the cremation.

The heavy scent of frankincense hit me as we walked into the funeral home. *'To hide the smell.'*

My stomach dropped. One step, then another. I stopped. A familiarness washed over me. The room was large, open, yet thick with a cloudy haze. The music played too slowly and a bit too sharp.

He was laid out at the front of the room, flanked by dozens upon dozens of flower arrangements. His casket was shiny white, and beautifully carved. The déjà vu was undeniable. My pulsing heart filled my ears.

Both my hands clasped the warm chrome rim. *'They should turn up the air conditioner.'*

The gold of my wedding rings caught my eye. "You don't have to do it you know." He had joked with me the morning before my wedding. He was so handsome in his tux, young and perfect.

I looked down and sucked a deep breath. His suit was dark, casual, made for office work. They had remembered to wrap his scarred hands in his communion rosary. The hue of the suit and the black of the beads failed to conceal the gray of his skin. His face was no longer sun-kissed was but bloated and held a blueness to it, and the ashiness of his hands…

His beautiful almond eyes were not closed in a restful sleep. His grimaced mouth, his jaw clenched tight, promised never to tell us why. Somewhere in the depths of my soul, I knew I had seen him like this hundreds of times. He'd be so pissed if he knew how badly the undertaker had messed up his perfect hair. My fingers reached for his arm. Frigid, stiff, solid, and void of life. I jumped as if I had been burned.

I turned and ran as fast as I could. *"No!"* My heart and my head thumped in unison. My hands covered my ears as I squeezed my eyes shut. *"No!"* Tears burned my cheeks. I ran past the doors into the bright day. I ran around the corner of the building.

Just as the grief overtook me, Kevin laid his hand on my shoulder. He turned me around and I collapsed into his embrace. After twenty-nine years of the nightmare the hug I longed for a thousand times over, finally came.

****

MICHELLE ANGONE

Michelle Angone is an internationally published author. She has written on women's issues in UK's "Riot Angel" magazine as well as several small print zines using short fiction, poetry, and essay.

A reluctant academic, she has majored in just about everything from nursing to philosophy. What she lacks in diploma she makes up for with certificates and initiations. She is a priestess of several paths and a student of the mysteries.

Currently, she is a homeschool mom, teaching paganism to children whose families fall outside the typical homeschool norm. As a lover of the arts, Michelle has been a lifelong vocalist, occasional aspiring performer, and a former children's choir instructor. She enjoys speculating on the world around her, be it the seen or unseen.

Her curiosity tends to cost her many hours of endless research into the occult and conspiracy theories, and wherever the two collide. This pastime rewards her with lots of aha moments and even more laughs.

Michelle lives in North Georgia with her husband of thirty years, her children, an acquired granddog, and her baby cat. A herd of deer rely on the Nana and Bog Witch for their morning and evening meals. Once a day, a group of juvenile delinquent crows demand corn tortillas from her in exchange for their silence and her sanity. Although a bit outspoken and more than a little bit opinionated, Michelle enjoys a quiet life in her witchy cottage in the woods.

Time Warp

DR. RUTH A. SOUTHER

Traveling through Missouri is always an adventure, but this time, it was insane.

"Holy Bejesus, do you see that?" I reduced the speed of my van down to a crawl on the winding AA road through the foothills of the Ozarks.

"Yeah." My shotgun rider leaned forward for a better look, as did I. "Is that a meteor?"

We watched a bright green 'something' creep across the dark sky, leaving a fuzzy trail behind it. Circular, it radiated intricate cones of color that fed the tail.

"I don't think so—it's moving too slow for a meteor. And that color? When have you ever seen one that green?"

"Never," she replied in a breathless whisper, talking more to herself than to me.

We stretched forward, practically pressing our faces against the windshield until the whatever-it-was disappeared behind a ridge of trees. It seemed closer than any shooting star I'd ever seen. *Did it hit yet?* I realized I was tense, waiting for the sound of an explosion. It never came.

"I don't like this." Elizabeth spoke in a low voice. "This is bad juju."

"It was probably something to do with the military." I hit the gas pedal and moved the van forward at a normal speed.

She shrugged. "Maybe."

The four folks in the back of the van paid no attention to either the phenomenon or the fact we almost came to a halt on the road. They were excited to get to our destination, a spiritual retreat center in the heart of the Ozarks.

We were close, and it'd been a long drive — six hours from Springfield, IL, but we were dedicated to The Grove and our experiences there. Plus, we'd stopped along the way at a roadside concrete art shop to pick up a statue fountain — Venus on the half-shell — for the west altar.

It was huge and sat in three pieces in the far back of the van. The concrete storefront was along the interstate, full sun and quite warm for October. We were grateful the statue was bone dry because it was already heavy enough with no rainwater weighing it down.

It was Cilia's birthday, and we couldn't wait to see her face when we gave it to her. I wasn't sure how we would get it out, but at least I could drive to the ritual ground and drop it off; We wouldn't have to figure out how to get the fountain there with a tractor, and that was a good thing.

With the green meteor tail gone, we continued through the foothills. The further we went, the denser the trees became, and the hills grew steeper. There were no street lights in this part of the state, only the far-off glimmer of a pole light near a house.

There is a real danger of animals leaping out on the road, particularly deer, but also raccoons, possums, rabbits, and the occasional hunting dog. One time, I thought a big stick was across the road, but it turned out to be a giant black snake. I caught the very tip of its tail, and it took off to the other side like a bat out of hell. I've never seen a snake move that fast, and I hoped it wasn't injured.

As we wound around the narrow road, always aware of speeding vehicles coming our way, we kept looking for another green light in the sky.

We didn't expect the light to be a white, bright spotlight right over the top of the van. When it appeared, it scared all of us. The ones in the back had no choice but to see this one since it was so close.

"What the hell!" Marie screeched from the rear of the van. She sat by the sliding door with its big window.

The squawks from all of them were deafening.

"Is it military?"

"I don't hear a helicopter."

"Maybe it's a pole light."

"There's nothing here, not even a farm building."

"Yeah, yeah, I see it's all forest, but…what else could it be?"

"It's a fucking alien, I'm telling you," shouted Elizabeth.

"It's not an alien." Once again, I braked. I wanted to have a good look at this thing. "Sure seems like it's hovering right over us. Can anyone see what it is?'

A chorus of "No!" came from the backseats.

"Someone roll down a window and look out." I really wanted to know what it was.

Again, "No!" echoed throughout, bouncing off the sides like a bunch of tennis balls.

I crept along the road, and the silent light followed us. I kid you not. The light stayed with us with every curve and bend, downhill and uphill. I'll confess right here that I've always wanted to meet an alien—oh, and ghosts, but that's another story. This seemed like a bona fide invasion, and I was excited. This section of Missouri was known as the UFO capital of the United States, and I'd witnessed multiple unidentified flying objects on these trips.

Everyone else was terrified. Again, the cacophony of voices rattled through the van.

"What are we gonna do?"

"Speed up and see if it goes away!"

"What if they get us?"

"How will anyone know?"

"Will they find the van, and we'll just be gone?"

"We're all gonna die!"

"We're not going to die," I growled. "This is ridiculous. I'm going to see what that is once and for all." I brought the van to a dead stop and opened my door.

"I swear to goddess, if you get out of this vehicle, I'm going to lock your skinny ass out and we're driving away," Elizabeth shrieked.

"We need to know what we're dealing with."

"I. Don't. Care. Get out and you're walking the rest of the way."

With the ceiling light on, I could see the glint in her eyes; she meant it. Everyone else had gone quiet, waiting to see if we would get into a fight.

"Fine." I pulled my foot back inside and slammed the door. As I did, the bright light jerked to one side, dipped, and disappeared.

"Are you all happy now? My one chance to meet an alien, and you all ruined it."

"You wouldn't be saying that if they took you hostage and did all kinds of tests on you and then dropped your body back on earth and you didn't remember anything. You might even be one of them at that point, like body snatchers. Uh-huh, that's what you'd be, Souther."

Elizabeth, always the practical one.

"Oh my goddess, you're so dramatic. All of you. Shut up, and let's get to the Grove."

Miles passed with no further distractions until we came to the turn-off for Bunker, MO. We drove right through the center, past all the pickup trucks with shotguns in the back windows that were parked at the bars. We stopped at a gas station and convenience store to fuel up and get any last-minute snacks.

Except the town wasn't there. Even though it's a small place, we should've seen the lights by now. It was just an empty, dark stretch of road. As my headlamps struck the landscape, I couldn't help but slow down *again*. This was turning out to be the weirdest trip to The Grove, and that's saying something as the Ozarks host some pretty spooky happenings.

"What in the holy hell now?" I was close to hysterical laughter. I began to wonder if we would ever reach our destination. Little did I know that wasn't a joke.

"The trees are upside down!"

I'm not kidding.

"What the…? I've never seen anything like this." Elizabeth peered through the windshield. "It was that damned alien, I just know it. We've been transported to some other realm."

At that comment, hysteria broke out in the back.

The tops had dangling roots as if trying to reach the ground below, appearing almost like hair draped around the trunk. I would understand if these were willow trees, but they weren't—they were maple trees. Silver maples are all over Missouri; I'd seen them so many times I could identify them.

The thick trunks made the bottom look even odder than the top. The lower half of the branches spread out and held the tree up as if made of plastic. When the headlights hit, I saw through the branches to the surrounding black clouds.

By this time, I'd come to a full stop in the road as we stared silently at this dismal tunnel of upside-down trees. At the far end, or as far as I could see, was a terrifying black maw of clouds that appeared like a beast waiting to swallow us.

This was pre-cell phones; however, I had a GPS—until it froze up as it was wont to do in the Missouri hills. We were relying on an old-fashioned map and written directions.

"We should turn around," Mary said from the back. I could tell by the quiver in her voice she wanted to turn around. Mary was scared of everything, no matter where we were. I shrugged away her fear.

"What? Before the Martians get us?" I admit my curiosity was bubbling up despite the strange scene before us. "They already tried, remember? Just about an hour ago? I don't think we have to worry about them."

"I want to see what that is," called out Ryan. "Let's not be afraid of some weird shit. I mean, we do weird shit at the Grove all the time."

Oh, now he was being brave after practically pissing himself over the UFO.

"Not *this* kind of weird," quavered Mary.

At least Ryan was on the side of 'let's explore.'

Clearly, Mary was not.

"I have to pee," announced Kathy. "I have a nervous bladder, you know, and this is definitely making me nervous. This whole trip has been crazy. I may never come down here again."

Kathy always said that and always went back.

"Don't let her out. I feel in my bones this is bad. Really bad." It was dark but not so dark I couldn't see Elizbeth's expression.

My enthusiasm to check out the strange landscape ahead of us grew but appeared to be waning with the others as we sat in that van, staring down the foreign terrain. "I say we go through it and see what's on the other side. I mean, we've never seen anything like this before. What do you say, guys?"

"I think we should turn around," called Anne. "This is just too…too otherworldly."

"But we work with other Realms all the time," I protested. "Now we have the chance to drive through a portal."

"Oh, hell no," spouted Elizabeth. "I am not going through a portal when we don't even know what's on the other side!"

"That's the fun part," I smirked.

"Don't make me slap you." She raised her hand in response.

There were no road signs anywhere near us. I stared in my rearview mirror and saw the deep black behind us mirrored the darkness in front of us. In other words, it wouldn't matter if we turned around — we were in the middle of a crazy town.

Ryan turned on the overhead light as he searched the map for this particular road but could find no sign of it. "How did we get so lost? I can't even find this road on the map. What is it called? And what happened to Bunker? Did I fall asleep and miss it?"

"Nope." I waved my fingers in the air, indicating a 'poof' explanation.

"That's ridiculous. How can an entire town just disappear? We can't be that far off. We stopped at a little park fifteen minutes ago to check the route. I mean, wasn't it just…." He turned and pointed out the back window. "…there?"

"Yup. Yup. Not there now, though," Elizabeth huffed. "We're goners. They'll never find us. We're already on the other side. Now it's not the aliens I'm worried about, it's the damned Fairies!"

"Stop it, you're scaring me." Mary tugged on Elizabeth's hair, something she hated more than anything.

Elizabeth turned and smacked Mary's hand. "Don't touch me, or you'll find yourself standing out on the road waiting for the ghost train."

"Ghost train?" Kathy's voice was a choked squeak. "There are ghosts?"

"Or worse, the Wild Hunt. You never get away from the Wild Hunt." Elizbeth's eyes gleamed with mischief. There was nothing she liked better than teasing Kathy, who believed everything Elizabeth said.

"Quiet, everyone," I shouted. "There are no ghosts, no Fairies, no portals, and no aliens. We aren't lost."

"Well, then, where are we?" Mary was taking small, gasping breaths.

"Everyone, just calm down. I know where we are."

I lied. I had no idea where we were, but in truth, we couldn't be that far away from the turn-off to The Grove.

"If we just follow this road, we'll come out in the right place."

"Are you sure?" Elizabeth's voice was suspicious.

"Yes." With that, I put the van in gear and inched forward. We were going through the jaws of whatever beast lay in wait for us. I was both excited and scared. Would I finally get to see an alien? Would we be propelled into the Faerie Realm? Would we end up in an alternate Universe?

We stared at the trees as we grew closer. I drove slowly just in case I needed to slam on the brakes.

As we approached the thick swirling mass at the end, I sent up a silent plea to Lilith, my patron goddess, to keep us safe. And please let the aliens be friendly. And speak English. And maybe give us a ride on their spaceship.

If it was the Fairie Realm we were entering, I sent up another prayer that they would be nice to us travelers and guide us back to the Mortal world. I knew they wouldn't. They'd keep us.

Sigh. Now my friends had me imagining the worst.

Everyone grew quiet as the van nosed into the voluminous bulk of who knew what. Everything went black, and even my headlights could not penetrate the darkness. Avalon, my sturdy, well-maintained vehicle, gave a little shudder as if it, too, was nervous.

"We're all gonna die," whispered Anne.

"Shut up or I will beat you stupid," Elizbeth gritted.

Everyone else maintained their composure, and yet I think there were some involuntary tears happening in the back. I dared not take my eyes off the road to check, though. I leaned forward, my fingers so tight on the wheel my knuckles ached.

"So here we are, heading into The Mists of Avalon." I had to laugh. It was our favorite book, hence the name of the van.

"Mists of Hell, more like," growled Elizabeth. "I knew I shouldn't have come on this trip."

"How could you know that?" Ryan snapped back at her. "Are you psychic?"

"Yes, you son of a sheep-shearing, dung-sweeping ass."

"You'll be the first one the aliens take, miss smarty pants," Ryan replied. "You have more meat on your bones."

"Ha, they want to hear you squeal like a pig!"

"*Stop it!*" I gave a loud huff. "If there are aliens, they will take us all, so stop bickering."

"We could be driving right into their spaceship." Mary pulled her jacket zipper all the way up, like that would stop an alien.

"We aren't. Look." We were out of the storm clouds without a drop of rain falling on us.

Ahead of us was a clear, star-studded sky—still very dark as it was a new moon, but the tiny glittering lights sprinkling the heavens brought relief. I felt everyone relax, as I, too, let go of my fear. "See, we're fine. Now let's figure out where we are and how to get back to Bunker."

"I thought you said you knew where we were," Kathy squeaked.

"Pull over," Ryan commanded. "So I can look at the map."

"We are *not* stopping." Elizbeth leaned around and shook a finger at him. "We'll figure it out."

"Fine." Ryan sat back with folded arms—I could see him in the rearview mirror, and his mouth was a tight line of resistance. "Get us all killed."

"By whom?" Elizabeth sniffed. "Crazy mountain men with rifles…." Her voice trailed off as she thought about what she'd just said.

With everyone falling silent, I kept driving, going a little faster now as we were all eager to get to The Grove.

I was startled when a white car with Florida plates came out of nowhere and barreled around us, quickly disappearing. "That was odd," I muttered to myself as there had been no other traffic, none whatsoever until now, and only that single white car.

"Look, look, lights!" Mary bent forward with a relieved gesture.

Indeed, as we drew closer, we could see it was a huge plant operation of some kind. The area was dotted with coal mines, so that wasn't surprising. It had smokestacks, large round open containers with heaps of coal, a long track reaching a railroad car, and more outbuildings.

I was comforted knowing civilization lay close by as I craned my neck to see if anyone was around, although I did not recall ever passing such an operation. Over the years, I'd traveled most of the rural roads near Bunker.

After we passed the coal mine and saw the closed gates, thinking the night shift still worked, we moved on to a curvy road that felt like going downhill. Trees, the normal kind, sprang up around us as we took the twisty, hilly pavement that did not appear familiar at all.

A half-hour passed with no turns or even the opportunity to turn; We simply followed the bends on the two-lane and trusted we would eventually be somewhere near our destination.

Out of nowhere, the white car with Florida plates came screaming around us again and headed off into the distance. Soon after, the same coal mining company came into view.

"What the hell? I realized we were back where we were an hour before.

"We're lost," announced Elizabeth.

"We're not lost," I growled. "Just…uh…circling around."

"The aliens got us, and we didn't even realize it," moaned Ann. "They're gonna probe us, I just know it."

"Ain't nobody gonna probe me." Elizbeth reached for her 50-pound handbag. "I'll clock those SOB's right up side the head, I swear I will."

"We should've turned back there." Ryan's voice was a little too smug for me. I was about to stop and kick him, and maybe everyone else, out of my van.

"Nobody is getting probed, and no one is gonna clock anyone." I thought, *and if she did hit them, and it is aliens, we'd all be incinerated. Sheesh.*

"And what road do you think we could've turned on, Einstein? There wasn't one! Now, everyone, just shut up and let me think."

I kept driving, of course, as there was no other alternative, and we once again drove around the same winding roads. The white car passed us for the third time as the lights of the mining company came into view. I would not admit it, but I was beginning to panic.

How would we get out of this weird time loop, alien dreamscape, or whatever it was?

On the fourth time of witnessing the same stupid white car and mining company, I'd had it. I pulled over to the side of the road amidst the loud disagreement from my companions.

"Everyone, just take a breath, please. Are we not magical ourselves? Do we not know how to create sacred space? And shift energy? We do. Let's just close our eyes, put out our energetic feelers and find our way to the Grove."

Five minutes later, with screeching tires, I did a U-turn. I'll be damned if I was going to keep following that loop of road. We passed the mining company going the opposite way, and the white car with a Florida plate passed us, also going the opposite way. Half an hour later, we drove into Bunker, the small Missouri town on our usual route.

I breathed a sigh of relief. We were out of the crazy and onto our destination, which we arrived at twenty minutes later. As we stepped out of the van, a huge wind blew in and we were pelted by acorns. They hit hard, and we all ducked with our hands covering our heads.

"What the hell now," I muttered.

The door to the retreat center banged open, and everyone inside poured out.

"Where have you been?"

"Why are you so late?"

"We thought you were in an accident!"

"Yeah, dead alongside the road."

The wind stopped at that moment and no more acorns fell.

I held up my hand, asking for silence as I tried to explain what happened. "It was so weird; we got lost and couldn't find our way back for a while, and just now, the wind and the acorns...." I pointed up to the trees.

"What do you mean? There was no wind, and that's not an oak tree," the owner said. "And you are three hours late! We were all so worried."

"Three hours? That's impossible...." Or was it possible? We all looked at each other, shaking our heads. A ride on an alien ship or a huge portal time loop? I was now very creeped out. My chest felt tight, and I attempted to change the subject. There was no way to explain what happened to us, even to this crowd.

With a deep exhale, I said, "Anyhow, we have a present for you."

We threw open the back van doors and gathered around our Venus altar with pride. And there, in the shell, sat a puddle of water. Not damp, not a trickle as if the concrete had been wet, a pool.

It was at that moment I knew the supernatural truly exists. I always felt it, sensed the magic, the shifting energy during ritual, and even glimpsed things that were not of this realm, things like the white stag from Fairies pawing at the ground in the woods while steam escaped his nostrils or hearing the Wild Hunt pass by and seeing shadow figures walking between the trees. I explained those things away by calling it ritual-induced hallucinations.

This, though, was something different.

No drums, no meditation, no powerfully charged ground to dance on.

Nope. Just six people in a van traveling to a Mystery School, minding our own business.

Color me a believer, now and always. My life and perceptions have been altered forever.

RUTH SOUTHER

Ruth Souther is a metaphysical and natural arts practitioner in Springfield, IL. She is a Master Shamanic Breathwork Facilitator, Master Reiki Practitioner, Hypnotherapist, Ritualist, Priestess, and Minister. She holds a Master's in Shamanic Intuitional Practices and a Doctorate of Shamanic Psychospiritual Studies and is an Initiated Priestess.

She facilitates Vega's Path Elemental Priestess, Universal Priestess, and Elemental Mystery School, a new addition as of 2024, which takes her Priestess Path program to Nashville and Teotihuacan, Mexico.

She authored The Heart of Tarot (an intuitive guide to the cards), Vega's Path: The Elemental Priestess, and three novels: Death of Innocence, Surrender of Ego, Rise of Rebellion, and many more stories are percolating her mind.

She is a facilitating member of The Edge of Perception (NFP spiritual organization) and, along with other members, creates a safe space to offer rituals and ceremonies.

In the summer months, you'll find her in Michigan at a family-owned cottage on Lake Gilead, surrounded by kids, grand and great-grandkids, and many cousins. It's her happy place where creativity flows just as the water ripples.

At home, another lake beckons her to boat, kayak, and enjoy all the wildlife that wanders, flies, or creeps into the yard and waterways. A cold beer on a hot day, floating on the pontoon with family and friends aboard the boat, is the most delicious way to spend a day.

Reach Ruth at: ruthsouther52@gmail.com
www.vegaspath.com or www.Facebook/vegaspath
Edge of Perception | Springfield IL |

Ruth is a contributing author and board member/Chief Editor of Crystal Heart Imprints—an independent cooperative press supporting and guiding authors and artists in their creative projects.

Visit www.crystalheartimprints or Book Cooperative Association | Crystal Heart Imprints | United States for more information.

Voices In The Wind

Eye To Eye With Hurricane Ian

BEVERLY OBERLINE

Who is screaming? Please tell me there isn't someone out there in this storm. I can't see anyone—but—what is that noise? It sounds exactly like someone—no, more than one—many people—screaming! What is happening?

The hurricane grew wilder as I watched its approach through the window. The shingle roof on the long paint company building across the alley shuddered and whipped around in the wind, held only by its straps. Rain blew in horizontal sheets.

The palms twisted, shaking and buckling, bending wildly forward and backward. Their movements made me think of the crazy tube men used in advertising.

Unknown objects began hitting our building. The hurricane proper had barely begun. We had hours to go. It would only get worse.

Somehow, I had to shut it out and make it through.

Closing my eyes, I began deep and evenly spaced breaths, gradually willing myself into a meditative state. Shutting off the noise from outside, I began to feel lighter, my conscious self lifting away from my physical self. Soon, I welcomed the floating sensation of astral projection. I could see my actual body, seated in my chair.

Looking down at corporeal me, I knew my heart to be on the verge of panic mode. My lungs wanted to gasp and hyperventilate with anxiety. Despite those visceral instincts, my rhythmic, deep breathing kept me seated and still in the chair.

The violent weather continued outside. Adrenaline spiked through my veins, a fight-or-flight cocktail. Only years of regular meditation practice and breathwork—using yogic breathing patterns—allowed me to keep my breathing at a slow, deep, intentional and measured pace. There is no denying I felt scared, but I also accepted a certain inevitability: whatever was going to happen would happen.

All these coping mechanisms worked pretty well until I heard those voices in the wind.

A Little History

I have lived on Pine Island in Florida since March 2019 and love it here. Yes, it is the decimated Pine Island you've seen on the news in September 2022 and later on the cover of Time Magazine's Year in Review. The "authorities" planned to outright condemn the whole place until our people started building and repairing the washed-out road anyway. The island was nearly destroyed, but we refuse to be victims. We are building back together with the help of thousands of wonderful volunteers and organizations. That's where I live and I'm so proud of it and of all our people.

Around 2014, I visited a close friend and co-worker, Teresa, who lived on Pine Island and I fell in love at first sight. The island was not over-developed and had a slow pace, an Old Florida feel that I loved.

This place also has a long history of fierce independence. It was originally inhabited by the Calusa (or Caloosa, spellings vary). They were such ferocious fighters that most other inhabitants left them and their territory strictly alone. The Spanish conquistadors were so impressed with their tenacity and fighting that they wrote about them in their campaign histories. Shell mounds still stand here, which the Calusa built. Much of the shell all over the island comes from other mounds, which were leveled.

Maybe it's the water, maybe it's the sun. Maybe the Calusa left something. Maybe it's being a barrier island, the last point of land before the big water. Whatever it is, there is a sense of crackling magic all over this island.

I decided then, whatever it took, I would move here.

Upon returning to Illinois, I utilized intense visualization, manifestation rituals, and positive energy to generate the result I wanted. It wasn't long before Teresa was looking for a roommate. With generous, practical help from the folks who love me, I became that roommate. My dream of living in Florida had come true.

Most everybody immediately visualized lazing on the beach when I said I was moving to an island. This is an island created from mangroves, though, so there are not a lot of beaches. The lazy days of bikinis, boat drinks, and baby oil are way back in my rearview mirror. I'm here for the palm trees, warm temperatures, and island breezes.

Naturally, one of the big concerns about moving to a southern coastal area in the US is hurricanes. But everybody has some kind of natural disaster in their area, so you might as well just accept the odds if you like where you're living, and I do. I love it.

My first couple of hurricanes were Category 1 or Category 2 and mostly rain and wind events. Honestly, they were nothing more than extended versions of a loud Midwestern thunderstorm in July. They were a little windier and a little wetter. They lasted longer but were not scary.

In late September 2022, however, Hurricane Ian was predicted to become a Category 4 as it moved through the Gulf. The weather prognosticators kept talking about wind shear coming south off Alabama and Mississippi, which would slow it down. That meant their actual prediction was a Category 2 at landfall up around Tampa. That's not far from us—just a couple hours up the road—but the difference between being in the bull's eye and in one of the outer bands is often enough in hurricanes.

It's late for a hurricane, too. Though the season runs through November 30, a late September/early October hurricane is not all that common. It made it "remarkable." We didn't know then how remarkable it would be.

Decisions

September 23, 2022—Friday afternoon. The approaching hurricane's landfall is predicted for the following Tuesday, late in the day. I'm pulling things together for a "go bag" in case we need to bug out. I heard the clear voice in my head, the one I don't dare ignore, and it said, *Buy a weather radio.*

Oh yeah, I forgot, my old one croaked.

Amazon had one that could get to me on Monday; plenty of time. It had an additional AM-FM band which I didn't think would matter, but soon enough that would be our only connection to the outside world for days.

The period over the weekend was watchful waiting. This was accompanied by numerous and varied opinions from friends, old-timers, sea captains, weather people, folks who have been through many hurricanes, and folks who have been through none. It may sound odd, but the watchful waiting is unnerving in its boredom.

Are there things to do? Yes, and we did them.

We battened down the patio furniture on the back porch.

We moved the glass table top behind the big storage cabinet.

We locked the shed doors.

We took down wind chimes.

We tied or brought in anything that could blow away or become weaponized if it did.

We did laundry, so if or when we seriously packed a bag, we'd have clean clothes—and clean clothes to come home to.

We cooked, ate, and shared what we could of the food in the refrigerator and freezer.

We made a last trip for extra supplies, animal food, food for us that required no refrigeration, and batteries.

We put as much gas in the car as it would hold.

We waited and we watched.

I replenished my altar. I called in all the magical and metaphysical help I could muster from guides, ancestors, deities, angels and archangels. I said prayers. I asked for protection and safety for those I loved, human and animal. I asked for our little home to remain whole. I opened my heart and sent it out to the Universe. I put a message on social media asking for protection and prayers for our little piece of paradise.

During my move, someone remarked that at least with a hurricane, I'd have more warning than a tornado. Give me a tornado any day. You can duck and cover and it'll be gone in fifteen minutes. This thing has the longest telegraphed punch in the world, and then it won't fucking leave.

Fast forward to Tuesday morning, September 27, 2022. This storm has taken on a life of its own. Not only is it not slowing, it is growing. Each time they show a satellite or hurricane hunter's view of it, it is bigger. The state of Florida is 447 miles long and about ninety miles wide where we are. So, with a storm 400 miles wide, like this one, it means most of us, in some way or another, will get clobbered. But they're still predicting a Category 2 at landfall, with landfall still designated for Tampa.

Huh?

Yes, I can hear you now, see you shaking your head. Simple good sense tells you this thing will not politely put on the brakes and slow from a CAT4 to a CAT2 just to hit Tampa. But we listened to the reporters on the weather channel. They're supposed to be the experts.

As well, we were both waffling and dragging our feet. Teresa didn't want to leave her house. I didn't either.

Built with love and care, the folks she purchased it from had it blessed. Add in Teresa's Creek and Cherokee juju, my Norse, some good old-fashioned hoodoo and witchery, and it has a pretty serious metaphysical bubble. Some people locally call it the "castle house" because it has a turret. Painted a cheerful pale yellow with blue and white trim, it's framed with tropical palms, bromeliads and bougainvillea.

The open interior has skylights, stairs leading to a loft, and charming stained glass. It is unique, beautiful and unexpected.

All of its physical attributes are lovely, but it is the soul of this house that is amazing and welcoming. While Teresa's taste runs more toward traditional and mine toward Southwestern, oddly enough, her sage greens and dusty roses work perfectly with my desert cacti, turquoises, and corals. Our combined home has become an eclectic blend of Illinois, Alabama, the Southwestern US, Florida, mermaids, witches, wolves, and alligators. It truly is a magical place.

More importantly, it is a hurricane code house: Made of cement block, it has hurricane windows—windows made to withstand extreme wind speeds—and it's raised slightly off the level of the road in front and set on a foundation, which is essential given that we are on an island and need protection from the surge.

Storm surge is water from the ocean that is pushed toward the shore by the sheer force of winds. It combines with normal tides and can cause extensive damage.

Water was our primary concern as predictions of devastating surge heights increased. Wind-wise, this house had withstood Charley's 150-mile-an-hour winds and Irma's 143-mile-an-hour winds without a scratch. It was the surge predictions that would tip the scale.

The road we're situated on is called Stringfellow. It is the main north-south road running the length of the island. There's only one way on and one way off this island. Pine Island Road crosses Stringfellow at "The Center," home of our only traffic device—a four-way stop sign—and runs through a little art enclave and the village of Matlacha (say: MATT la shay) to the mainland. There's a drawbridge on the road over Matlacha Pass, but when winds are over forty-five miles per hour, the cops won't let you cross it. So, we had a choice to make.

Seems silly, doesn't it? It's a hurricane, ladies, GTFO! Yeah, well, it just isn't that easy.

First of all, where do you go? By Monday, the news reported no hotel vacancies of any kind across Alligator Alley and on to the East Coast. The storm was headed north where I-75 turns into a parking lot during evacuations. I'd far rather stay in the house than be parked on the interstate with all of our animals trapped in a car during a hurricane.

South of us are the Everglades, with hunting camps and cabins. But it floods like nobody's business, leaving you stuck there with all the gators and mosquitos even if you do make it through the storm. West is straight into the Gulf—and straight in the path of the hurricane—now stalling to a ridiculously slow speed of eight miles per hour with interior winds pushing 140!

Secondly, if we do go, what do we take? The animals for sure, so that's two large cat condos and one cat crate, plus the Shih Tzu who rides with Teresa. Then we decided that if we chose evacuation, we would go in my SUV and leave Teresa's sedan for fear of getting separated or breaking down on the road and being unable to put everything in one vehicle.

But we would need more than just the animals.

Clothes, toiletries, shoes, medications—it's an enormous amount—enough to last for an unknown number of days.

Add batteries and battery-operated lanterns and other devices because the power *will* go out and all stores will be closed for the immediate aftermath.

Blankets and pillows because we're not entirely sure of the sleeping arrangements, but we know they don't involve freshly made beds.

Cash. With the power outages, ATMs will not work and all purchases will be cash only for days, possibly weeks.

What about good jewelry? Leave it, hoping we'll be back in a couple of days, or drag it along?

Important papers?

Keepsakes? Everything we own is potentially about to be destroyed!

It's overwhelming.

And it's nearly impossible to process, thinking of the next thing and the next. I began to think we'd need at least a box truck to get it all, if not an eighteen-wheeler. It's also painful because the choices being made may mean the last time I touched something I consider precious might have been the last. We simply had no room and we knew what that might mean.

We had almost convinced ourselves to stay, each in our own private way. Our friend, Mike, had asked if he could shelter at our house. His rental was at the island's south end, down several feet off the road and backed up by a canal, so he would most certainly have the excessive flooding predicted for the storm surge. He brought his furbaby, Miss Kitty, and they settled in.

My business partner, Misty, and her family were sheltering in our shop in Cape Coral, about twenty miles inland. Our landlord and her family had sheltered there from other storms, so we knew the building to be solid and sturdy. She invited us to come over, and we decided if we did leave, that's where we would go.

Tuesday, midafternoon. The raging storm is traveling so slowly that landfall predictions are pushed to Wednesday afternoon. Still, the skies are the color of late evening dusk, though it's only about 3 o'clock. Rain is becoming more persistent. It is not pouring down but plenty steady, enough to soak you in a minute. Looking at the weather channel again, I was starting to feel antsy.

Misty voice-texted me at that moment and said, "Don't wait too long to get off the island."

That's all she said. But Misty is an island girl right down to her soul, and she got stuck on the island during Charley because they waited too long. I'd heard those stories, and there was that little something in her voice making my spidey sense go all jangly.

Just about the moment I was going to tell Teresa I thought we had to evacuate, she called to me from the other room and said she'd been looking at wind speeds and timing. The winds were predicted to reach forty-three miles per hour at four in the morning, and neither of us wanted to wait. If we were going, we needed to do it now or not at all.

All right, we agreed. We're evacuating.

The decision is made. It was more difficult than I would have ever thought. But there was no time to think of all the possible loss. Now, we had to move with purpose.

We asked Mike to come with us but he chose to stay. He helped us load up the car and sent us on our way.

With my heart in my throat, we headed inland. The cats were meowing in protest but our Shih Tzu, Lucy, was fairly calm. I can only imagine Teresa's emotions as she left this home she had loved for fifteen years. I've only been here since 2019, and I had tears in my eyes. Driving away from all we knew and held dear, watching our friend waving from the porch, not knowing if we would see him or the house again—we were genuinely driving off into the unknown.

Okay, Bev. This is real. I am driving into a hurricane. Now is the time to welcome in the metaphysical protection and divine intervention requested and to trust the magic I've lived and breathed for decades.

I grew up in the Midwest, learning to drive in every kind of weather. My dad taught me how to handle most situations, and I'm confident in my driving ability, but it's a good thing we left when we did. The wind speed was under forty-five or we couldn't have made it across the bridge.

The word on the island telegraph is that the cops will keep you from going across the bridge. Lee County Sheriff's Office says they won't stop you, but they will recall all first responders when sustained wind speed exceeds forty-five. The simple truth is it's foolish to try to cross any elevated and open surface during high winds.

Whatever the wind speed at the time we left, I had trouble keeping my vehicle on that bridge and then the road. Every gust tried to hydroplane us across the lanes. No wiper speed existed that would keep the windshield clear, and I silently prayed there were no other cars we were about to be blown into. Traffic was understandably light, but there were still others on the road.

The car was silent except for the cats protesting now and then. Lucy remained surprisingly quiet, snugged up against Teresa's leg. They all seemed to have an intuitive understanding that we were deep in the shit.

My hands hurt from gripping the steering wheel. I could feel Teresa sending me driving vibes as we both tried to see something—anything. We could only see sheets of rain as we drove through them, as we came upon the next one, or it came upon us. It was impossible to tell which as the wind seemed to be coming from every direction. I just hoped I didn't hear a sickening crunch or feel a jolting stop that meant we had hit something… Or someone.

We white-knuckled it to Cape Coral and got to our shop, Sister Moon, where Misty and her family welcomed us. We were all soaked to the skin as they helped us unload the car. It was wet and slick on the open stairs as the rain blew in from the bottom and top.

But, at last, we made it inside. Our shop is on the second floor, putting us above the projected surge. We were with close friends. We changed from wet to dry clothes and began getting settled into what is normally my shop office. We felt safe. We breathed collective sighs of relief.

The sky continued to darken, and the rain intensified.

My office room contains a small table, two chairs for Tarot reading, and a massage table for my Reiki clients. There's a fairly good-sized easy chair, an ottoman, and a six-drawer chest for storage. We rapidly filled the space to beyond capacity with our traveling menagerie. We worried about our friends who chose to stay on the island, but were happy and relieved to be dry and safe and with good company.

Despite her protests, I decided Teresa should sleep on the massage bed and I would sleep in the big chair. We turned the AC down as far as we could stand it, knowing that it would quickly get hot once the power went out. We watched the wind and rain out the window. Like the storm itself, everything seemed to move in slow motion, but the increase in wind speed and volume of rain was steady and obvious.

By Wednesday morning, our world had become shades of gray. Day was notable only by a slight lessening of the grayness. It was impossible to know what time it was without looking at a clock.

By early afternoon, we still had phone service and knew from weather updates that the hurricane was getting close to landfall. Noise from the wind ratcheted up and up again, and kept on, becoming louder and louder.

Suddenly, the lights went out. Then back on. They flickered a few times while we heard electric circuits humming outside and transformers popping in the distance. Then, they were done. That was the last time we had power for two weeks.

One thing about a metaphysical shop, we have lots and lots of candles. Misty had just finished a large pour for an upcoming sale so we had altar candles everywhere. I kept an altar on top of the chest in my office and it now contained a half dozen tall glass candles. There are stones and crystals up there as well, so the result was sparkling and quite pretty. It reflected in the windows and gave a warm, comforting feeling. Blurring my eyes slightly, I looked at the image in the window and tried to forget—for just a moment— what was going on outside.

We were also using personal battery lanterns that are lightweight and extremely bright. We had ice in coolers, gallons of water, food, and snacks. Despite the oncoming danger, we felt ready.

I can hear the Universe laughing.

In 2004, Hurricane Charley hit almost the same place as Hurricane Ian in 2022. But Charley moved much faster than Ian, and he was much smaller. The entire hurricane of Charley fit into the eye of Hurricane Ian. A local TV meteorologist posted that image—tiny Charley inside massive Ian's eye—just before the power went out. It was one of the last visuals any of us had on our phones. My thought when I first saw the picture was, *We are so screwed.*

Hurricane Ian had slowed yet again, moving at an abysmal seven miles per hour. Just think of that math. The storm itself is 400 miles wide. It's moving forward at only seven-miles-per-hour, but the wind speed inside the storm is 150-miles-per-hour.

The storm is almost sitting still but its internal winds are vacuuming up whatever it passes over. Everything it has picked up—giant yachts and sailboats, cars and trucks, pieces of homes, enormous trees—is now battering the land like an angry giant with a monstrous scrub brush. It is also sucking up tons of water from the Gulf into its intense rain. Combined with the incoming tides, surge waters ran inland for miles and miles.

We are about twenty miles inland. It may not be enough.

Hurricane Ian

Hurricane Ian slammed into Cayo Costa, a beautiful pristine key ten miles northwest of Pine Island, at 3:05 p.m. on Wednesday, September 28, 2022. Wind speed inside the storm was 155 miles per hour at landfall, only one mile per hour shy of a Category 5 hurricane.

I knew Hurricane Ian would be much more than the CAT1 and CAT2's I had experienced since moving here, but my mind reacted the same as it did the first time I saw the Grand Canyon. My eyes saw it, my retina registered it, and my brain said, *No fuckin' way.*

Way.

Throughout, I sat there in the big easy chair in front of the window. Teresa perched on the massage table, leaning against the wall with Lucy, and the cats had found spots where they felt safe in this new and strange place with all the nervous humans. Ben, our sharp-dressed-man Tuxedo, claimed a spot in a corner behind a little open bookshelf. Monet, the Torty diva ballerina, was parked under the legs of the little metal table. Shadow, our little fire-breathing dragon black cat, stood watch on the back of the easy chair.

I knew I should not be in front of the window. Truth is, there is nowhere in our shop without a window except the tiny hall and the small bathroom. But I also knew there was nowhere else I *could* be. It defies logic and explanation. I felt held in the chair, almost by a giant hand. I could barely lever myself up to use the restroom. I felt I had to witness it, somehow.

I didn't understand until I heard the voices. When the realization dawned that these were the voices of those who perished in hurricanes back through time, my eyes filled with tears and sadness flowed from my heart. The horror worsened as I soon understood these voices included those losing their fights for life in this hurricane, at this moment.

We who can hear them are their witnesses.

It went on forever—the screaming sounds, the howling wind, the sheets of rain, the sheer noise of the thing, the violence—the storm forever seeking the slightest chink in our building's armor so it could come in and tear it apart and scatter us to the four directions. It went on and on and on and on.

Rain pelted the window. The cats meowed now and then. Periodically, Lucy barked at something unknown or unseen. Teresa and I stared at each other, wide-eyed, with breaths held at every loud bang or thump on the roof. Brutal wind gusts hammered the building so hard we wondered how it could hold. In the following seconds, our collective breaths expelled as we understood we were still whole, here, intact. Before we could catch another full breath, the cycle began again.

We didn't speak much; hardly at all. Every ounce of our energy was focused on our safety, taking care of the furkids, and holding our building in a protective space.

It is brutal to the psyche to be forced to simply watch. We prepared as well as we could. The only thing left to do was await the outcome. We were at its mercy.

The authorities say the storm was over us for something like twelve hours. It felt like twelve years.

Imagine a twelve-hour day where you are subjected to the same, repetitive phrase without pause, and you had no way to shut it off and nowhere to go to escape it.

There was only a short break for the eye to pass during that time, maybe thirty minutes.

For the remainder, the winds blew and blew. We heard shingles tumbling off the roof and then saw them fly away into the mist and the darkness. An eerie light was over everything. Even through the night when it should have been pitch, you could still see the tops of the palms twisting, shivering and shaking.

I felt so bad for the trees. They were blowing backward and forward, not even a second of rest, just blowing and blowing and blowing. It left you breathless.

The roof of the building across the alley from us alternately fascinated us and frightened us. It undulated, it flapped, it rolled up and back down again. We could see it straining against the tethering roof straps as it tried to fly away with the wind. We held our breath each time and thought surely it would let go. Fortunately, it did not.

With each of those held breaths came other thoughts: *Will that roof blow into our building? Will our roof hold? Is our roof strapped? If the roof goes, will the building fall? Will we be sucked out into the storm?* With every loud noise we thought, *Is this it?*

Through it all, like a demented soundtrack, were the voices.

For seemingly endless hours, the voices in the wind screamed. It reminded me of Legolas hearing the "fell voice" on the wind while trying to get over Caradhras. It soon became clear these were not evil voices. They were pitiful. They were sorrowful and crying, howling and screaming in terror. They begged for help and, if there was no help, for release.

I heard them every single time the wind whipped around the corner, and at 150 miles per hour, that is a lot of voices. It chilled me through my bones. I saw clear visual impressions of people in clothing from the era of the terrible Galveston hurricane in 1900.

Teresa heard voices too, but she heard more detailed speech, ancient old Spanish dialogues, and something she somehow knew was Calusa. She saw their faces, the conquistadors and the Indians.

She also had the impression of the folks who did not have the economic opportunity or ability to move themselves out of harm's way. So many were taken in disproportionate numbers, just like with Katrina in New Orleans. This systemic societal injustice still exists and she could feel their collective anger.

I saw others in the dress of various decades. There have been centuries of hurricanes here with countless thousands of fatalities and they all wanted to be heard.

One friend of ours said she heard a "chorus of voices" throughout the storm, and yet another said she heard "demons screaming" in the wind.

Later, when the adrenaline ran out of my brain and I could put coherent thoughts together again, I began to wonder if we, like rabbits, emit that one last horrible cry as we leave this realm. Whether we vocalize it or hear it in our heads, I think it imprints on our souls, and those of us who walk between the worlds can hear them at certain times. Air from the lungs passing over the vocal cords causes the vibration that makes the sound, after all. Why shouldn't we emit one last vocalization as the air leaves our bodies?

It wasn't words in particular, and nothing was recognizable as "conversation." But what we heard was formed by the vibratory activity of human vocal cords.

There were thousands upon thousands of those unformed sounds, the kind we all make when hurt. Many were cries of shock, then pain. We heard furious screams of frustration. Some were pure primal howls.

There were others, moans of pain and whimpers of futility. I heard snatches of prayers and entreaties, pleas to somehow be saved. Most of it was incoherent, screaming in horror at the awful realization of the situation and its likely fatal end.

Groans, sobs, wails, keening, and pleading were the continuous background. These are the sounds humans make when we are being battered without ceasing by the ferocious wind, rain, and all the deadly debris within it.

I heard this throughout the hurricane as it blew. I saw flashes and short visions of folks being overwhelmed by collapsing buildings, blown off balconies and roofs, and slipping from capsizing boats.

Teresa recently told me I kept asking, "When will it stop? It has to stop." I have no recollection of asking that aloud, although I do remember thinking it. Until she mentioned it, I had no idea I gave actual voice to it and still can't summon the memory to consciousness.

For twelve hours, the cacophony of screaming wind, blowing rain, and flying debris went on. Over it all were the wailing voices and I could do nothing but listen.

I've never heard anything more heart-rending in my life. I hope I never hear it again.

At some point, the sky lightened, and the wind lowered. For a moment, we could almost see a patch of blue in the west. But we knew it to be a false hope as it was only the eye passing over us. Too few short relieving breaths and then, the blow began again in earnest, this time from the opposite direction.

The wind, as it will, had been finding its way in throughout the storm. Windows and doors were shut, locked and bolted where possible, and still the wind came in. My office door banged back and forth in its jamb as though someone was smashing it from the other side. The other doors in the shop did the same.

Now, with the wind from the opposite direction, the noises continued and the wind shrieked. You read that in novels, "the wind shrieked." Have you ever heard the wind truly shriek? It's not a thing you want to experience. It sounds evil and it sounds mean. On this side of the storm, the wind became demanding and angry. All the energy within it hammered wind and water and every material thing it could get its hands on full at whomever or whatever was foolhardy enough to stand in its way. It screamed with all the power and spine-chilling vehemence of a banshee. There could be no doubt it was heralding death.

I know why psychological torture is effective. The continual pounding of unknown objects hitting the roof, the worry of whether the roof remained sound, the whining screaming wind, and the breathtaking headache-pounding adrenaline ride that goes with it cannot be easily borne for very long.

With the passing of the eye and now facing the eye wall—what is called the "dirty" side of the hurricane—we were looking square into the storm surge.

The realization that this moment had finally dawned caused our fear to intensify as we worried anew for our many friends riding it out on Pine Island.

Misty called us to the front of the building, and as we looked down, we watched the parking lot begin to fill with water. All of Cape Coral is built on and around canals. Some of them go out to the big water, and some of them go nowhere. (Honestly, nowhere, but that's another story.) All of them have water, the one thing at this moment no one needed.

Storm surge is an abnormal rise of water generated by a storm over and above the predicted astronomical tide. The weather talking heads predicted a five-foot storm surge, then nine feet, then fifteen, now twenty. A single-story house with a flat roof is fourteen to fifteen feet high.. A two-story house with a pitched roof is twenty-five to thirty feet tall. A twenty-foot storm surge anywhere on inhabited land would be devastating and deadly.

By now, with the power out, only the weather radio remained. Other than hurricane and tornado warnings—and warnings about the coming surge—it didn't have a lot of new information. We could only watch and wait.

It was during this time that I became aware of very brief, almost nanosecond flashes of blinding, brilliant light. My mind could see this somehow, cutting through the winds. It took a minute, but I realized the rare times I have seen those flashes, they have been associated with the Archangel Michael and his flaming sword. I won't give the hurricane sentience, but I knew whatever malevolence may have been taken up in the whirling winds was now being dispatched with savage efficiency.

In one or the other of the weather run-throughs, they began to predict a lowering of winds to forty to seventy-five miles an hour. In other circumstances, that would sound awful. To us, it was a tremendous gift. A 75-mile-an-hour wind after a 144-mile-an-hour wind is nothing but a stiff breeze. It meant less debris loosened and less chance of severe roof damage or broken windows.

It meant that the storm was moving away.

Best of all, when the winds finally began to lessen, so did the voices. I only heard them now and again if the wind whipped tightly around a corner.

Admittedly, I was blocking them as best I could, trying to not listen, to not hear. Throughout the storm, I was shocked out of my meditative state either by some unknown sound or our conversation. I would return each time to my rhythmic breathing and there I conjured my favorite concert moments, wolves howling, loons calling, whatever I could concentrate on for a few seconds not to hear anything from outside.

By now, I was worn out and numb. Holding the concentration required to alter my consciousness was starting to slip beyond me. That unchanging, pummeling wind wears you down mentally. It made me feel helpless. At this point I begged for it just to *stop*.

After another few hours of forty to seventy-five mile per hour winds, it dropped to thirty-six miles per hour, and finally, it was still.

It was Thursday morning. We'd been pummeled by this storm and the howling voices since late Tuesday night. We had no power. We had no internet. We had no phone service. We had hurricane snacks, water, juice and soda. We had a toilet and buckets of water to flush it.

We were frightened for our friends on the island but could do nothing.

This part was over.

We were alive.

All of us, humans and animals, fell into an exhausted sleep.

Aftermath

Sleep didn't last long. We had too much adrenaline still pumping and we needed information. Cell service was out all over Southwest Florida. Hot spots and wifi didn't work consistently. Our phones would light up but no messages could download. Only rarely could we call out. Misty's phone would work in fits and starts. She came into the room and said, "Bert's is gone."

Bert's was a large, well-known bar just across the bridge in Matlacha. It did a land-office business all the hours it was open. Snowbirds and islanders alike spent many happy hours in Bert's. Our response was, "What do you mean, gone?"

"Gone," she said. "It is no more. It is gone. Blown away."

"No, that can't be right. Can it? Surely not."

"It's gone. Nothing left but pilings."

Throughout the storm, I saw with my third eye a bubble of protection around us and the house on Pine Island. All my family, friends and witchy sisters and brothers sent us every kind of protection and love throughout the storm. Peering out of my mind's eye, I could see the bubble placed around us and the one around the house. Imagine being in one of those clear bulbs you buy to make a holiday ornament. We were in our personal snow globe—except with bending palms and no snow—but still, protected, and safe inside.

Was this only wishful thinking? Bert's was maybe seven miles from our house by road. It was probably no more than three miles as the crow flies.

Now, I tried again to visualize the house. I saw it standing, still within that bubble. I saw Teresa's car at the fence with trees from the lot next door blown over it.

A few minutes later, Misty returned and said, "The Bridgewater is in the road."

"Whaaaaat?"

The Bridgewater was a sizeable hotel right at the approach to the drawbridge over Matlacha Pass and next door to Bert's.

Teresa said, "How can it be in the road?"

"It's in the road. Their red metal roof is lying across the road. I just saw a picture of it."

Oh, this is bad. This is very bad.

Throughout this time, we were trying to take advantage of the brief moments the phones were working to call or text anyone we knew who had stayed on the island. We did not know then, but there were over 1500 cell towers down in Southwest Florida. Service didn't exist. That Misty's phone worked at all was miraculous.

Not long after we tried to wrap our heads around the information about Bert's and the Bridgewater, Misty said, "You guys, the bridge is out."

"What bridge?"

"The bridge. At Matlacha. It's gone. You can't get across."

Do you remember me mentioning there was one road to get on and off the island? The bridge she's talking about is on that road.

The frustration at the inability to communicate is unimaginable. I could see texts from family and friends wanting to know our status but what we typed could not be sent in return. Trying to find information about our friends and our home, about the island itself, was an exercise in futility. Any activity on the phone became a dead end nine out of ten times. Worse, with no power, the only way to recharge the phones was to run the cars, which required burning gas. Everything seemed to be a catch-22.

At the shop, with no power anywhere in Cape Coral, we could not make hot coffee but still had ice so we had iced left-over coffee. The second day, the ice had melted but we had some canned double espresso shots. Those worked pretty well, even at room temperature.

Now, the little AM-FM band on the weather radio began to pay off. Knowing the barrier islands, coastal areas, and much of the county had no power for TV, our local news and weather stations joined in and went straight to simulcast radio, focused on all things hurricane, twenty-four/seven. They welcomed folks calling in to ask for help and kept lists for referrals. They broadcast locations and links where people could get food, medical assistance, showers, baby food, animal food, water, gas, and anything and everything.

I was impressed with this broadcast group and the way they responded. Some of the on-air personnel also lost their homes but still showed up. It created solidarity. They truly did empathize with what people were going through. They didn't have to imagine it because they were going through it themselves.

People were also calling in and telling stories of escape and survival that would make you marvel or tear up and shudder. To hear any one of them will confirm your belief in magic and miracles.

An eighty-something friend of ours spent the storm sitting on her kitchen counter with family members and their two little dogs parked in the sink, watching the water rise higher and higher. Her brother, in his seventies, had a leg wound and was forced to spend hours standing on the folding ladder into the attic to avoid the bacteria-laden water.

Mike stepped out of our house to film the surge and the wind yanked the door out of his hands, slammed it shut and locked it. He was able to wade in knee-deep sea water to the back door and find it unlocked, but it was the longest walk of his life, not knowing if there was a way back into the house.

Another friend went to the home of an older couple to shelter where they all thought it would be safe. Instead, it took all three of them holding the door to keep it from blowing open throughout the storm.

How does any of that happen if not for magic and miracles?

And then it is silent.

Moving through the following days, surviving only with whatever is available, hammers home the realization of how vulnerable we are without our big growling electronic grid. Once it's gone, we are genuinely at a loss.

Gasoline sat in the underground tanks but the stations were without power to pump it.

ATMs had cash but no power to run them and no communication to reach the banks. Everything is cash only. No cash? Sorry, can't help you.

Restaurants were throwing out food because they couldn't cook it or keep it.

Mail could not be delivered as most roads were impassable.

What few phones could connect found the service so unreliable as to be no service at all.

The internet was down. You can't just say, "Google it," and look up the hurricane damage or what streets are open.

Without working traffic lights—and no cops directing traffic—you're on your own.

Every single thing becomes such an effort. Once you are down to a half tank of gas, you'd better start looking at topping that off. We drove miles between available stations. Each of them had lines reaching around two full blocks. Stress is high—if the station runs out of gas before you get to the pump, you run the risk of running entirely out of gas because you've burned it all waiting in line!

It was the same for free food. Many restaurants powered up generators and began cooking everything that was still good to give it away. But if you were more than a few miles away, the food might be gone by the time you get there or the line so long it's not worth burning the gas to wait.

And those non-working traffic lights I mentioned? Consider all the cowboys, the road ragers, the forever undecided drivers out there... The police asked everyone to treat each traffic light as a four-way stop. Ha! Reality looked like the Wild West.

Tempers were past short. A woman trying to make a U-turn through a gas station lot found herself staring down the barrel of a pistol. Another woman who'd been waiting hours in the queue for gas thought the first lady was trying to cut in, so she pulled out her gun. Fortunately, that situation was defused and no one hurt.

Add to all this fun stuff, the fact that I'm just stunned. My body is still running on adrenaline, though it's now wearing on my nerves almost as much as the storm. It's like a hard hit to the head. I kept shaking my head to clear it, blinking my eyes wider because my brain said the destruction I saw could not be what I saw. We started calling it "hurricane brain."

It's a very schizoid existence. Some things are awful and unbelievable. Others make you smile and laugh, like our bathing experiences.

We bathed in a bucket. In truth, Misty made that more than tolerable; it was enjoyable. In the warm months, an open-air bath in Florida is fairly pleasant.

She set up a little spa in the stairwell where no one could see (we were the only folks in the building). Somehow, she put together fluffy towels, every kind of bath, body, or hair product you could need, and she was available to pour, rinse, or hold up the towel. After a night and day of stress sweat, it was refreshing, elevating our moods despite the mess and destruction around us.

Another dear friend, Lucy, lives just down the street from the shop. She invited us to a tub shower once their generators were cranked up. It was a little chilly but it was wonderful!

The first four or five days were just involved with finding actual food.

As restaurants and gas stations began to open with generators and limited menus, we could get most everything needed. But with partially blocked or flooded roadways, it still took hours each day to locate, gather, and bring it back.

Our good friend, Jess, sheltered with her family and friends in Fort Myers. They watched their cars float away on the surge as they scrambled for the attic. Fortunately, the water stopped just in time and they were safe, but their vehicles were long gone.

The next day, without even knowing where their cars ended up, they all went to work. They gathered food and formed a pop-up food pantry. These good folks continued it for several weeks, and helped us and hundreds of others immeasurably. They made food available and ensured we could pick it up or someone would deliver it.

One of Jess' co-workers spent a day driving back and forth from Miami with her SUV packed with ice for delivery. Because of the region-wide boil order, there was not a cube to be had on our side of the state.

The surge had overrun the water treatment plants and broken water mains, destroying roads. That resulted in the boil order, which resulted in no available ice. Restaurants could not use their ice machines to make ice, so they served refrigerated drinks in cans and bottles.

The only ice available was being brought in by refrigerated trucks. Like everything else, it was rarely worth the gas for the trip only to find out the truck was already emptied.

Teresa and I will never take ice for granted again.

Finally, the Publix a block from our shop opened. We still couldn't cook or heat anything, but fresh subs and sliders tasted like three-star Michelin fare at that point!

One of the only messages to get through to us, sent from a dear friend, was a NOAA satellite picture of our house. It was standing with no obvious damage. There were trees blown down everywhere but not directly on the house. So we had hope.

No Current Plans to Repair

About this time, the admin of a Pine Island recovery group on Facebook posted a copy of a notice from the Lee County EOC that Pine Island was "decimated," that the infrastructure was "devastated," and that the island was "uninhabitable." Worse, there was "no current plan" or "any long-term plan" for the "foreseeable future" to repair the bridge at Matlacha, our only way of getting on and off the island.

Teresa and I both screamed, "But our house isn't devastated. It's standing. We can see it. What do you mean we can't go back on the island? Everything is there. They can't just take it!"

We also learned folks were being "evacuated"—airlifted—off the island to shelters with their pets and what little they could carry. This happened not necessarily "at gunpoint," but without option by uniformed individuals wearing side-arms (you can call that whatever you like). A close friend's husband was removed from their home this way, so I know it to be true. (The powers that be are trying to walk that back now, of course.)

We knew anybody with a boat would be shuttling people back and forth to the island, regardless of what anyone (who thought they were) in charge may have to say, and we began in earnest trying to reach our friend Mike so we could sneak back and get at least our keepsakes and computers, and whatever else we could carry. Sure enough, there was a veritable flotilla of watercraft, from canoes to construction barges, willing to shuttle folks across the pass.

Before we could arrange that, however, dock and bridge companies from the island began rebuilding the road, and the radio and TV news covered it wall to wall. Backed into a very public corner, Lee County reevaluated its stance and reopened the island to residents and rebuilding.

Bright Spots In The Darkness

As you might expect after an experience like this, it takes a minute to settle back into your usual self. For a good bit, you're walking the knife edge between hysterical tears and hysterical laughter.

In the first few days after the storm, when we were finally able to get some text and phone messages back and forth to folks on the island, Teresa decided she wanted her laptop.

When we initially evacuated, everyone thought "a few days," so we left our computers at home, presuming we would be back in less than a week and back to work. (There's more universal laughter. Can you hear it?)

She got word to Mike to pack up her computer and get it barged over. As noted, our local bridge and dock builders were barging folks across Matlacha Pass to get to the island for work and repairs and bringing in supplies, whatever was needed.

So, the computer was padded and packed (in a Captain Morgan box, of all things) and brought into Cape Coral. All we had to do was go get it.

Honestly, I thought she was nuts, but Teresa said having her computer, whether she could work or not, would make her feel better. So, off we went on this side quest.

Quest it was!

As mentioned, Cape Coral is built on and around canals. It also has one of the most confusing street configurations I've ever come across. There are multiples of everything. For instance, there may be a 16th Street, Place, Court, Terrace, and a Lane. They usually run parallel, but not always. Sometimes there's a canal in the way. Other times it's the same street but with a different name.

We had to go approximately five miles to pick up this computer at a house address. Teresa put the address in the GPS on her phone and off we went. Our conversation went something like this.

T: "Turn right in 500 feet."

B: "There's a canal in front of us."

T: "No, in 500 feet."

B: "There is no 500 feet unless it's 500 feet of water. There is a canal in front of us."

T: "Are you on NE Eighth Terrace?"

B: "Yes. That's what the sign says."

T: "Then why is there a canal?"

B: "I have no fucking idea. I didn't lay out this street system. Clearly, whoever did was doing some really good drugs."

T: "There shouldn't be a canal there."

B: "And yet…canal."

While Teresa and I love each other like sisters, we can also fight with each other like sisters, so this degenerated fairly quickly.

B: "Don't try to read the map on the phone, just read the directions that are written out."

T: "That's what I've been doing!"

B: "That can't be right! Every time you tell me to turn I can't because there's a fucking canal where there should be a street and then the streets are all backward. I don't know why you want your stupid computer anyway, you can't even work! We don't have wifi or internet at the shop!"

T: "I can work on the wifi across the street!"

B: "You know you can't! It's not secure!"

T: "It makes me feel better, okay? It makes me feel better to have my computer!"

B: {groans, rolls eyes, swears}

T: "Just put me out! Just put me and my dog out right here if you don't want to go get the computer!"

B: "Where, here in the middle of bumfuck Florida? Then what? You can't walk back to the shop. You don't even know where you are and you still don't have your fucking computer!"

T: "What are you doing?"

B: "I'm turning around and we're going back to where we turned off Santa Barbara. I know where that is and we can begin again. We are burning up gas and don't know if we can even find any more today."

T: "I hate this fucking town! Why do we have to drive all over East Jesus just to get my computer?"

B: "Good question. I don't have the answer, but right now, we're going to start over."

About this time, we went past a sign for Tropicana Parkway, one of those big reflective signs, with a post on either side. Half a block later, we went past a regular old corner street sign for Tropicana Parkway, but it pointed in the opposite direction.

Hmmm?

I stopped and backed up, turned another corner and stopped again. Then I began to laugh. I laughed and laughed and laughed.

My laughter earned a good cussing from Miss Teresa and a loud barking from Miss Lucy. In near hysterics, I could barely tell her what I had realized.

Every single street sign had been turned ninety degrees by the wind. They were all still standing and looked perfectly normal, but the sign saying we were on NE Second Place pointed to NE Seventh Terrace and vice versa.

Teresa had been reading the directions and I had been following them to the letter, but the street signs were precisely backward. It wasn't until I passed the big sign for Tropicana and then the little one that I realized what was wrong. When we looked at where we'd been, it fit perfectly. Then we both howled with laughter and the dog, though confused, joined in.

Within 10 minutes, we were at the house to retrieve her laptop. I'm sure the nice lady there thought we were either entirely insane or complete idiots, giggling and babbling about the weird roads and how confusing it is to get around in Cape Coral.

Manifesting Our Power (In The Most Literal Sense)

Our office is located just a block or so from a hospital; if the power goes out, ours comes right back on because we're part of that grid. But in this particular emergency, there was so much damage to the infrastructure, repair was being done only to the absolute "must haves," so we were still dark.

When we first opened, someone gave us a "shop witch." She is a former mannequin, now with dyed green skin and a witchy outfit. We stand her in the hallway and have her hold signs about our classes or special sales. We call her Matilda.

The first few days after the storm were unseasonably cool and we were able to have the windows open. But as we returned to normal fall Florida weather, there were just too many of us crammed in a small space for "fresh" air. We needed air conditioning and soon. We also needed power for medical necessities like Teresa's CPAP machine and refrigerating Monet's insulin.

Power trucks went up and down the street every day and night, but still, our lights didn't come on.

Then Misty had a brilliant idea. She took Matilda and stood her in the parking lot holding a big sign that said, "Three Hot Witches Need Turned On." Folks going past started pointing; some stopped to take pictures and within a few minutes, one of the cable trucks stopped. The guy read the sign, chuckled, and drove off. About five minutes later, *hello*, here comes a truck from the power company. Misty was on the balcony and confirmed we were definitely "hot" and needed our AC. They laughed and a very short time later, on came the power.

We didn't realize until several days later that they had not powered the block but parked a giant generator at the power pole that feeds our building. The power guys were keeping fuel in it twenty-four/seven so we "hot witches" could stay cool!

Reality Bites

Driving through Matlacha on our first trip out to the island was tear-filled and sobering for both Teresa and me. It started out as an old fishing village and much of its charm came from those old fishing shacks made into boutiques and quaint vacation rentals. They were built on fill dirt and pilings. In places, there is now nothing left but pilings. The dirt has washed out nearly to the road. The buildings are either gone or partway in the water, smashed and beyond salvage.

As Misty told us, the Bridgewater Inn, a sizeable hotel, ended up in the middle of the road. Bert's, the long-time popular bar beside it, is simply not there. Restaurants on both sides look like old Western movie sets: there are front walls and signs, but you look through the door, and there's the water out back. Just a front wall is all that's left.

There are areas where there were little vacation places and boutiques, but it's so completely obliterated your mind can't picture what used to be there. There were a couple of older mobile home courts and both endured catastrophic damage. It is obvious people were lost throughout the area, and anyone like us can feel it.

There was a particular place where Teresa almost couldn't breathe as we drove through it. She said she kept seeing the opposite shore in the midst of the storm. There were just a few points of light and she could taste sea water coming into her mouth. She told me, "She drowned. She was drowning. She knew it. I felt it." It took months for that visceral response to begin to lessen for her.

Completely by chance, we recently discovered that someone had drowned in that very spot. Moments after that information was discovered, Teresa heard a very clear voice say, *There is clarity on the other side.*

Within seconds after that, the heaviness and despair she had been feeling for this unknown person began to lift. While she will always honor and remember her, she can now get through the spot without losing her breath.

Our hearts were in our throats the first day we got to our island. Except for Matlacha, Little Pine Island—the connection to Pine Island—is mostly reserve land, so there were downed power poles and trees but not a lot else blocking the road between Matlacha and us.

But the trees broke my heart. Our verdant jungle, our tropical paradise was no more. Broken and felled trees were everywhere. The few palms still standing had torn or crooked crowns. The pines were stripped bare of needles. Spanish moss and air plants—usually hanging everywhere—had blown away. Whatever remained standing was bleached white by the surge water, raising helpless bare branches to the sky.

When we turned at The Center to go home, we both held our breath, wanting to know and afraid to know. Imagine our relief when, as we came down Stringfellow, we could see the top of the roof through the trees, and it was whole! We turned into the drive burst into tears of joy and happiness to see this sweet little house exactly as I had pictured it in my third-eye vision—and from the NOAA photos—standing, intact!

Palms from the lot next door had broken our fence but were not on the roof. Teresa's car looked intact. We lost some trim. Most of the fence was crushed or gone, and what remained was unusable. But the house withstood the storm.

We are blessed and we gratefully and humbly give thanks to every kind of answered request from people who love us all around this country.

We drove south into Saint James City proper, where Ian came ashore on Pine Island, and it was terrible. There are large boatyards and many of those boats were stacked up like cordwood in the road. There were damaged homes, poles broken, and wires and transformers strung everywhere, pieces of roofs and debris in the street, mobile homes obliterated, businesses flooded.

Please understand that the term "debris" isn't a little bit of trash, in this context. Any single pile of "debris" is longer than your car, twice as tall, and often unrecognizable as to its original purpose—boat, truck, jet ski, pool cage, roof. Driving through it was sobering and challenging to absorb.

We made our way around, located friends, and assured ourselves of their status as alive and well. We breathed many sincere thank yous to all that kept us and ours protected and safe.

Power on the island was not restored until mid-October. Neither of us can be without AC long, so we could not live in the house even though it was standing. More friends stepped in and set up a week for us at a hotel, just for a break from us all being stacked in the shop like sardines. We were packing to make that move when Mike called and said the power to our home was restored.

It seemed like we had twice as much stuff this time as we did on the first outing, but we jammed it in the Santa Fe and drove back to Pine Island. We pulled into the driveway, and I think we both exhaled fully for the first time in three weeks.

We were home. Whatever else there is, we'll handle it. Right now, home is enough.

Cleaning Up

We can travel back and forth now without crying, but only just.

Pine Island and its communities of Bokeelia, Pineland, and Saint James City are tearing out and rebuilding. The south end of Saint James City was hit the hardest and it will be a good while before everything is done there.

The folks in Matlacha are also determined to rebuild. Matlacha sits on Little Pine Island, and we're kind of geographically joined at the hip, so we are all one big community. It is heartening to see the rebuilding of lives and property. Business is returning to both places.

Try to imagine the mountains of debris and pieces of life piled up on the sides of the road. "Mountains" is not an exaggeration for the size of the stacks. Initially, most of them were taller than an eighteen-wheeler and went on for miles.

Everywhere you look you see somebody's antique dresser, Grandma's mirror, or a chair that belonged in a child's room. There are broken dishes, warped records, soaked photos, and every kind of cloth item saturated with saltwater and sewage.

Photo Credit Annie Wenz

No one mentions it on the news, but when the surge overruns the treatment plants, the sewage joins the surge. Anything— absolutely anything—that the surge has touched either needs serious bleach/cleaning or it's trash. Most of it has become trash.

It took from October to March to haul it away.

Survival, Loss and Magic

I am happy to report our friends have made it through, for which we are incredibly grateful. While our damages will take time and money to repair, the good news is that *we can* repair them. The previously mentioned foundation kept us out of the surge.

Teresa's car is totaled from the water. She bought another— new to her—and named her Evangeline.

Mike and Miss Kitty survived but had to move. They were able to relocate to the northern end of the island and have been settling into their new place.

Our good snowbird friends are all right and have been back to start repair work. The hugs when we all met again were tearful with relief.

Some of our friends lost everything but what they were wearing. We have cried with them and for them and our hearts continue to hurt as they try to find a way forward.

People died because they had medical issues at the height of the storm and the first responders could not get to them.

Other folks were lost to the sea, the surge, and the storm all over Lee County. We may never know all of their names or exactly how many.

Shortly after returning to the island, we had a friend who went to sleep on her couch and didn't get up again.

Her health hadn't been the best in recent months, but I believe the hurricane was the real catalyst. Just too much stress and strain, worry and fear about the future, and her body couldn't take it.

Truly, everyone who was affected by this storm has PTSD. It is amazing the time it takes to simply get things straight in your mind, even as to chronologic order, because there are days it feels like one long nightmare. Fortunately, several health professionals are offering means of counseling and opportunities to vent.

But that's when you truly, deeply need to believe in the magic and then see it happen.

There is pure magic in the folks who were moved to travel here from all over the country to help and in those who fund the charities that fed thousands of us for nearly two full months for free. There is magic in friends helping friends and supporting each other, in folks still checking in, knowing we're not okay, but we'll get there, who want us to know they still care.

All that is purest magic—it is grace, it is love, it is joy—and it is what will get us through.

I consider myself blessed to have an active life between the realms with many guardian angels, guides, and a host of ancestors. In addition, I am privileged to be friends and sisters with some of the most powerful and loving witches and priestesses there are on this planet. I called on all of them and said we're in the way of this thing and we need your protection, and whoa, did they ever send it!

Whatever grace is given from whatever quarter, from my animal guides to the surprising appearance of Archangel Michael, is humbly accepted with deep gratitude.

The magic here is the magic of community. Given the vibrant tapestry of folks here on the islands—Pine Island and Little Pine Island—whether it's about politics or incorporating, differences of opinion can get loud and angry.

But when it's all falling apart, and you're wondering whether you can ever get past it, here comes a cheerful-looking fellow with a chainsaw over his shoulder saying, "Is this the house where you needed some trees cut up? I can take care of that for you!" And then he does.

You just have to let the magic happen.

Before and After

I am forever changed, as is Teresa. Despite our sturdy little house, any real chance of greater than a CAT3 will see us headed north, tout suite. We are actively creating a working bug-out plan that can be put in place and get us and all we need, battened down, stowed away, packed, and on the road within four hours. If it's a false alarm and we spend a night at a hotel somewhere, we'll make the most of it and enjoy breakfast out the next morning.

We both have PTSD (along with everybody else). There is a wonderful coffee klatch group with weekly meetings on the island now. It's been enlightening to both of us. That PTSD is some sneaky shit. You think you're all right until you realize how much you are not. But, we're getting better, and that's the key.

The animals, too, are different. They hang around together now. They didn't do that quite so much before Ian. The storm took Lucy's hearing, or most of it. We think probably the pressure did it, and she may even have had a little stroke. She's fine now and her usual feisty self. Lack of hearing may be a blessing in disguise as there is less for her to hear that requires barking.

Family and friendships, while never taken for granted, are cherished even more. The sweet gestures from people who have reached out to check on us mean so much. We received so many unexpected gifts: magic beans (coffee), gift cards, cash, and the offer to give us a week at a hotel. Folks who called or dropped a card just to say hello and let us know they care and the ones always available by phone or text twenty-four/seven have all helped us as we make our way through this larger-than-life event. They warmed our hearts and lifted our spirits and we are so grateful.

My magical, metaphysical life is deeper and more alive than ever. I have seen it work and will forever be thankful to all who added their energy and beliefs to keep us safe and well.

****

BEVERLY OBERLINE

Beverly's spiritual journey has been long and rewarding. She is an intuitive Tarot reader, having studied with her dear friend and mentor, Dr. Ruth Souther, for over a decade. She is a working and traveling Initiated Priestess of Vega's Path Priestess Process.

Beverly is a seasoned Holy Fire Karuna Reiki Master, a Shamanic and Drum Reiki practitioner, and has received second level Munay Ki rites.

She has been active with, and served on the BOD of, The Edge of Perception Collective in Springfield, Illinois, offering public and private ritual for all seasons. Bev is an ordained minister of the Sanctuary of Formative Spirituality, a not-for-profit organization committed to spiritual freedom and the support of individual beliefs. Founder – and alpha wolf - of Wolf Spirit Energy, she teaches and reads Tarot and practices Reiki and other energy modalities in Southwest Florida.

For the past three years she has worked in collaboration with Sister Moon Apothecary and More, offering Tarot readings and in-person Reiki, and distant Reiki, Tarot instruction, and her Becoming the Crone class via Zoom. Dubbed "Spiritual Sherpa" by a sister-friend, she offers metaphysical guidance, spiritual growth and understanding to all her clients. Her meditation, "Spirit," is available on Gulf Coast Meditations' Awaken The Spirit Within, with the text published in Writing Is Our Superpower.

Her experience enduring 2022's Hurricane Ian and its aftermath is included here. Bev continues her public ritual work with the The Edge, as well as expanding her writing horizons. She is always in search of new modalities and wisdom to add to her metaphysical repertoire.

Her email is SoulSherpa2023@gmail.com, call or text at 239-940-1404, to schedule in-person Reiki, or Zoom for

Tarot readings, Distant Reiki and classes. Her Spirit meditation is available via Spotify at:

https://open.spotify.com/track/3wBXBMp5v28bYU 4XRrHpWQ?fbclid=IwAR1vI86InuV5Snaampu6957V CHAZ8joc-et5_eJPbmETcAMNZF-26lAhgZ

Lesbian Lament

PEGGY PATTY

I offer a rhythmic singsong
so not to ruffle feathers.
Deep truths are often hard to hear
of the matters we have weathered.

I don't pretend I'm a scholarly author.
My lesbian history is very personal.
We witness vast joys and some losses.
Some damage is irreversible.

I've detailed my memoir in prose before.
Some say I'm just complaining.
So here's my attempt at a lightweight poem
to make my life struggles more entertaining.

My goal in life has always been
to disperse the fog of illusion.
It tends to hold many lies
and to render a wrong conclusion.

Activism flows in Lesbian bloodlines.
Scratch history's surface to disclose.
We, women struggle to aid other women
as rape shelters begun by Dykes show.

Have you ever had to hide your Spouse,
cause it's too dangerous to reveal?
Why are gays required to pretend
doing that is no big deal?

Smart Lesbians remain super vigilant
not to leave core safety to the fates.
Physical & financial dangers befall
when the world won't condone your mate.

Forty years I've remained vigilant
while navigating through my life.
A constant maneuver round folks who say
I must never have a wife.

Our Love was considered illegal.
We surely didn't want to be martyrs.
As white females, we clearly had it easier.
That was just for starters.

I didn't want to be arrested in the 80s.
After graduation I ducked out to another state.
Southern dykes weren't so lucky.
Some were prosecuted to meet their fate.

In '86 Challenger Spacecraft exploded.
We lived 300 miles apart.
By that Fall we'd created a home
as permanent Sweethearts.

We'd potluck with other Lesbians
since that's where we'd feel free.
Was rude to ask someone's job or last name,
because safety was not guaranteed.

We rarely touch each other in public
going on now 38 years.
Traumatic things have happened
to our close friends and our peers.

We've been forced to watch in total dismay
as friends' careers are threatened or destroyed.
Holding tight to our partners and our mental health
we're firm to not become paranoid.

When we're out, we must constantly be wary.
Be cautious of how we talk.
To intimidate us out of our neighborhood,
glass shards jammed in our sidewalk.

When a bullet rang into our living room
we knew we were caught in a bind.
Local cops warn us to "never call again."
Said they wouldn't protect our kind.

As we were in physical peril
it's apparent we needed to lie.
My girlfriend borrowed her dad's shotgun
though she couldn't tell him why.

We secured new employment
and fled in the Chicago suburbs direction.
Oak Park was the *only* place in Illinois
that had *any* lesbian legal protection.

When marching in '93 National LGBT protest
at our Nation's Capital we felt brave.
We treasure a fading Polaroid
that captures us being depraved.

We share a sweet kiss on the National Mall
with White House backdrop in the picture.
Honoring radical acts of same-sex love
anti-gay laws were still legal Scripture.

Snapshot proves we could be arrested.
It captures us being criminals.
Sodomy laws were still in force in most states,
though the jail time might be minimal.

We were on guard to dodge jerky landlords
who might oust us without regret.
Sneaky Director snitched to my boss
so my job threatened at the outset.

After 23 years of hiding,
'09 Iowa wedding was our legal prize.
Precious few mid-west relatives graced our event
which wasn't a surprise.

I don't disclose I'm married to a female
though the year is now 2023.
We're on alert for multiple dangers
to monitor our physical safety.

As I rhyme this little ditty,
I sometimes wonder who cares
if the Supreme Court invalidates my marriage
though we've been together 38 years?

We love our beautiful brave Butch Dykes.
Our Lesbian culture's treasure.
They're always the canary in the coal mine.
Their resilience is beyond measure.

Dignity challenges remain just as clear.
Dykes equal only 1% demographic.
If you scan any smut channel
Lesbian word is still pornographic.

Safe Lesbian places
have all, but disappeared.
We're told, *"You don't need female space
since all prejudice has been cleared!"*

The *Lesbian* word is still dirty.
Dyke is filtered off the top.
Many remain hiding undercover
or censor their language on TikTok.

Youthful Lesbians often exclaim
the sexist battle still occurs.
They struggle finding each other
while dodging sexual predators.

We share survival skills with young females
by our insistence to thrive.
One blurts out, she'd never met a Lesbian
over the age of 25.

She has only imagined
Lesbians either die
or they will become Bi,
before they reach 35.

Struggling young Lesbians
tell us what they need.
Visibility and respect.
A safe space just to Be.

While navigating the world for respite,
we bump into the Unitarian Universalist church on the
way.
It's crucial to watch what they actually *do,*
not listen to what they *say.*

I'm appointed Welcoming Congregation Chair
and voted Vice President of their Board.
But when push comes to shove
it's clear I'm meant to be ignored.

As Dykes, we're required *not* to complain
or be banned from their "open" door.
We are told we must be grateful
and sing Unitarian praises galore.

"Safe space" becomes just illusion
when Lesbians are accused of sass.
Church leaders clamp down on our dignity
to pull a classic Spiritual Bypass.

During newly married lesbian couple celebration
we hear liquored-up key Unitarian quip,
"I really don't understand.
Which one is the woman
and which one is the man?"

I'm shocked into stone silence
behind a Unitarian closed door.
Leader's view, *"Gay men just want sex."*
I flee fast before I have to hear more.

Now, I'm a private person.
I've survived decades in my career.
But their casual cruelty aimed at us
proves church leaders continue to be insincere.

We endured 3 days of anti-lesbian rants
as Unitarian Teacher aims to enlarge.
He writes to over 700 his hate-speech about us.
A Class 4 Felony could now be charged.

Cover-up begins by fibbing leaders
insisting to target us, as their Facebook task.
Male Teacher types, *"I hate her and all lesbians like her.
She can kiss my heterosexual ass!"*

Their Facebook posts mock us Lesbians
as more church members join in to jest.
We attempt to calm their dysfunction
but they laugh at our distress.

We are easy targets.
A bullseye on our back.
We mustn't reveal their hypocrisy
or they will attack.

We're lectured the church guarantees freedom
which allows Unitarian members to ridicule our sex
life quite a bit.
They're rewarded to type on FB that *we're crazy.*
Unitarian Teacher posts that we're *pieces of shit.*

Unitarian leaders direct *we should apologize*
and *we must ignore* blatant lesbophobia.
We're told everyone's prohibited
from criticizing their church utopia.

Church members are obligated to believe it's healthy
when same male Teacher isolates children from view
to instruct his version of Lesbian Sex Ed to kids
behind Unitarian closed door at the venue.

New "Church Rule" demands *our silence,*
or they'll gaslight us, if we dare cause a fuss.
Leaders tell us in person and in writing,
we're required to cover-up what they're doing to us.

Cautious women trust us with their shocking
Unitarian secrets.
Plead with us to never disclose.
So we can't use their disclosures to defend ourselves
as the emperor wears no clothes.

National Church declines to protect us from attacks.
Tell us that they're sad to confess no power to aid.
Local Unitarians can choose to ridicule Lesbians
as those "woke" Headquarters' officers fade.

We're admonished we *must not* tarnish
their local LGBT image, carefully crafted.
If we show that their image is really a fraud,
then their reputation might be shafted.

A staunch Unitarian member *reports us*.
How dare we *reveal* our ordeal to friends on the Web!
We're accused of breaking some new "Church Rule"
as their shaming us becomes more widespread.

A *Rule of Silence* is imposed to gag us.
While on Facebook, tricky leader is free
to type what a horrible woman I am
to expose heterosexism targeting me.

There's NO misunderstanding between us.
Their Message received is crystal clear.
Local church mails certified letter *banning us*
proclaiming: *"You're both prohibited from Unitarian
grounds here!"*

No one else is ever to blame
except banned Dykes deserving to be cowed.
Leaders publish, *"You're hurting the Church's
reputation!"*
We dare speak the real Truth out loud.

Dilatants say they can't understand
why we'd be so sore.
Can't we just suck it up
and be their patriarchal whores?

You have not lived my life.
I admit I haven't lived yours.
Genuine kindness and respect are vital
for us ALL to be on safe shores.

Unitarians pride their church being "Liberal".
They "virtue signal" an open rainbow gate.
But diversity flows into one big melting pot,
and everyone must bow to their culture that's straight.

If different sexual orientations are honored
except the one that excludes males,
the blatant message is unmistakable
when misogyny is so thinly veiled.

The church pretends to be "progressive".
Hyping they're spiritual AF to a tee.
However, hiding their dirty secrets
is what their Leadership enforces it to be.

We are Unitarian roadkill.
Most avert their eyes driving home.
Their ethics are as genuine
as rainbow cake made of Styrofoam.

We turn to the "liberal" community
who feign that they're so sad.
We forward the vile hate-speech we received
but they think it's not so bad.

Why would they choose to get involved
when the Church says *nothing's going on*?
Church whispers, we're simply disgruntled brats
who are manufacturing untrue facts.

Unitarians *advertise* "LGBT Welcoming Congregation"
so ugly homophobia *couldn't* happen there?
Sometimes cover-ups hide in *plain view*
when folks don't actually care.

We experience Unitarian Universalist much like a cult.
Better submit to what they say.
They try to intimidate us into silent on their nasty
treatment
or we will be thrown away.

This is our lived experience.
Church leaders declare their actions never occurred.
Are we living in a parallel universe
or are their past written documents erased or blurred?

Cover-up of the truth remains uncorrected to date
since no one's affected, but us.
Women's experience isn't important to them
and Lesbian lives, even less.

Has anything changed in the last few years?
Not a single thing whereas,
still never any written apology to us
though leader gaslights claiming he has!

Some call us whiny Dykes.
Misfits to be ignored.
Local church labels us as liars,
in their emails, call us more.

But *facts* are certainly stubborn things.
As a trial attorney I find them welcoming.
I've kept copies of their written homophobic rants.
We wait for the apology that's never forthcoming.

Karma of the church will do its' work,
as we put on needed balm.
Though a wolf in sheep's clothing
is celebrated to continue on.

If Unitarian Universalist Enforcers wish history
portrayed them a lot better,
higher minds might've intervened
before sending us their *banning the lesbians letter.*

Some may view this Report as fake.
Most say we didn't get far.
We deserve the harsh treatment
for having guts to stand for who we are.

We uncovered some slimy Unitarian secrets.
You may disagree.
But your reading the ugly hate speech targeting us
would prove to be *the key.*

As lesbians we've *never* received an apology for
being shamed at LGBT Welcoming Church.
That's a Fact.
We still wonder why Unitarians so easily turn their
backs
when lesbians are being attacked?

If you're a female Unitarian member or friend
I genuinely hope this doesn't happen to you.
We never dreamed we'd experience it either,
but the leadership's hypocrisy is a major clue.

Perhaps we woke some people up.
We certainly make Unitarians mad.
<u>We slog through their massive shadow-side.</u>
Our Shining Light is more than a fad.

I do not worry for money.
I do not worry for fame.
I worry for my Lesbian sisters.
Unitarian copycats play deceptive games.

I'm blessed to detail our harrowing trial.
Persistence to resistance, via me.
Elsewhere, I might be flogged or worst.
There's much danger in 2023.

So what are my words of wisdom
at the age of 72,
when the world rips at your dignity
and a kangaroo court convicts you?

It shouldn't have to happen to you
for you to think it matters.
Neutrality *always* encourages abuse.
Complacency leaves Justice in tatters.

It's not your beliefs that make you
a person of integrity.
It's your *choice of behavior*
that proves your credibility.

In the end, each of our lives matter
just to the people who care.
But a legacy may be left behind
if we model that Truth can prevail.

A legacy of never hesitating
to pay the price for an authentic life.
Speaking up *against shame-shifting*
where victims are falsely blamed for strife.

We stand on our ancestor's shoulders.
Centuries of Sisters risking their lives.
Standing in a world worse than this
they were determined to survive.

We're steeped in Lesbian history
and we won't let them down.
We invite you to join with us
if hypocrisy lives in your town.

When you're commanded to suffer indignities,
required to smile and never respond.
Remember others need to see you rise up
to help women resist being preyed upon.

Do not suffer in silence.
Don't allow your worth to be smeared.
Even when you're told *no one believes you.*
Do Not Let The L Disappear!

 As Bitch sings, *"That's OK.*
We know the man always gets his way.
But at the end of the day,
we're still here anyway!"

Gentle reader, perhaps you're scanning this poem.
Perchance, you just got bored.
If here, consider opening your heart up
when earnest souls appear at your door.

We all wish to spread our Light.
We're trying to be more awake.
But refusing to help another
is not an enlightened choice to make.

For we are your mothers and daughters.
We are your sisters and friends.
We are the women who illuminate life
and grieve at your ultimate end.

What has been done in darkness
can always be brought to Light.
Don't dim yourself to fit in.
Let your *Soul Shine Bright*!

Let's anchor our dreams into this 3-D
of our joyous vision of hope.
To manifest a delight filled reality
where we can do more than just cope.

If you've ever become acquainted
to that place adjacent to hell.
You're welcome to gather with us
as we sit in a Spell.

We Rise from the Ashes
Refreshed, and Renewed.
The Past is now Banished
to Vanish from View.

We're no Longer Hidden.
Our Gifts Open Wide.
We're Predictable as Water
as We Turn the Tide.

We're the Fire on the Arrow.
We're as Common as Earth.
In the Air, We're the Phoenix
as We Witness Re- birth.

What have I learned so far in my life?
What do I discern as a Fact?
Decide what you *know* is important in Life
and risk all for that!

PEGGY PATTY

Peggy was born on an Indiana farm where she delighted romping in the acres of oak and walnut trees.

Her fondest childhood memories include collecting shiny stones from the meandering creek.

She obtained a B.S in Social Work, and Masters in Human Services. Working in the women's movement in the 1970's inspired her to receive a Law Degree. She spent the next thirty years advocating for victims of violence against women in the Illinois civil and criminal court systems.

As an Assistant State's Attorney in an Illinois county, she prosecuted felony domestic violence cases, including attempted murder. And as Director of the Legal Institute at the Illinois Coalition Against Domestic Violence she provided legal assistance to victim shelters across Illinois.

Peggy's a Reiki Master for 25 years who enjoys facilitating Retreats. She organized volunteers to offered free Reiki sessions to patients at the Simmons Cancer Institute in Springfield, Illinois.

Passionate about the rejuvenating power of vibrational sound, she facilitates SoundBaths, Crystal Bowls Meditations, and drum circles throughout the Midwest. She loves presenting workshops on the healing effects of Sound Vibrations on the Body, Mind, and Soul at state and national women's conferences, including the National Women's Music Festival and the Illinois Women in Leadership Symposium.

Peggy's instructed medical students at the Southern Illinois School of Medicine's Integrative Medical course "Power of Vibrational Sound" several years.

Holding many Healing Vibration certificates, her highest reverence honors her Sound mentors encouraging her, "Let the Sound Teach You."

Peggy and her spouse Phyllis received a certified letter banning them from the Unitarian Universalist Church in Springfield Illinois because they wouldn't obey to cover-up shocking written homophobia and sexism targeting them by church hierarchy and members. She appreciates having illusions clarified.

Connect Peggy Patty on Facebook or by email at earthbeat3@gmail.com

Musings on the Journey of Being an Author in Mystic Memoirs

The metaphysical journey of immersing myself in the details of my esoteric memories is a wild ride. It feels very expansive and healing, but also apprehensive. It's a bit scary attempting to describe on the computer screen actual energetic occurrences. Very personal and sacred experiences. Can I relate to others the unseen aspects of the universe with sufficient awe and skepticism?

When I began analyzing what I'm writing on the page, an unfamiliar idea popped up. Maybe it's reckless to put my real name on these articles? An odd question, since I don't consider myself to be timid. However, in those moments, it seems reckless not to be anonymous.

Slowly I began recollecting the times in our not so distant past when it was dangerous to disclose our "knowings" such as these. Especially in written form.

I ask myself one question. *Did I experience these events, or not? If placed on trial, would I deny my written accounts of them?*

My stories are as real as every other experience in my life. They deeply inform my life.
They are Truth, as I know it.

You need not look elsewhere for the Secrets of the Universe
For they are already Inside You.
Each Person is Powerful Beyond Measure.

I Head Down The Path In The Smokey Mountains

Dwight Harriman

Prologue:

I've been a mystic all my life, and I had been formally practicing as a shaman for over a decade when this event happened. It was hardly my first meeting with the Divine, although it is one of the most profound and one that continues to unfold. This is one of my favorite encounters. Writing this story has deepened my experience in ways I didn't expect.

The Setting:

It is August 2010; I know the date only because I have an email with the date. I don't work in linear time much. I have gathered with my fellow apprentices in the Smoky Mountains. We have rented a cabin for five days; we share the cost, the food, and the cleanup. We will meet three times this way. We are apprenticing with a shaman named Peter Calhoun. He's one of the most amazing men I have ever met.

There are so many stories I could choose to tell for this book from my work with him: Asking the weather for a favor and having it granted? The healing ceremony that's all about forgiveness? The many different journeys I have developed from his teachings? Learning that no shamanic event ever starts on time? Those will all be in my own book.

The Assignment:

"Everything is living," Peter said one morning. "Everything has a spirit. Even things most people don't consider alive- like stones, the land, and bodies of water have a spirit. This is the invisible landscape you can learn to sense. As a shaman, you must learn the invisible landscape and be as comfortable there as you are in the tangible physical world. Your assignment today is to connect to one of the spirits of this place." I knew my destination immediately.

It was a waterfall about a hundred yards off the trail. This is my spot. I know this with a surety that only comes from Spirit. Mature birch and hickory trees provide a welcome shade on the trail. The air is cool and crisp during my hike to the falls. Leaving the trail, the way looks treacherous. The flat, well-worn path gives way to much more rugged terrain. There is no fear, though—I had passed this way on another day and had seen the passage to the falls laid out before me. I see the handholds and footholds to the falls as if they were highlighted for me.

Reaching the water, I sit on a large stone, staying clear of the spray. This is not a giant cascade of water, but dozens of small cascades playing through the stones as they fall to the stream below. There is not the roar of a large fall that makes conversation and thought impossible, but a kind of bubbling laughter. I can talk here. I can also think, which becomes a problem.

The Meeting:

Running water, whether a tiny creek, a giant river, the ocean, or this waterfall, has always comforted me. Today, though, I am nervous and agitated. I have meditated for years, but that practice doesn't help me now. I attempt to relax and center. I am unable to. I reach down to the pool of water below me. I scoop a handful of water up. I splash it on my face. I instantly relax. For a bit, I am calm and centered. I wait for the contact I know is coming.

Two minutes later, I am again nervous and agitated. I attempt to relax and center. I am unable to. I reach down to the pool of water below me. I scoop a handful of water up. I splash it on my face. I instantly calm down. For a bit, I am calm and centered. I wait for the contact I know is coming.

After another two minutes, I again feel nervous and agitated. I reach for the water for a third time. As I'm reaching down, I hear a voice saying, "This is going to take a lot of water." The words come, kind and gentle. This is not a rebuke, just an amused River Spirit. "What is wrong?" he asks. (Spirits don't necessarily have gender, but I have always experienced this one as male.)

I respond with a truth I did not know until I said it aloud. "As a shaman, I spend so much of my time in nonlinear time and space that I am afraid I'll get lost and not find my way back."

"Don't worry; come back here, and I'll put you in the right place."

Instantly, I could breathe again. The knot in my stomach unraveled and disappeared. The splashes of physical water that gave me temporary relief are replaced by the permanent relief of a never-ending flow of water from a River Spirit. The fear fell away. How could it remain when a River Spirit has my back? That fear has not returned.

As we continue our conversation, I realize I hadn't discerned the path so much as remembered it. The path to the falls lay so open to me because I traveled it many times in many different lives. Not all were human. Another shaman taught me that we all have a Spirit Animal for each cardinal direction. All of mine—Buffalo, Hawk, Hare, and Octopus—had been there as well. They had all drunk from the river. Octopus drank when it was part of a giant inland sea millennia ago. The others drank much more recently.

This is a sacred space for me. A tangible place where I connect to the Divine. The melody of the falls, the cool air, and the shade of the trees combine with my memories of the encounter to create a sense of peace within me. Physically, my heartbeat and my breaths slow; mentally, I let go of the mundane and sink into the experience. I feel held by Spirit here. This is a place I return to in lifetime after lifetime.

It occurred to me as I write this that I can do a journey to discover when I first encountered this place and this Spirit. I resolve to do this soon. As much joy and connectedness as I've received from this encounter, there is a way to deepen my connection.

The Agreement:

I ask for his name, and he tells me it has no human translation. River Spirits' names are a combination of location, connections to other bodies of water, and the amplitude of their waves at their peak size. I can carry the name in my soul, I just can't transcribe it. Or begin to pronounce it. He asks me to take his greetings to any and all other natural bodies of water I come across. I, of course, agree. I have done so ever since.

When I cross paths with a river, a creek, a stream, a pond, a lake, a sea, or the ocean, I raise my open hand with the palm facing the water and say, "I bring greetings from this River Spirit." His true name is in my soul, and they hear that. For a few moments, I become a conduit between the two. The surge of energy flowing through me recharges me. After the connection breaks, I place my hand on my heart and absorb the good vibrations. I will also place my hand on any part of my body that needs a little boost. (As I write this, I realize I have never given that blessing to someone else. Along with the journey to the first encounter, I have resolved to do that at the next opportunity.)

For me, the experience is always changing and evolving. I prefer to make the greeting when I can see the water, although that isn't necessary. Sometimes, especially when physically depleted, the connection is made, but I don't get the sensation of being the conduit. Other times, vast bubbles of joy and laughter move through me. There are times when my hands pulse with energy afterward.

I frequently make the connection when driving. Once, while driving at night, I missed a creek, and it shouted, "What about me?" I, of course, sent the greetings and an apology for missing them initially.

I live in the Atlanta area and cross over the Chattahoochee often. The Hooch is a magnificent, healing river. Being a channel between those two powerful Spirits is always a wonderful experience. I do as much of my work outside as I can. The parks and trails along the Chattahoochee are some of my favorite places to work with others. I bring others to these sites so the river can heal them.

I need only make the connection once to fulfill my agreement, but I almost always do it whenever I encounter a body of water. "Almost always" because I am human and do forget. When I go crystal mining in Arkansas, I have my hand upraised with my palm out every few minutes, as there are rivers, creeks, and bayous galore.

Surprisingly, some bodies are not as responsive. Some are old and quiet; they do enjoy the recognition. A few have power and strength all out of proportion to the size of their current state—they were much larger and more powerful rivers in the past. They will be again. I love to connect with the smaller creeks when they are filled with recent rain and are joyously and noisily larger.

I have even connected to rivers that no longer have a physical body. I discovered this a few years ago by looking at a valley and thinking that a river must have flowed there at one time. I was correct. I now regularly find and greet these ghost rivers. The same energy and intensity can be there. I send greetings, and they respond enthusiastically, happy someone has acknowledged them.

While I have connections with the other elements as well, none are like this. None have the depth and connectedness I experience from the simple act of carrying a greeting. This has never felt like an obligation. It has always been an opportunity to go deeper in my practice. My life is richer because of this continual Spiritual Messaging.

The Council Fire:

In my practice, I have a council fire. It is a Shamanic Journey where I journey, build a sacred fire in the other realm, and ask my guides to circle around the fire to be with me. There are up to a dozen, although not all of them may be present on any given circle, and there is usually an open spot in the circle for any guest. I teach a class where I take people on this journey, and they get to meet their own council.

My council is an eclectic mix. There is an Orisha, a Celtic Goddess, a Greek Goddess, a Christian Saint, my Octopus, Two Wells that represent the lineages from my parents, a giant alien that looks like a praying mantis, a couple more that don't wish to be named, and, the River Spirit. I visualize him as a column of water. The others can be intimidating; he is always a calm, reassuring presence.

The Journey:

This council fire has the specific goal of learning about my first meeting with the River Spirit. To prepare, I set sacred space: I light a candle and burn a little sage; I listen to a recorded shamanic drum session with earbuds to reduce outside distraction; I set my intention. With a series of deep, slow breaths, I ask for the Spirits to gather around me and with me.

When setting intention while leading others on journeys, I use my rattle to create circles of sound. When setting intention for my own journeys, they become circles of light. I hold my breath momentarily, then draw three golden circles in my mind's eye. I ask the Spirit of the Ocean, the River Spirit and my Octopus to be with me. I ask the same for the Spirit of the land, the Spirits of the plants, the Spirits of the in-between—those that are neither plant nor animal—and the Spirits of the animal kingdoms. I invite the Spirits of ancestors, guardian Spirits, and any beings from any realm that come only for my good to witness. I ask for angels to watch overhead. I ask for the Great Spirit to be with me. For Great Spirit, the circles become the infinity symbol.

Once sacred space is set, the journey starts beside a campfire. There is a river that runs beside it and a mountain on the other side. I strip myself of the mundane world's garments and burdens. A backpack carrying all my concerns for myself drops to the floor, as well as a small cloth bag for any overflow from the backpack. There is almost always overflow.

I dress as a shaman with leggings, a shirt, and moccasins. I gather my drum, rattle, abalone shell, staff, and necklace. Every lifetime as a shaman, including this one, these are my tools. I head up one of the trails on the mountain. At a small pool of water, the reflection keeps changing. It changes from Australian Tribesman to a member of the First People, back to myself. It's fascinating, but today, there are different priorities.

I keep walking, until I am at the Sacred Grove. This is an ancient group of trees. Today, they are Live Oaks, my favorites. They are shapeshifters. On some visits, they appear as Lepidodendrons, trees from 350 million years ago, to remind me they are truly ancient.

This is sanctuary. Here are my Spirit Animals and my inner children. Today, I also realize a potential solution for two clients dealing with severe entity attacks. *Use the two wells in this realm.* The realization is to send the water from one of the wells to each person and cleanse their spaces. I do so.

The journey continues to a sacred fire, where the council waits. This is the launching point for discovering my first meeting with the River Spirit. I greet the beings around the fire, and then, as is often the case in my journeys, I am immediately transported elsewhere. Octopus grabs me with a pair of tentacles and pulls me deep into another place.

I find myself as my octopus in an ancient sea, discovering what will become a freshwater spring and the beginning of the river. Octopus seems to be doing a ritual to call forth an opening for the River Spirit. Then, time and space blur as the scene shifts. A buffalo, more correctly, an ancestor of the buffalo, comes to the river, lays down, and dies peacefully. The scene shifts again, and this one is not peaceful. A Cherokee man fights a battle and takes an arrow in the chest, bleeding out into the river.

The scene shifts to a hare being killed by a fox at the river, then to a hawk diving to take a fish from the river and being itself taken by something large and scaly. My connection to this place has been paid for by blood.

After that series of traumatic events, I am shown children playing here, all types of animals drinking and coexisting, and my latest visit to the river. There is much peace and joy in this spot as well. The deaths helped to make this a sacred place for me, and thankfully, that type of sacrifice is no longer needed.

This part of the journey ends, and I surface, going through time and space again: First, as a stone, then a fish, then an otter, and finally, myself. I surface in a pool of water. Octopus took me through the pool to start the journey, but the descent was so rapid that I couldn't notice any details.

Now, there's a sacred pool to go with the sacred grove and the sacred fire.

I realize I'll need to do another journey to have a place of sacred air. I also understand that I'll need to do a journey to determine my first encounter with the other members of my council. Writing up the experience has both deepened my relationship with the River Spirit and enriched my practice in ways I honestly didn't expect. Having told this story so many times, I did not think I could add this much to it.

As the journey ends, I use the last few moments to send light and love to those who need it, thank all who helped me in the journey, and then gently come back into my body, the chair, and the room. I turn on the light, open my laptop, and begin recording my experience.

The Sharing:

I meet with a fellow practitioner along the Chattahoochee. I explain what I want to do and she immediately agrees to help me. We walk along the trail for about a mile; this takes us away from most of the other people on the trail. The trail branches here. There are paths down to the shore after the branching; that's where we're heading. Finding the well-worn path to the shore I was looking for, we head down, avoiding the vines and the thorns. We come to a small opening in the brush with a clear view of the river and room enough to sit. We chat for a little while as I determine how I want to do this.

I decide to hold my left hand up to the river and have her hold my right hand with both of hers. I send greetings from one river to another. It works! She feels the connection as well. Shamans call this being a hollow bone. It is letting the energy of the universe flow through you without resistance. Tears of joy fill her eyes as she becomes a hollow bone.

She now has the ability to take his greeting to other rivers as well. I say that she is under no obligation to do so, that is only my agreement, but she insists she wants to. She later shared with me that, as she drove home, she raised her hand to a small river by her house and said, "I bring greeting from the River Spirit." She said tears of joy came again when the river happily acknowledged the greeting.

Epilogue:

One more bit. I was at the Tennessee River two years ago after visiting a place called Te-lah-nay's Wall. It is the most amazing place of the divine feminine I know.

Every step along the wall brings a quiet peace. It deserves its own recounting as well. It will have that in my book. I was on my way to a crystal mine in Arkansas and had stopped by the wall and the river. At a state park, I approach the river with my hand upraised, palm facing the river. "I bring greetings from the River Spirit."

The river answered me with a bemused "He flows into me."

I said, "I know, but I told him I would bring greetings to every natural body of water."

He smiled. I made a river smile. I love being a shaman.

****

DWIGHT HARRIMAN

Dwight has been a mystic all of his life. He has been formally practicing as a shaman for over 25 years, deepening his relationship with Nature and Spirit through a melding of various paths.

Called by visions as a child, his early mystical leanings ripened through long-time recovery work, his studies of religion, the study of anthropology, and through his shamanic practice. He sharpened his intuition with Tarot cards and is a Reiki master.

Dwight earned his degree in anthropology with honors from Georgia State University. He studied for years with different shamans including an apprenticeship with elder, shamanic healer, and visionary, Peter Calhoun.

Dwight has worked with thousands of people in private sessions, in workshops and in his Shamanism 101 classes which he designed to make shamanic practices

accessible to everyone. Each one has a journey or meditation able to deepen a person's relationship to Spirit and to themselves. Class titles include Past Life Spelunking, Meet Your Dragon, Shed Your Skin (to give up limiting beliefs), Council Fire (to meet your Spirit guides) and Meet Your Higher Self.

As the Atlanta Shaman, Dwight's greatest joy is helping people shed limiting beliefs and step into their own personal power. He believes everyone has gifts they can share with the world. He delights in helping people find and develop these gifts.

He loves nature and works outdoors as much as possible. He mines crystals and creates wonderful and powerful shamanic tools with them. The same insightful eye that makes him such a good shaman has recently led him to create amazing nature photography.

Contact Dwight

www.atlantashaman.com or dwight@atlantashaman.com. If you're in the metro Atlanta area, he can frequently be found at the metaphysical store Forever and a Day in Woodstock. View his photography at www.dwightharrimanphotography.com.

When Pele Calls

My Relationship with the Volcano Goddess

SONJA GLAD

March 6th, 2023

Sonja, it's time to get up.

"Mmmmm. You know it was a rough night, right?" I answered the voice in my head.

My fuzzy mind wasn't quite awake. I pulled a pillow over my head, blocking the rays of sunshine streaming in through the kitchen windows of my studio apartment.

Come on, Sonja. The sun is shining. It's time to get up and go for a walk.

I looked over at the clock on my bedside table. It read 8:08. My eyes widened in curiosity. 808 is the area code for the entire state of Hawaii, so I thought there might be some significance, perhaps even some magic brewing.

Closing my eyes, an image of Pele, the volcano goddess, popped into my mind. I imagined her long black hair highlighted with the reds and oranges of flowing lava. She wore a crown of red ohia lehua flowers. Her hands reached out to me.

Digging my knuckles into my sleepy eyes to clear my vision, I asked, "Is that you, Pele? Are you the one waking me up?"

My intuition *dinged* as my heartbeat quickened—a physical reaction confirming my suspicion. Yet I still felt confused. She had never awakened me from sleep before.

I remembered the first time she spoke to me in her alluring yet deadpan tone.

It happened four years ago while participating in a plant ceremony in a sacred place next to a deep crevasse on the northern slope of Mauna Loa, the largest volcano on the planet. The Hawaiian High Priestess who officiated the ceremony had told us stories about Pele throughout the previous week during a professional training I attended.

The priestess handed each of us a coconut shell cup filled with kava tea. Taking a tentative sip, I held the bitter, muddy-tasting liquid in my mouth. As my lips began to numb, the kava tea slipped down my throat. I held the cup to my lips once more and emptied its contents into my mouth, eager to finish the unpleasant-tasting liquid.

Relaxing my body on a blanket on the hard lava surface, I let my mind float away as the high priestess began her drumming and chanting. The chanting and drumming helped me sink deeper and deeper into a meditative trance.

That's when I first heard Pele's voice.

You have three years to get ready to come back to me for three years.

"Who is this? I don't understand."

You have three years to get ready to come back to me for three years.

"I can come back and visit the Big Island in three years, but I can't come for three years. No. No way. Where is this voice coming from?" It felt like the earth, or more specifically, the volcano, was pulling me into it.

"What a wild trip. This sure isn't like any other Shamanic journey I've ever experienced. Is it the kava making me have this auditory hallucination?"

No hallucination. The plant medicine only helped open the door for you to be able to hear me.

You know who I am.

Slowly, an image of Pele materialized in my mind. I looked deeply into her almond-shaped eyes and watched her lips curve into a slight smile. Her hands were cupped in front of her heart, and I couldn't tell if the fire was in her hands or if her hands were framing the fire coming from within her heart.

You know me as the goddess of volcanos and fire, Pele-honua-mea, but you may call me Pele.

I felt a tug on my heart and my chest tightened, squeezing the air from my lungs. My breath caught in my throat as I silently cried in reverence. Tears streamed from my eyes, pooling in my ears.

Sonja, Pele's voice beseeched me, *listen. You have three years to prepare. Then you need to return here for three years.*

"I can't do that. There's no way I can leave family and friends and work for that long."

Yet a seed was planted in my soul that day. Both a strong yearning to follow Pele's calling and a deep sorrow at what that might mean consumed my thoughts and emotions.

I kept my thoughts to myself. Who would believe me? How could I possibly go for that long? How would

I tell my wife? I sank into a state of perpetual anguish, heartache, and depression.

Pele showed up several times before my departure from Illinois, constantly encouraging me. *Come. Come. Come.*

It always happened when doing Shamanic Breathwork, Shamanic Journeying, or in a deep state of meditation. A sea turtle usually accompanied my journeying, gently guiding me through the vast ocean expanse that separated me from my future. I finally realized there was no choice but to listen to her call and follow her command. When the fiery volcano goddess speaks, what could I do but obey?

I now live in Hawaii on what I call a three-year sabbatical. I've almost made it through my first year. My other home, where my family lives, was over four thousand miles away. I missed them. Last night wasn't the first night since my trip to Illinois over the holidays, where I'd laid awake for hours.

"What in the world am I doing here, away from everyone I know and love?" I wondered.

Yet since my arrival in June '22, three years after her call, Pele continued to whisper in my ear. Now that I was in her domain, her sense of urgency and command had diminished.

She invited me to visit her just a few months ago. Mauna Loa had erupted through a fissure in the summit caldera in the exact same place where we had held our ceremony three and a half years earlier. Pele hadn't erupted there in almost 30 years.

Within 40 hours of the lava breaching the surface, I was there, bringing her flowers, chocolate, and prayers of gratitude.

Seeing the spectacularly powerful, fiery night-time light display filled me with awe. A mix of water vapor, carbon dioxide, and sulfur gases rose from the fissure and engulfed the sky. Smokey clouds lit up the night as they reflected the oranges, yellows, and reds of the lava spilling down the slope.

Hearing her voice wake me up this morning surprised me. After all, I wasn't in any spiritual or meditative state. I'd been sleeping.

"Okay," I sighed with resignation. "Since the sun is shining this morning after days of clouds and rain, I guess I'll get out of bed and go for a walk," I told Pele grudgingly.

But not even the volcano goddess herself would make me skip my usual morning routine.

I rolled onto my belly for my first yoga pose of the day, one called crocodile, where you just lay prone. After ten breaths, I pushed myself into cobra for another ten breaths.

Next came the cobra wave, or belly-on-bed pushups, which I did ten times. Then, child's pose for ten breaths and ten cat-cows before rolling onto my back and elevating my legs.

I started to think about the day ahead. "It's too late to make it to my 8:30 yoga class."

I made sure you wouldn't be able to go, Pele snickered at me. *Who do you think disrupted your rest so you'd sleep in? You need to go for a long walk.*

This was definitely Pele's bossy voice in my head.

After going to the bathroom, I flipped out my yoga mat. "If I'm not going to my yoga class, then I'm gonna do at least a few sun salutations," I informed Pele. A feeling of rebellion kicked in. I was not a big fan of being told what to do.

"All right, Pele, I'll go on your walk even though I don't feel like it. But first, I'm going to do what I need to do."

Standing there naked on my mat, I imagined Pele with downcast eyes shaking her head. Her long hair looked alive as it swayed back and forth, like lava flowing from the crown of her head and down over her bare shoulders.

I lifted my arms over my head and inhaled. Exhaling, I bent over and touched the ground. I pulled halfway up before folding in again. With hands on the ground, I stepped back into plank and inhaled. Then, exhaling, I lowered my knees, chest, and chin to the floor. On the next inhale, I pushed up into cobra before elevating my bum into downward-facing dog.

"I'd really just rather stay in bed, but I'll go. But only when I'm good and ready," I grumbled.

Noticing my passive-aggressive tone, I gave myself some grace, knowing my best may not be great right now due to lack of sleep and my depressed mood.

I decided right then and there to change my attitude and have some gratitude. After all, not everyone got a wake-up call from a goddess.

Five breaths later, I jumped my feet toward my hands and folded in again. With another deep inhale, I rose to a standing position with my arms over my head and my palms meeting in prayer. Slowly lowering my still joined hands toward my heart, I gently brushed my thumbs against my crown chakra, third eye, and throat chakra, then settled them at my heart.

Forgoing the rest of my yoga practice, I quickly rolled up my mat and put it back in the corner by my free-standing clothes closet. After putting on some clothes, I headed to the kitchen to put together my breakfast of oats with walnuts, shredded coconut, papaya, and unsweetened chocolate almond milk. Breakfast would be ready upon my return.

I filled my water bottle and grabbed my phone and keys before putting on my socks and tennis shoes.

Almost an hour after my interesting wake-up call from Pele, I finally walked out the door.

It was beautiful out. Pausing, I looked around. The greens seemed greener than yesterday. The sunshine cast some leaves in shadow while others radiated with glowing vibrancy. The bright red, pink, and orange hibiscus blooms had unfurled their petals, spreading them wide open.

Days of cloudy skies and rain had forced the hibiscus blooms to stay closed. Now the petals unfurled and proudly displayed their fire engine red stamens with clusters of brilliant yellow pollen sacs. They seemed to be vying for my attention.

"Look at me."

"No, look at me!"

Feeling exhilarated by the lush environment and the shining sun, I turned up the street and walked with purpose toward the main road of the subdivision. Turning left, I continued toward the ocean, almost a mile away.

"A feather. Oh, and there's another one." I hadn't found any feathers in weeks, probably because it had been so cold (65-68 degrees Fahrenheit) that the birds couldn't afford to let any of them go.

"Thank you. Thank you."

More feathers.

"It's a feast of feathers! Thank you, thank you, thank you, thank you!"

For me, finding a feather was a reminder of the gifts from the universe. I hadn't seen any since my return to the Big Island a month ago after being gone for seven weeks traveling to Illinois, Florida, and Mexico. I'd noticed the lack of feathers and wondered if the gifts from the universe had dried up.

Walk toward Kahena Beach. Pele instructed me.

"I got a late start, so maybe I can go down to the ocean's edge by that pull-off before the beach."

No. Go past the beach to the little path after the last house on the left side of the road. She commanded me.

"I won't be home till after 10:00 a.m. if I go there. That will push back breakfast, then lunch, and mess up my eating plans for the entire day. But I can roll with that," I told Pele and kept walking.

Getting to the ocean, I turned right. My eyes drifted to the left toward the water as I kept a lookout for something spectacular.

"Will I get the gift of seeing a whale today? Surely, there's something big in store for me as I'm doing what I've been told to do. After all, I am following your orders, right?"

My eyes followed the curve of the land to the point where the black lava cliffs met the dark, cerulean ocean waters. The unusually calm waves created only a narrow white border between land and sea. In the past, I'd seen them jump much higher against the cliff walls.

Intuitively, I recognized the distant point on the horizon as my destination. It was farther than I'd ever walked along the Puna coastline.

Ambling past Kahena Beach, I turned left on the road that took me past the oceanfront houses. After the last house, I turned left again and carefully descended the narrow, jungly path. It was steep. I gave a little prayer of thanks to whoever added the ropes, giving me something to hold as I climbed down the treacherous trail.

Stepping out onto the lava bluff, I paused and breathed in the salt-kissed air. Before me, the powder blue, expansive sky opened wide. I walked to the edge of the cliff and looked down. Thirty feet below, the ocean's waves gently licked the lava walls. Black and tan boulders were visible beneath the surface of the clear water. I suspected it was low tide as many rocks were visible above the water's surface.

A few weeks ago, at this very spot, the waves splashed up over the 30-foot walls, filling the tide pools scattered around. No way would I have approached the edge then, but today, it felt safe.

I turned right and started walking southwest along the ocean's edge. Coming to where I usually went into the woods, my intuition told me I wasn't supposed to go that way. I stayed on the lava rocks, cautiously putting one foot in front of the other on the uneven terrain. Having a healthy respect for my environment, I walked at least ten feet from the edge.

Go closer, Sonja, Pele encouraged me. *You don't want to miss it.*

"Miss what, Pele?" I paused and looked out over the calm ocean waters, searching for a whale or maybe a pod of spinner dolphins.

"Are there sea turtles down there?" My fingers were crossed, hoping against hope to see just one turtle's head pop up above the water's surface. Gingerly stepping closer to the edge, I looked down.

No turtles. Disappointed, I stepped back several feet, turned to my right, and kept walking.

After walking for a few more minutes, I paused and slowly turned around 360 degrees. No one was in sight either in front of or behind me on the bluffs. I slipped my arms from the sleeves of my t-shirt, pulled it over my shoulders, and let the shirt hang down around my neck between my breasts. I continued walking as the sun's warmth penetrated my exposed back.

Looking to my right, I was once again tempted to meander into the coolness of the woods, take my shoes off, and let my feet soak up the energy from Mother Earth. But I didn't.

There was a feeling of edginess walking within five feet of the cliff's steep drop-off, unlike the calming sensation of walking amongst the ironwood pine trees on the soft, needled ground beneath them.

Up ahead, I noticed a sea arch. Seeing it made me wonder if there was empty space just a few feet below where I tread. My anxiety escalated until I remembered I was on a sacred quest, following my inner guidance system. I'd grown to trust my intuition and follow when Pele called, so I shook off the anxiety and kept walking.

Just ahead. Look to the left, Pele guided me.

There was a six-foot depression in the lava against the cliff's edge. It was about twelve feet across. Seeing an easy descent, I thought it would be possible to climb down there but decided to keep walking.

"I'll bet there's a better place just ahead," I reasoned with her.

After taking just a few steps, something stopped me. It felt like a huge invisible hand pressing against my chest.

Turn around. Go back, Pele ordered in no uncertain terms.

"Ahh, shit," I mumbled and turned around to head back to that slight depression in the lava landscape. I found the easiest path to this lower level and descended into a relatively flat alcove that fronted the wide-open ocean. Little black crabs scurried over the edge. It was dry.

Take off all your clothes, Pele instructed me.

"Okay, Pele," I replied hesitantly.

Looking around and still seeing no one, I removed my shoes, socks, shirt, shorts, and undies. I moved to the flattest part of the little nook and sat my bare derriere down. My legs stretched out before me. My feet were less than two feet from the edge.

Lay down. Hat and glasses off, too, I heard and tried to get comfortable laying face up and butt naked on the hard, uneven surface. I took off my sunglasses and hat and felt exposed at a whole new level. I was never without sunglasses and a hat when outdoors. Reaching my arm over my head, I deposited these final shields, although they lay within easy reach.

Closing my eyes and tuning in, I became more aware of the sounds of the waves rolling into shore. The rocks jostled as they were pushed back and forth by the waves. Occasionally, a light misty spray filled the air as the waves hit the rock wall many feet below.

My mind and body relaxed into Pele's lava arms.

Last year was about adjustment. This year is about doing. And next year is about being, I heard.

"What?"

Last year was about adjustment. This year is about doing. And next year will be about being.

"That's it? That's the message you want to give me, the gift that's supposed to put my mind at ease. You've got to be kidding! Surely, I'm in Hawaii for some higher purpose than that. Adjust? Do? Be?

"I know this past year has been about adjustment, and I'm so grateful you made it easy for me. I thought it would be so much harder leaving home. And it wasn't, partly because I had no doubt that my coming to Hawaii was you calling me here.

"The whole process flowed seamlessly, from telling my clients I was closing down my office, to moving away and finding the perfect place to stay while here. It was so easy, almost too easy. I'd started to think my whole time here would be easy."

I imagined Pele sitting at my side, reaching her hand toward my head and stroking my loose hair.

"Emotionally, it's been more difficult since I returned to Hawaii after the Christmas Holidays. Spending time with my wife, family, friends, and spiritual community made me remember what I'd left behind in Illinois. Now I'm all alone again."

I felt her finger gently wipe away a stray tear as it slipped from the corner of my eye.

"I do still feel joy in the moments when I'm out walking or going to a yoga class. But the in-between times are harder, lonelier."

I thought back to last month and my two-week pet-sitting gig on Maui. While it was beautiful there and a wonderful opportunity to spend time with Chi, Tiki,

Sissy, and Maumau (the three dogs and one cat), I came back to the Big Island feeling broken hearted once again. I'd fallen in love with little ChiChi, and after the

struggle of leaving my own pets in Illinois the month before, it just felt like another huge loss.

"Yes, this past year has been about adjustment, I'll give you that," I conceded.

"And oh, yes, this upcoming year is about doing. No doubt there! I'm going to be very busy with multiple pet-sitting jobs and the retreat I'm planning with Daniela," I told Pele.

"And that trip you want me to take by myself to the Philippines and Indonesia. By the way, why? I want to know what you have to teach me by going there. Alone."

I'd traveled by myself many times for work trainings but vacations just seemed to be something you shared with your spouse or friends. But none of the people I'd asked had wanted to go due to costs or travel time. So alone I would go.

"I know. I know," surrendering to my history with Pele and her greater wisdom. "I'll just have to wait and see and rest in the trust that whatever it is, it's for my highest good. But a girl gets curious sometimes, you know?" I said, seeking Pele's understanding of my plight.

"Okay, so besides traveling a lot, what am I supposed to be doing this next year," I asked.

Draw and write. Write and draw. This experience is something you need to write about. When you get back to your apartment, start writing. And draw. Lots of drawing. Draw and write. Write and draw, Pele chanted in a sing-songy cadence.

"Okay, but how is this new? I just finished my third collaborative book chapter, and I'm all set up to start my next children's book. This message just seems to be what I already know and what I'm already doing."

Oh, Sonja. All right, Pele told me in a grudging tone.

"All right, wha… ?"

Out of nowhere, I was startled from a state of deep relaxation by what felt like a huge bucket of water being dumped on me. Gasping, I sat up in shock and swallowed the salty water that had entered my mouth. I coughed heartily to clear my lungs from the aqueous assault.

"What just happened?" Confusion set in as I looked around, dazed and feeling like I'd just been baptized by the ocean. Taking note of a few details I'd overlooked upon my descent into the alcove, I began to suspect the ocean's waves were no stranger to this recess in the lava landscape.

The lava was smooth, most likely from a regular attack of waves. There were sea grasses clinging to the wall beside me. And there, a few feet from where I sat, were a grouping of Hawaiian Opihi Limpet shellfish clinging to the rock's surface. These clams needed water to survive.

But the alcove had been dry when I first arrived. The waves gently crashing into the lava wall many feet below. How had Pele timed the wave to descend on me right at that precise moment in our conversation?

All at once, laughter started bubbling up from deep within me.

"I guess you thought I needed a great, big slap in the face to shift my attention. Well, Pele, it worked. Okay. I get it. Doing. Drawing and writing.

"And by the way, thank you for the gift of confirmation." Was that Pele's voice I heard chuckling in amusement, or the waves softly slap, slap, slapping the wall?

Sitting up taller now, I scooted a foot or two further from the edge and leaned back, letting my arms support me. I soaked in the sun and the experience I'd just had.

Laughing to myself, I wondered if another wave was going to come, grab me, and carry me over the edge and out to sea. I'd heard those kind of things happened here. And no one would ever know until my dead, bloated body washed up on Kahena Beach. I scootched back some more.

Shifting gears, I continued my conversation with Pele.

"I can do 'adjusting,' and I can do 'doing,' but 'being' scares the shit out of me. Are you going to do something to me that will make me just *be*?"

My heartbeat sped up as I imagined 'just being.'

"Will I break a leg, get cancer, have a stroke? Does it mean no walks, hikes, or snorkeling? Will I have to stop playing pickleball and going to my writing group? What does *being* even look like? Sitting on a bench watching some ducks by a lake? Don't leave me hanging like this, Pele. What do you mean by *being*?" I desperately begged Pele for an answer. And I wanted it now.

Oh, Sonja. Haven't you learned yet? I've been showing you over and over.

You can only see the path ahead when it's just a few feet in front of you. When it's time, you'll know what 'being' means for you, Pele explained.

"Okay, Pele, I've trusted you thus far and survived."

But my words didn't belay my racing monkey mind. My heartbeat was still rapidly thumping with anxiety.

I told myself to get a grip and shook my body a little. Then, I searched for a way to calm my frantic thoughts.

"Let's come back to the present moment. Just take a few breaths. Look around at what you see, smell, taste, hear, and feel. You can do this," I encouraged myself.

Taking a fuller breath, I saw the great, big Pacific Ocean. With another inhale, I focused on the slightly fishy smell in the air. There was still the taste of saltwater on my tongue. I listened and heard cliff birds calling. And with another deep breath, I felt calm once more.

One stage at a time, my dear one, Pele reassured me.

A few minutes passed. It felt like this experience was complete. I put on my sunglasses and tie-dyed baseball cap.

Now somewhat dry, I put on my clothes and shoes. Climbing out of the alcove, I saw the other side of the sea arch, only it wasn't just one arch as I'd thought it was, but a double arch.

"You don't see that every day. I need to remember this place." Looking around, I took in the rest of the landscape so I could remember how to find it again.

By now, it was after 10:30. I tried to avoid being out in the sun between 10:00 a.m. and 2:00 p.m., so I wandered into the woods as soon as I saw an opening. It felt cool compared to the blazing heat of the Hawaiian sun. Gratitude for this experience filled my heart, creating within me a desire to remember it forever.

"After I get back to my apartment and have breakfast, I'm definitely going to write about this," I told Pele.

And I did. Then, I joined another writer's group and started attending a weekly watercolor painting class.

"I hear you, Pele. Hear and obey. Thank you, thank you, thank you!" Humbled, my spirits were raised, and my mind was at ease once again.

****

SONJA GLAD

Sonja Glad has a Master's Degree in Human Development Counseling and a Doctorate Degree in PsychoSpiritual Studies.
She is a Licensed Clinical Professional Counselor, a Shamanic Minister, a Reiki Master, a Breathwork Facilitator, and a Soul Collage Facilitator.

Sonja has written and illustrated two children's books, WooHoo For Sensitive Somjay (2021) and Feel Your Feelings, Feel Them All (2023). Her next children's book will be released in 2024.

She has also contributed a chapter in three other collaborative books, Shaman Heart, Turning Pain into Passion and Purpose (Chapter 10), The Chaos of Covid

(Chapter 8), and Shaman Heart, Sacred Rebel (Chapter 10).

Sonja currently lives on The Big Island of Hawaii and visits her other home in Illinois. She is happiest when she can be outdoors. She loves reading, writing, painting, practicing yoga, hiking, snorkeling, pickle ball and exploring the world. Learn more about Sonja on her website: www.sonjaglad.com

Lord Bat

Guardian of Palenque Miracles & Mysteries of Sacred Mayan Energy

PEGGY PATTY

Holding my breath, I stand frozen in Nadene's cozy living room. She is waiting patiently for my answer while pressing the photo into my reluctant hand.

"Who's the odd man hovering on the left side in this picture?"

Glancing down, I recognize the sole shot I snapped while alone inside a sacred Mayan Temple's "initiation room" in central Mexico three weeks prior. To my naked eye, the mysterious image only shows sunlight streaming onto a stone floor from a small rock window.

But Nadene sees something more.

Her blue eyes are perplexed while shaking her short blond hair. "He's standing right here looking at us in the picture."

I remain firm. "There's nobody in that picture. It's just the dark, hazy walls."

Why am I so hesitant to confirm the prominent shadowy figure peering at me from the left side of the photo when Nadene is so insistent to point it out?

I am in the midst of discovering a puzzle that is not easily solved.

At least by me.

I'd just returned from my second spiritual adventure in two years, exploring the sacred energy of Mayan feminine sites in Mexico. The golden age of the Mayan empire was from 250 AD to 900 AD, during which many of their elaborate pyramids and temples were created.

For unknown reasons, I'm fascinated with this intriguing culture and its spirituality.

Why am I drawn to explore the Maya, one of the most advanced ancient civilizations to ever flourish in Mexico and Central America?

Yes, the Maya designed incredible architecture expressing sophisticated knowledge of astronomy and the natural world.

But is there something even more profound?

Modern archeologists marvel at the intricate skill of the mathematicians and artisans who crafted these magnificent cities with their interconnected stone roadways. Cities that survive the intense ravages of time. A keen understanding of wet and dry jungle terrain is evident in the portions of the surviving ancient roads, spanning hundreds of miles and connecting masterful trade routes.

Fourteen centuries later, delicate Polychromos-colored decorations still grace stunning reliefs that depict historical and cosmic events in the magnificent Mayan temples and pyramids.

Today, we can view how vast stone pyramids crumbled while twisting roots beneath the thick forest canopy did their damage to the ancient structures. Over more than a thousand years, the forest swept in, reclaiming the cities that were mysteriously abandoned to deteriorate into the earth one by one.

What happened to the cities' inhabitants, who seemingly disappeared from history's sight?

This mysterious collapse of their political system of city-states around 900 AD remains unclear. But remnants of their ancient culture continue to exist in the lives of more than 7 million Mayans. Now, many people live near the poverty level in a region where tourism praises the accomplishments of their ancestors but tends to ignore them.

One of history's greatest riddles is what forced the abandonment of the Mayan pyramids and temples, resplendent with their intricate hieroglyphs and delicate carvings. Hundreds of books have been written speculating on the cause. I've scanned dozens of them, looking for a plausible explanation.

I find myself returning time and time again, seeking answers in hidden passageways, lingering behind tour groups, seeking answers to questions I can't even put into words.

It seems, perhaps, peeking into the mystifying Maya is my passion.

Unfortunately, my first trip into this ancient world ended badly.

On the last day, I'm chanting vibrations inside a stone temple built atop the highest pyramid at Coba in the Yucatan. The sun blinds me while stepping back into the intense midday heat on the summit. I fail to get my bearings in my attempt to scan the jungle treetops below.

Stumbling toward the descending front steps, I fall on uneven stones. I gift myself with a badly twisted ankle at the top of a Mayan temple.

Not my finest hour, especially since I still have to get my body down from the top.

Finding myself in this predicament is both humorous and troublesome. My new friend, Nadene, is on top of the Coba pyramid when I injure myself. She watches me, probably with some amusement, as I descend from the top of this 120-step structure by sliding down on my tush since I can no longer stand up.

It is a bit comical, as my ego is bruised, along with my foot.

Unable to walk after smashing my ankle into hard rocks in front of my fellow travelers, I'm escorted by a local villager from the ancient archeological site on a bicycle taxi. At least my injury occurs only ten blocks away from my hotel.

Why am I so inept? No one else is injuring themselves on this trip.

Definitely the low point of my first Mayan adventure, since I don't like to make a spectacle of myself. I'd rather stay in the background when I'm in unfamiliar territory.

After returning home to Illinois, I schedule a holistic session with my good friend Jan, a respected energy healer. I'm anxious to seek her perspective on my unusual calamity during my first adventure exploring energy sites in Mexico.

Laying on Jan's soft table, I sheepishly begin, "It is weird, Jan. I sprained my ankle on the top of the Coba pyramid so bad that I had to be bicycled out of the site by a local man. It was embarrassing!"

I let my mind drift back to the painful memory of my clumsiness, plus my descent down the venerable temple on my posterior.

After reflecting for a moment, Jan quietly pronounces, "Once, you were part of a processional to the top of an ancient structure. Then, you were ritually sacrificed. Not the exact pyramid you fell on, but another one during a different time period."

Instantly, my mind snaps back into the present moment.

Wait a minute. What happened?

I'm baffled.

Why was I so gullible to climb a pyramid when I knew I would be killed at the top? Am I one of those naive "true believers" who does everything I'm told to do by the hierarchy?

Feeling stunned, I stare at the white ceiling.

Was I really that clueless? Can't I read the room to sense something's up?

My quick and cool reaction to Jan's startling disclosure is a bit odd, even to me. Why don't I have any curiosity about the ritual itself? Instead, I'm laser-focused on the physical logistics of how I got on top of the temple in the first place.

I blurt out my confusion, "Why would I voluntarily climb to the top if I know I'm not coming down alive?"

Jan's calming smile soothes me. "Well, Peggy, they told you it was going to be somebody else."

All of a sudden, I begin laughing out loud. Intuitively, the truth of her statement was crystal clear.

Oh yes! This is how any sacrifice would be done. Everyone in the ritual that day would be told the sacrifice would be someone else. Damn those sneaky group dynamics!

In a flash, a phrase from an old high school poem pops into my mind as I lay absorbed in the moment on Jan's massage table.

Never ask for whom the bell tolls; it tolls for thee.

I rush home to research the poem. In the 1620s, author John Donne published the metaphysical concept that we are all socially and spiritually interconnected.

Donne wrote:

No man is an island, entire of itself; every man is a piece of the continent, a part of the main; if a clod be washed away by the sea, Europe is the less, as well as if a promontory were, as well as if a manor of thy friend's or of thine own were; any man's death diminishes me, because I am involved in mankind, and therefore never send to know for whom the bell tolls; it tolls for thee.

I've not thought about Donne's poem for 40 years, but always felt the truth of it.

At a deep level, I know we are all interconnected. Perhaps my Spirit learned this the hard way on top of a pyramid a couple of thousand years ago?

So why am I flying back to Mexico a second time to explore even more sixteen centuries old Maya spiritual sites?

Perhaps something is calling me?

With excitement, I book airline tickets for my second trip with Nadene. Since becoming friends at our first sacred site exploration two years earlier, we had kept in close contact. She lives just three hours away, so we're eager to plan our air travel together in anticipation of our continued spiritual adventures with Mayan Master Teacher Miguel Angel Vergara.

From the beginning of the first trip, I've not been so foolish as to think I could just go wandering around ancient spiritual sites without guidance.

Master Teacher Miguel has been studying, teaching, and living the wisdom of the Maya for over thirty years in Mexico. As a Mayan Priest, he leads journeys in

Mexico and Guatemala with his heart-centered style of teaching that makes his tours to Mayan sites come alive. His seminars on shamanism, astronomy, and the meaning of Mayan glyphs connect rapidly and profoundly during our first trip into the world of the ancients.

On our initial trip, Miguel always gave a patient response to our questions about this enigmatic culture. He never rushed or was flippant in his reply, when we asked some very uneducated curiosities about the ancient world based in colonialism. As North Americans, we're steeped in historical interpretations depicting ancient civilizations, including the Maya being very violent. He would just sigh.

Miguel's expertise as a shaman/guide illuminates the deep spirituality of the culture. His books on Mayan Goddesses and other sacred knowledge are deeply rooted in expansive metaphysical concepts.

His premiere teaching is striking.

Mayan knowledge is not a religion. It is a Way of Wisdom.

Miguel teaches us early in the trip that the Mayan spiritual feminine sites we will explore are "active energy sites, not ruins."

"The Masters of Light are still waiting at the sacred spiritual sites to teach and guide us, if we will connect to them."

So captivating. But what does that really mean? I hope Miguel expands upon these active energies at sacred sites.

I find Master Miguel's teachings very intriguing and entirely plausible. But somewhat theoretical.

Nadene and I are eager to learn more Mayan wisdom from him. We're journeying with another group of spiritually curious adventurers to four different Maya feminine spiritual sites, this time in Central Mexico. On our last trip, there were many intriguing experiences around every corner. What's in store for us on our approaching journey?

After several months of physical therapy from my tripping debacle on top of the pyramid, I am walking without pain.

Then it happens again!

I twist my ankle, falling on stairs, just three weeks before my second Maya adventure is to begin.

What is going on with me? Why do I keep tripping and hurting my ankle? I'm only in my late fifties. Am I getting too frail to travel?

This time, I damage my left ankle while descending the concrete steps outside a local Catholic retreat center after a Reiki Retreat weekend where I had led a drum circle.

Such a weird coincidence. I am headed back for more Mayan quests with another injured ankle? I don't want to deal with this!

I choose not to dwell on the circumstances surrounding my last serious ankle injury at Coba in the land of the Maya. It is a troublesome memory since I'd been told some ancient folks did sacrifice me once.

Perhaps I'm not physically able to travel on such a strenuous trip again. Hmm. But I still wanna go!

Seeking to put my worries aside, I dutifully follow my MD's orders to purchase a large, complicated cloth ankle brace, which reaches up to my knee from the medical supply store. I hope for the best. My current sprain on steps outside the Catholic retreat center is a bad one, and I'm worried.

How many acres will I be trekking at these Maya archeological sites? Can I physically keep up with our group? My ankle is so swollen now. Damn, can I scale ancient uneven stone buildings each day with an immobilized ankle like this?

Putting negative thoughts aside, I continue packing for the trip. After all, I paid in advance for the complete tour arrangements: meals, lodging, plus my airline ticket. I cram a bunch of older clothes in my suitcase to wear on the trip.

I am not losing that prepaid money. I sure hope I won't be sidelined to a hotel once I get there.

Determined that my new ankle injury will not interfere with the promise of an intoxicating trip, I continue to push ahead unless I get a hard "no" from my body. Doubts fill my mind about the strength of my ankle. Surviving the extensive walking tours of the Mayan archeological sites is a must.

Am I being reckless in ignoring my recent injury? I'm usually so cautious.

Trying to be diligent to baby my foot, I arrange for a wheelchair. Nadene volunteers to navigate me the length of the grueling concourses at the Chicago airport. My wheelchair is a godsend with each step of the trip. Harried passengers dragging their heavy luggage rush around me to meet unknown deadlines.

Countless blocks of unyielding cement at the crowded Mexico City airport become effortless as Nadene wheels me past weary travelers. I rejoice when officials in crisp white shirts and tired faces wave us to the front of a fifty-feet-long Customs line. Overwhelmed with gratitude, my body begins to relax.

Nadene is quite pleased not to have to wait in long lines, also.

Maybe there IS a benefit to a weak ankle!

We're relieved our tour bus isn't difficult to find, and I leave my wheelchair behind. Soon, we're relaxing in our hotel for a needed night's rest.

The following day our twelve-person tour group gathers with Master Teacher Miguel for a delicious breakfast buffet of eggs, sausage, and overflowing fruit. The air is rich with anticipation to begin our profound ten-day journey into the land of the Maya. None of us goes back for seconds.

After our nourishing meal, I remain obedient to my injured body's needs. I strap on my bulky ankle support and head for our bus along with Nadene. Our first sacred Mayan site is only 90 minutes away, and I'm pumped.

As our bus pulls into a small gravel parking lot, I watch local families with small children wander by with colorful blankets. Several community vendors selling treats set up small tables on the grass nearby. We're eager to depart the bus to begin exploring our first spiritual site on the trip.

Oh, yes, this is a Sunday. That's why the families are here.

It's so easy to forget basic moorings when on an international quest.

Upon arriving at an ordinary-looking entrance gate, I slip near the front of our group. I can't help but notice the heat of the sun. Safety first. I perch a tan floppy hat on my head, hoping not to become a piece of burnt Mexican toast. Clutching my lightweight blue backpack with my reusable bottle of cool water, I venture forth with my leg stabilized by my prescribed tight white cloth wrapping up to the knee.

I chuckle, entering the grounds.

What a fashion statement I must make. I've never cared about such things, so why start now?

The old archeological structures in the football field-size area are all but erased by time. Looming at one end is a pyramid in sore need of renovation. The jumbled piles of three-story-high ancient stones look precariously amassed as if by a careless giant.

Nadene sighs, "I wish that old rusty sign wasn't chained across the bottom of the steps leading to the top."

Glancing around at the rambunctious kids playing with friends, it's clear why climbing the cluttered steps rising to the deteriorating temple is closed to tourists.

My shoulders slump as I frown, "Yes, it does look dangerous to climb, but so disappointing."

As yet, we are unaware of the exquisite gems awaiting our explorations in the coming days.

I hear the laughter of children playing on several of the large grassy mounds around me.

The heat isn't bothering them. It's obvious they weren't raised in the upper Midwest winters.

Slowing my pace, the relentless sun bears down. My body's temperature begins rising, along with my irritability. Dragging around the brace on my leg prompts me to survey the grounds for a shady spot to cool off. I envy the handful of shady green trees along the edges.

Why aren't there any benches? Obviously, everyone is made from more robust stock than North Americans. Am I the only one miserable here?

Beads of perspiration form on my face. I feel myself baking in the uncovered field. I adjust the brim on my hat and soldier on. Light sweat begins trickling down my back and forehead.

Pausing in the sun, I envision how ancient Mayans might have inhabited the ground where I stood.

I wonder how many buildings had thatch covering the roofs for cooling? Or perhaps they just spent most of the time outside anyway. We certainly don't live much of our lives in nature now.

Miguel gathers us in a circle directly in front of the pyramid on a high treeless mound in the open meadow. He begins officiating a short Mayan ritual honoring sacred energies while my mind relentlessly searches for a nonexistent lawn chair in cool shade.

The sizzling hot afternoon sun continues to beat down on us in the grassy circle during the ritual. We're captivated by his gentle, authoritative voice calling the Lords & Ladies of each of the Four Directions in Mayan cosmology.

The sound of Miguel's invocation begins to fade in my ears.

The heat has found a victim. I feel my knees begin weakening. Closing my eyes, my body starts to sway as I succumb to the Central American sun.

Careful! Am I going to faint on this grass in front of everyone? Get this ankle brace off right now. Maybe I'll feel a little cooler.

Glancing at the ground, I shift to the side. My right leg takes a step back from the ritual circle. Unable to deny that my consciousness is draining from my body, I plop on the soft ground.

Cursing to myself, I begin struggling to unwrap the tight cloth brace layers.

Damn, how does this thing come off? I'm close to fainting, right here on the grass in front of an ancient pyramid.

My fingers tug at the cloth. At last, my fumbling is successful and the fabric falls to the ground beside me.

Tossing the contraption behind me, I join our circle again. As a faint breeze touches my face, the oppressive heat rises off my body. Feeling relief, I hear Miguel conclude the Mayan ritual.

To avoid another heat crisis, I buy a refreshing icy snow cone from a vendor to cool myself off when we gather back at the bus. Settling back in my seat, I wonder how soon I'll be forced to deal with that darn constraining apparatus.

It is astonishing! *I never wear the ankle brace again.*

I scale at least ten temples during the next eight days. Plus, I trek for what seems like hundreds of miles. Though I remain vigilant of my walking stance throughout, I never again feel the need for the ankle brace.

Looking back, I'm amazed. I have never worn a support device since peeling it off during a Mayan ritual that day in February 2009!

After shedding my brace at the first spiritual site, we head back to the hotel for our much-anticipated spiritual lecture from Master Teacher Miguel in a lovely outdoor alcove.

Miguel's soft, authoritative voice always shares deep Mayan wisdom in earnest.

"Spiritual sites are certainly ancient archeological treasures. However, these grounds, with their revered pyramids and other buildings, should never be mistaken for ruins. When we are on these sacred grounds, we're walking in real energies."

Little did I recognize the profound meaning of Miguel's teachings at the time.

My usual practice is to wait for any potential "teacher" to prove themselves to me before I go "all in" with them. However, I notice I'm prepared to trust

Miguel's wise truths before he even starts his presentation.

We find our seats in the quiet alcove with a small fountain in the center surrounded by flowering bushes.

Poised in our soft chairs encircling Miguel, we lean in close to absorb his teachings. Wearing a white shirt and blue jeans, he begins writing key spiritual concepts on a large easel with a black marker.

"We are vibrational beings. Each of us is part of the great dance of Life. It's crucial to adjust our frequencies, especially those connected to our minds. Reharmonize the body, soul, and spirit as One."

My ears perk up at the word "vibrational." I become laser-focused on his message.

Yes! Hope he shares more about the power of everyday frequencies. Love to hear more of his thoughts as a Mayan shaman.

Since English is not his first language, I'm concentrating on every word. No one wants to miss a single concept. We glance around to compare our notes with each other. I feel in the presence of a Master offering us an extraordinary gift because of his generosity of both knowledge and time.

His dark eyes are solemn. "Invoke the name of deity daily, pray, and chant mantras. Singing raises our vibrational frequency. Acknowledge all the gifts you have in your life, like food, clothing, and housing.

These make you responsible for reinforcing your positive thoughts and emotions for the benefit of the earth."

I struggle to keep up with the wisdom in his teachings.

"It's important to tell Mother Earth in a loud voice that you love her and respect her. There is a responsibility now to work for the planet."

My notebook is filling with my frantic scribbles. I begin to squirm in my seat. His intense presentation proceeds without any breaks. My entire body is tensing up while I shift from side to side to ease the tightening in my lower back.

Miguel is still going strong in explaining engrossing spiritual concepts in Mayan metaphysics. Despite that, we, mere mortals, need a bathroom break.

A low murmur from the back of the room makes it to the front. Everyone agrees we need twenty minutes to stretch our legs.

Tearing myself away from the lecture, I glance at my watch.

Wow, it's two hours later! His teachings are so mesmerizing.

After walking a bit among the blooming botanical beauties around the alcove, we fill our water bottles to the max. We settle back into our chairs, anxious to capture more Mayan wisdom.

The air around us fills with reverence when Miguel introduces us to the Divine Mother Ix Chel (Ee Shel). She's the feminine divine messenger in the Mayan wisdom tradition—the Mother Earth "Rainbow Mother" goddess of earth, moon, and healing.

Mayan Teacher Miguel shares, "Cosmic Mother Ix Chel represents the untapped power we possess. We lost touch with the vast capabilities of our awareness years ago. The Divine Mother has the power to transmute our emotions. All we need to do is ask."

I furiously scribble notes of Miguel's in-depth teachings. A slight cooling breeze brushes my skin. I desire to capture every word. I strain my head forward and cock my head.

Nadene bravely offers a question during a pause. "How do we ask for help?"

Miguel is explicit in his response. "Do mental alchemy when negativity is present. When we replace anxiety, we get peace. Imagine something beautiful. This will change the energy."

Is it that easy? Can just using sacred practices with our imagination help bring about a more sane and loving world?

My mind wants to believe it's that simple. My heart already does.

Miguel shares an ancient glyph of Ix Chel. Her image is of an old woman pouring a pot of healing liquid onto the earth. The coiled snake on top of her head refers to the kundalini symbol of risen energy in her crown chakra. The ancient drawing highlights spiritual energy ascending through her body, which resides at the top of her head.

I stare at the intriguing image as Miguel goes deeper. His spiritual knowledge is steeped in the venerable wisdom traditions of the East and other sacred philosophies from around the world.

"The divine feminine figure, Ix Chel, is also portrayed with a lily in her hair, symbolizing the priestess who connects with love consciousness, akin to Christ Consciousness, and other ancient spiritual traditions. Her left hand touches the earth where power rises. When we tune into the powerful nurturing energy of Ix Chel, she opens us to the mystery of our divine essence."

Deep respect is in the air as Mayan Priest Miguel expounds on these spiritual truths. We know we are in the presence of a man whose extensive knowledge of a revered past is a precious gift to us.

Miguel shares that he will show us how to show reverence by leading us in discreet sacred rituals honoring Mayan spirituality/cosmology before we enter each spiritual site on our trip.

Again, he highlights, "These are active energy sites, not ruins."

Our next day's journey is to the fascinating Mayan archeological treasure of Palenque.

At the gates of the ancient ceremonial grounds, Master Miguel leads us in a Mayan ritual to show respect. No need to draw the attention of others to our ritual. On his silence signal, we turn toward each other to make a circle before entering the revered site. Miguel softly intones a concise, sweet ritual honoring the sacred spiritual energies of the four directions within Mayan spirituality.

With one graceful motion, he removes a few grains of corn from the small woven cloth bag hanging at his side. Placing the seeds in each of our hands, he instructs us to scatter a few corn kernels in each of the four directions to acknowledge the spiritual energies.

Corn is honored in Mayan culture, representing a gift from the Gods. It's the foundation of Mayan civilization because it is the core of life.

We are now spiritually invited to enter the esteemed Palenque grounds.

Palenque flourished from 400 AD to 900 AD. Archeologists estimate less than 5% of the city is explored now, leaving more than a thousand structures still covered by dense jungle. The rest of the vast acres of this spiritual and social site from the Maya world remain uninvestigated in our time.

Sprinkled throughout the fascinating structures are elaborate glyphs from the sophisticated Mayan writing system similar to the Egyptian hieroglyphics.

The highlight of our Palenque trip is climbing the stone pyramid, where archaeologists discovered a burial temple at the base in 1993. A female burial chamber is buried deep in the base, which modern archeologists call the "red queen" or an "unknown noble woman." The body is so referred to due to the discovery of red cinnabar covering her entire body.

Archaeologists are still researching if she may be Lord Pacal II's mother or wife, the most prominent ruler of Palenque around 650 AD. The "red queen's" body is now at the National Museum of Archeology in Mexico City, along with the incredible offering of jade discovered with it.

Teacher Miguel shares that her real honorific name is actually "Lady White Heron." She is the female/feminine spiritual presence in Palenque.

Our excitement rises as we hike toward Lady White Heron's Pyramid. We see the Temple of the Inscriptions Pyramid dedicated to Lord Pacal II beckoning ahead, which is famous worldwide. His spectacular sarcophagus, covered by an enormous carved stone lid, including a full-sized jade mask covering his face, was discovered in 1952 inside the base of his Temple.

Miguel explains there is a complex of underground tunnels connecting both of their temples. Also, both pyramids are across from the sprawling so-called Palace of Palenque complex, consisting perhaps of a hundred rooms. The complex is deemed one of the most magnificent architectural structures in the Classic Maya era, with courtyards, stucco murals, and steam rooms.

Our small group is anxious to explore Palenque's exquisite architecture all around us. We slowly walk through the expansive complex of temples, ball courts, plazas, and other structures.

No one should travel to unknown civilizations without some expectation of experiencing energetic encounters beyond our regular lives. The veil of time and space can be lifted, and we may be offered a glimpse into the world of the ancient Maya.

However, I am uniquely "left-brained" in my daily life.

As a domestic violence attorney, I handled many hundreds of contested civil and criminal court trials and trained other attorneys to handle hundreds more. I taught attorneys, judges, and police officers to examine literal black-and-white evidence to decide what is rational, factual, and significant.

"Just the facts, madam," is what the court system demands.

My "feelings" are of no value to a Judge in my attempt to obtain an Order of Protection or child support for violence victims. My "intuition" certainly does not put milk on the table for their children. Only provable facts weighing in favor of justice for victims will do.

I'm skilled in discerning and crafting the delivery of facts to the court system so families have housing, food, and safety.

However, my actual encounters at Palenque defy any literal explanation, even though I end up bringing home black-and-white photo evidence to back up the occurrences!

Miguel leads us past spellbinding stone pyramids at least four stories in height on a winding path through a grassy plaza.

He begins sharing Palenque history while we pass six ancient, enigmatic structures.

"Here's the Temple of the Sun. On the inside walls are some of the most beautifully preserved murals here. On the right side is the Temple of the Moon where women would gather for ritual occasions. Later, we will stop to study some of the ornate figures in these 1,600 years old stone buildings. We will also walk through a Mayan initiation room."

In solemn silence, we follow the Mayan shaman down a wide dirt pathway into the midst of the venerable city over sixteen centuries old. We're facing what seems to be an unachievable task to peek into the mystery of the Maya.

Just past the tree line, I stop on the dusty trail. The scope of the city's Palace complex and fifteen-plus pyramids becomes apparent. My heart beats faster. I struggle to attempt to understand the scene before me.

I can't make sense of these foreign shapes of hand-cut limestone jutting to the sky. The pyramids seem to emerge from the surrounding jungle. How is it possible to connect this view to the modern world?

I might as well be on the moon.

My eyes widen in amazement while awe ripples through my body. I'm immersed in the wonder of an ancient culture, just as mysterious today as when Europeans first saw the massive decomposing buildings overtaken by the tropical forest in the 1500s.

Am I really standing here where thousands of people walked in rituals? I'm sure they were marveling at this unique sight, just as I am now. What were their lives like?

My gaze is drawn to the Pyramid of Lady Great White Heron directly ahead in my path. Hers is the primary Maya feminine temple pyramid highlighted by Miguel that day.

Our group gathers at the base of the first of many pyramids we'll climb on our adventure. The day before,

I'd removed my heavy ankle brace during the ritual in the sizzling sun. Feeling optimistic that morning, I had left it behind in my hotel.

Will I be able to climb all the way up? Was I foolish not to strap back on the cumbersome ankle support this morning? Guess I will find out if I can trust my intuition!

All twelve of us begin slowly lumbering up the nine levels of steep steps leading into the Temple on the flat top. I can hear solemn whispers of support while we proceed to each level of the Pyramid.

Oh yes. Miguel told us this is the ancient temple where Lady White Heron's body was laid in the base more than 1500 years ago.

I feel my energy surging. My careful movements allow me to climb halfway up with no ankle pain. A slow smile spreads across my face while moving confidently to each higher level. I reach the top platform of the Pyramid with ease.

Wow, I'm doing it. I'm able to climb all the way to the top!

Attaining the pinnacle of the Pyramid, I enter the dark stone Temple through a small stone door. Soon, all of our group fills the inside of the Temple after climbing the steep stone steps outside. Feeling a bit discouraged in the sparse rock space, I search for some exciting detail to photograph.

Everything is a bland gray color.

In a flash, a decision springs to my mind. I'll wait until I'm alone in the Temple before using my camera.

There are too many people walking around here. What shot do I want to take? It's all bland gray stones. Certainly, I'll find something.

I'm anxious to use my new candy-apple red camera with a 240-picture memory card purchased for the trip. I'd hoped it would be adequate for a ten-day spiritual adventure of sacred feminine sites in Mexico.

How many photos of ancient temples will I need to capture the charm and mystery of Maya spirituality?

I am about to find out the answer.

Lady White Heron's Temple Pyramid is very dark inside. The only natural light filters in through a small open doorway.

As my eyes acclimate to the dark room, I notice eight bare lightbulbs hanging precariously from a single strand of electric wire strung throughout the twenty-five-foot-long ceiling. The bulbs are the only light illuminating the darkness inside.

The visitor area is about twenty-five feet long and eight feet wide with an offset small room with a heavy stone platform. Viewers stand in this extended space to see the smaller stone chamber directly in front of the outside entry.

An old iron gate is locked outside the small chamber room to keep anyone from wandering into the six-by-twelve-foot chamber in front of us. We take turns peering through the iron bars.

Only one item is left in this small Temple room. A four-inch thick gray stone slab sitting ajar on a concrete base.

With no background information offered regarding the slab in front of us, curiosity builds while waiting in the cool air of the sacred stone structure.

Does Lady White Heron mind having her name changed and her body moved hundreds of miles away? I wouldn't be pleased. Maybe it doesn't matter. Hmm, I wonder what was under the stone slab?

Everyone in my group finishes their explorations and disappears through the small stone door. I watch my friends descend into the light down the front of the Pyramid.

Finally, I'm alone on the top of this ancient tomb!

Barely breathing, I spring into action with my camera. I no longer need to worry if someone will pass in front of me in the small rock corridor.

I need to hurry. It'll take my friends a while to get back down those steep steps. They can't get too far. I'll snap some shots and go join them!

First, I want a picture of the locked chamber inside the iron gate. I begin looking through the bars at the heavy stone slab within.

Now, I know the basics of photography. Don't point my camera lens near a lightbulb if I want to take a clear and accurate photo of a scene. I lift my lens to frame the stone slab.

Jerking my camera back in surprise, I'm startled by what I see.

What's that? A round blue orb!

Pulling my camera away, I stare into the chamber with my naked eyes. Everything looked normal. Well, as normal as looking into a 1600-year-old chamber on top of a burial pyramid is.

Holding my breath, I peek into the camera lens again. My senses are electric. A vibrant cobalt orb is taking up about a third of my viewfinder.

There it is again! What am I looking at?

I'm confused as my heart beats faster—so many questions.

Am I pointing toward a light bulb? Is there dust in the air? Moisture?

I scrutinize the front of the camera. Nope, no dripping water leaking on the lens. I glance at the calm day appearing outside the Temple door. Not a cloud in the sky.

Stepping back, I look around the camera to investigate the source of this shockingly beautiful anomaly. I cannot find any bright blue round objects anywhere! I'm certainly not pointing my camera at a light bulb.

Can I find other blue orbs in this burial Temple?

Since everyone is gone, I begin rushing down the entire length of the Temple corridor, taking photos.

Yes, there are more cobalt orbs in some of these pictures!

I'm amazed and disorientated at the same moment as I remain alone at the top of the Pyramid in this deserted feminine burial Temple.

It must be from some reflection in this dark Temple. But where?

I keep looking but can't see anything resembling a colored orb in front of the camera!

Tingling with excitement, I discover other cobalt orbs in the photos I am snapping. Very intriguing, indeed.

I would love to continue exploring the phenomena. My rational mind keeps looking for scientific clues in the stone structure to cause blue circles in my camera lens, but I don't have time to make sense of it all.

Plus, I'm getting nervous.

I gotta catch up with the rest of the group. Where on this earth am I? Somewhere in central Mexico, alone, on top of a burial pyramid. I don't even know where Miguel is taking us next.

Left with no choice, I hastily snap a few more pictures alone atop Lady White Heron's Pyramid. I pivot around to move toward the outside light coming from the only door leading out of the Temple.

Focusing on not falling on my face, I carefully navigate down the stone steps at the front of the Pyramid in the afternoon sun. I descend as fast as possible to the grassy lawn below. Searching the surrounding stone structures, I'm relieved to see Nadene viewing another ancient monument with the rest of the group.

Relief floods over me. I scamper over to join them at the base of another pyramid. I begin to wonder what the other travelers are experiencing.

Did my friends' photos capture any blue orbs? Maybe their pictures also show mystifying objects invisible to our eyes.

Absentmindedly, I tap my new camera.

Will I even see anything curious in these Temple photos once they're printed? Maybe the electric blue beauties will be gone, and all I'll have is my imagination to remember them by. I wonder.

On my way to rejoin my new friends, I notice a delightful small rose bush in full bloom on the side of the limestone Palace complex. One of the bush's bright blooms lays on the grass beneath it. I find myself instinctually reaching down and picking it up to admire. I love flowers.

I pause a moment. The rose is already fallen from the bush. My instinct tells me I should put it gently into my pocket, so I do.

Next on our walking tour of this intriguing spiritual site is another architectural marvel of Palenque - the Palace complex itself. This complex has perhaps a hundred connecting rooms plus two large courtyards built over several generations. The Palace is the largest building complex in Palenque. It was equipped with baths and saunas supplied by a freshwater aqueduct flowing like a maze beneath the complex.

Walking through the Palace, I enter one of the indoor open-to-the-sky courtyards. Numerous elaborate sculptures and bas-relief carvings are attached to the walls that still astonish modern archeologists with their intricate details.

Two sides of the courtyard have about nine rows of stone stadium seating with staircases. Plus, each side of the courtyard's walls still has the original life-size stucco figures attached to them.

Standing alone in the large Palace courtyard, I imagine what history these original stucco sculptures tell.

What happened here? Who were these people, and what were their lives like? Did they have family gatherings here, or was it always reserved for dignitaries?

Remembering the small ruby-red rose that fell from the bush in the plaza outside, I reach into my side pocket.

Good, I didn't crush it!

Looking at the rose on my palm, I notice I'm drawn into the middle of the grassy green courtyard.

Glancing around to ensure I'm alone, I silently place the rose in respect on the grass in the courtyard's center. I step back.

I realize I'm caught up in the moment, but I still don't want to look crazy to any onlookers.

Standing at the edge of the courtyard for a few minutes, I gaze in wonder at the distinctive red rose in the center amid the stucco reliefs.

I don't have a clue as to why I feel drawn to place it there.

Near the end of our ten-day adventure, Miguel led us to revisit Palenque. I'm delighted since I snapped the blue orb photos there. No other colored orbs had visited my pictures during the trip except there.

Today, we will view pyramids in a completely different section of this expansive sacred site.

We climb the Temple of the Sun and the Temple of the Moon. We also walk solemnly through the large ball court, which Miguel describes as being used for spiritual practices, not ritual sacrifices. He explains how all of these sites have specific aspects of astrological alignments, especially the ball courts.

So much history!

At midday, Miguel encourages our group to wander around Palenque individually for an hour to soak up the ambiance. Standing in one of the large plazas, I notice I'm facing more than six pyramids surrounded by dense green jungle.

I have no idea which intriguing direction to go first.

When the group disperses to embark on their solo journeys, I notice I'm following Miguel. He approaches the plant-covered steps, meandering to the top of a mysterious pyramid at the edge of the jungle entitled the Temple of the Foliated Cross.

I reach the top and sit near him. We are towering over most of the city of the Palenque from this vantage point, including the Palace complex and burial pyramids.

Miguel reaches into his cloth bag to pull out a small round glass container filled with oil. He dabs some on his finger and touches my 3rd eye with it. Then he places some oil on his forehead.

I sit in silence beside Miguel for several minutes. He leans over to point to the thick jungle canopy, "There is a portal above the Pyramid through the trees."

Squinting, I hope to view an anomaly in the distance.

I see nothing.

Guess I'm not enlightened enough to be wasting the time of a Master Mayan Teacher.

I begin feeling a stinging sensation of the essential oil on my forehead.

Ouch, is that burning my skin?

I grit my teeth.

I refuse to be a wimp before a Mayan Shaman! If it's not bothering him, then I will tough it out!

My eyes are drawn to the massive nine-level Temple of the Cross Pyramid directly to my right. Puzzled, I watch Nadene sprinting alone up the steep stone steps in front of the Temple. It's one of the largest pyramids unearthed from the jungle at Palenque.

Why is she trying to run up those steps so fast?

Later Nadine reminisces, "I'm not sure why I was rushing up there. I just needed to be near the front of everyone else."

I chuckle, reminding her, "Nadene, you were the only person on those temple steps when you were scamping up. There wasn't anyone else around you!"

Clearly, I'm not the only one having unique, energetic experiences at Palenque.

Ordinary time has little meaning at such a sacred site. I'm unclear how long I sat beside Miguel gazing over the top of Palenque from the Temple of the Foliated Cross.

The burning sensation on my forehead is lessening. I feel drawn to descend the rocky face of the Foliated Cross Pyramid while the hot sun continues to beam bright. Meandering across the grass plaza surrounded by pyramids, I have no particular plan.

In a flash, an idea pops into my mind.

Humm, I wonder if I can find the Mayan initiation room in the Palace that Miguel pointed out? I would love to check that out again! I didn't have a chance to get a feel for the stone bed at the end of the room.

I stroll toward the large Palace complex with its many rooms, courtyards, and staircases. This large stone complex rose three or more stories, with dozens of rooms now open to the sky. Over a thousand years of jungle conditions ravished the labyrinth of rooms, so many are left now with short walls and collapsed roofs.

Finding the "initiation room" seems like a fool's errand, but I feel a spark.

It would be so cool to find that exact room!

Early in the trip, Miguel led our group into this expansive stone Palace through the original massive stone entrance. I realize the twelve layers of entry steps would be too steep for me to climb again today.

Nope! I'm not climbing those coliseum steps in front of this vast complex again! Those steps were difficult enough to scale earlier. Yes, my ankles are holding up, but I've scrambled up at least ten steep pyramids this trip. I'm not going to push my luck.

I started focusing on remembering where the initiation room was located. Miguel had led us into a long, dark room with one stone window on the far end.

My memory of his pronouncement is distinct, "This is a Maya spiritual initiation room."

I slow my pace and allow myself to be drawn to enter the extensive stone structure through a side entrance close to the ground.

Is this the right entrance? So many massive stones everywhere. Hey, I'm walking beside the pyramid where I took the blue orbs photos. Why am I not going there?

I recall bright sunlight greeting me upon leaving the initiation room before, so I actually may be at the correct entry.

Are these the same steps Miguel led us through? I will not allow myself to get lost.

I enter a long, dark room and immediately notice the large stone slab bed at one end.

Yes, this is the same room!

Squinting at the slab, I rejoice.

There it is! That's the stone bed Miguel said was a part of Maya spiritual initiations.

As I become more accustomed to the lack of light, I study the bare rock room surrounding me in all directions. It feels like a stone cave surrounding me on all four sides, plus floor and ceiling.

I begin walking toward the ten-foot initiation limestone slab. Suddenly, I feel my body stop as if it has a mind of its own.

This is close enough.

Warily, I stand in silence about twelve feet in front of the initiation bed for a couple of minutes. Will I receive any mental or emotional impressions? Two or three visitors roam this large, empty cavern before they move on.

I open my imagination while exploring the scene before me.

What were those initiations like? Exactly where were people standing in this room? Geez, that stone slab looks uncomfortable. Nope, I am not gonna lay on the slab to test it out! Over 1500 years have passed since individuals used this room for rituals. Miguel emphasizes the depth of Mayan spirituality, but I imagine violence might have visited this place like any civilization if it devolves.

My somber thought gave the room a different feeling.

Yep, enough of that! Do I really want to know what that ten-foot slab was used for?

Abruptly, I turn around to change my mood. Deciding no spiritual initiation is in the offing today, at least for me, I move away from the stone slab bed.

Venturing further into the dark room, I notice a handful of visitors filtering around to reach a small stone staircase hidden on the right side of the room. The visitors seem to disappear when they reach the corner, which I assume leads up and out of the initiation space into other areas above, inside the Palace.

The only light in the room streams through a small two by two feet stone window, perfectly framing a single small green tree in the plaza outside.

I wonder if there's enough light in here to take a shot of that sweet tree framed by the rock window. This might turn out to be one of those artistic pictures.

Motionless, I wait until a young mom holding her small son's hand disappears into the right corner.

Just like when I took my photos at Lady White Heron's Pyramid, I feel a strong desire to be alone to use my camera.

Within a minute, I'm standing alone in the initiation room. I snap a picture of the light streaming through the window but immediately feel a peculiar sensation.

It's the feeling you get when you wonder if you are really alone. And if you're safe.

I want to leave this room. Now.

Electricity ripples down my spine.

I longer wish to take any photos. Panic floods over me. My only mission becomes finding the enclosed stone staircase, hoping it leads out of this long dark room with the small window.

Go. Now! There's no reason not to feel safe. There's no one else here but me. But I need to find that staircase. Why?

Alarm bells go off in my mind. I waste no time turning to see if someone's behind me. Bolting, I hurry toward an unseen staircase for no logical reason.

In truth, I flee with as much dignity as I can muster.

With each step farther from the initiation room, my body relaxes. A light, calm mood comes wafting toward me as the stone steps lead to a higher level. I'm relieved the ancient walls and ceilings are open to the bright afternoon sky.

Upon feeling the bright sensation of the sun on my face, I begin lecturing myself.

Well, that was weird. I must have a little anxiety from being alone in an unfamiliar country. I've never had anything happen like that before.

Fifteen years later, I can still remember the unsettling feeling overcoming me when I fled to climb the stone staircase from the initiation room.

Late in the afternoon, I realize I feel a little odd when our group gathers back together. Miguel gently leads us in giving our thanks and saying our goodbyes to the ancient Palenque site.

It is the last day of our trip, and I will be flying home to Illinois tomorrow.

I glance at my new friends. I can see we are all tired, hungry, and overwhelmed by our ten-day-long adventures.

However, at that moment, my tiredness seems a distant concern. Something that I can't pinpoint is happening.

Our group walks in silence toward the unseen exit somewhere ahead. I notice I'm allowing myself to slow my pace until I am the final member trailing behind the others. We are approaching the edge of this alluring spiritual site to head toward our bus.

Within a few yards of the gates, surrounded by jungle, I feel my feet abruptly stop on the dirt path. In the distance, I view a young Mexican woman standing inside a small ten by ten feet wood hut delineating the edge of the archeological grounds.

My thoughts become crystal clear.

I am not leaving here. If I pass the hut ahead, I cannot come back.

I remain standing inside the Palenque gates, watching my fellow travelers disappear out of sight. They are dutifully heading to our bus to fly home the next day.

Soon, no one is in view.

Even the young woman seems to have vanished.

It is just me and the power of Palenque.

My friends must be over three blocks away. Why am I still standing inside the gates to Palenque?

What am I doing? Why am I not leaving to get on the bus?

Miguel must have noticed I'm not with the group. His figure appears outside the gates about two blocks away. He motions for me to join the others.

I feel myself shake my head from side to side.

No, I am not leaving Palenque.

I continue to stand motionless.

Why am I doing this?

This foreign feeling is more than a passing regret about leaving a mesmerizing site. I am staying in Palenque.

Alone on the dirt path, I watch Miguel look my way and then turn to join the rest of the group.

A split second later, self-preservation takes over with fear gripping my body!

Am I insane? What am I doing? The only people I know in Mexico have vanished from my sight to board our bus parked god only knows where. I am alone here. This is reckless. My passport is on that bus!

My mind begins clearing. I realize I have no clue what I'm doing standing alone on a dirt path in the Mayan jungle, except for the slowly subsiding desire never to leave the gates of Palenque.

My strong, rational mind tells me I better get my butt on that tour bus so that I can head back to my life in Illinois.

I rush toward the exit of the archeological site. Not a single soul is around to view my hasty departure. Blocks ahead, I turn toward the shop-lined street filled with tourists.

Propelling myself down the street in a daze, I dodge a local woman with beautiful long black hair and wearing a colorful skirt. She is balancing swatches of bright multi-hued cloth squares on her head while holding bags of white embroidered blouses and belts for sale in both arms.

She must notice the panic on my face when I swerve around her to earnestly search for my connection to my life in the modern world.

After rushing several blocks, I see my friends loading onto the bus. The pounding in my heart begins to recede.

Thankfully, no one on the bus inquires why I'm the last person to get on. I have no logical answer anyway. The bus is quiet. Everyone is too occupied by their own Palenque experiences to even notice me.

Progressing through our week's adventures, we have all become believers in the "active Mayan spiritual energy."

After returning from Mexico, I schedule a holistic energy session with my friend Jan, the respected healer I had visited after my first Mayan trip.

Upon entering her comfortable home, I exclaim, "Jan, I had extraordinary Palenque experiences. I took photos of gorgeous blue orbs. I've been mulling it all over in my mind. It was… so intriguing there."

Jan's calm voice is clear after listening to me reminisce. "You left part of yourself in Palenque. You need to bring ALL of yourself back."

I begin to protest. "But it is so indescribable! I sensed so much happening, but it's somewhat unclear."

I search for the words "except for a lingering feeling…"

My mind drifts. I struggle to describe my reaction to the ancient site. I'm being pulled back to those unexplainable Palenque encounters.

For the first time in our relationship, Jan raises her voice. "No. You need to bring all of yourself back, now!"

Jarred by her strong directness, I comply.

I trust Jan's spiritual instruction. It's foolish to ignore it. I have no desire to stay at a spiritual site in another country, regardless of how fascinating it is.

I have created a life that I love in the present. It's only logical for me to use all my energy for this lifetime. As a Virgo, I respond well to the invocation of logic.

One can only imagine what experiences individuals have if they are open to the energies at Palenque and other Mayan spiritual sites. Nadene sensing Kukulkan on a pyramid's peak or other fellow travelers seeing orbs in the trees can strain credulity.

I, for one, will never question their honesty after my encounters on the journey.

A couple of weeks after my return from Palenque, Nadene and I get together to revisit our life-altering Palenque trip through our evocative pictures of temples, burial chambers, and stone ceremonial monuments.

I'm anxious to listen to Nadene recount her own experiences on the Mayan trip.

Sitting on her overstuffed couch, we examine each fascinating Mayan artifact photo. My prize snapshots are the beautiful blue cobalt orbs beaming brightly from Lady White Heron's Pyramid Temple.

Yes, the blue circle lights showed up! The orbs radiate in many of my temple pictures from the top of her Pyramid. But there are no blue orbs in any other picture from the trip.

Very interesting.

After staring at one image in my stacks of printed photos, Nadene turns to me. "Where did you take this picture?"

I glance at the four-by-six picture to prod my memory. The image shows a small window with lots of bright light streaming onto a stone floor with dark walls on all sides.

I slowly realize it is my photo of the unlit "initiation room" in the Palenque Palace complex.

"Hey Nadene, remember Miguel told us about the unusual "initiation room" at Palenque? That's where I went during our solo time the last afternoon. This photo is my artsy venture to snap light coming in from the window. But the photo didn't turn out, though. The room is too dark."

With a quizzical expression, Nadene leans over to me, "But who's this guy in the picture?"

I'm confused. I peer closer at the snapshot, "What guy, Nadene?"

She looks directly into my eyes, "The guy in the initiation room with you."

I feel my heart beat faster. I know I need to give a firm answer. "What do you mean, Nadene? There's no guy in this picture."

Nadene becomes more insistent. "Peggy, here's the guy's face. He is standing in the upper left-hand of your picture. Look, here he is!"

Handing the photo to me, Nadene points to the upper left corner.

I stand up and hand the picture back.

Nope. There is not a person there.

We burst out laughing. Something peculiar is happening here, but we have no idea what it is. It is more than a difference in my opinion or eyesight.

Remaining firm, I insist, "I don't see any guy, Nadene. It's only the pattern of the stone walls."

I am not lying to her. I have no intention of seeing any sketchy shadow guy hanging out in one of my pictures.

It would be a relief if Nadene would just drop the whole thing. But as good friends do, Nadene senses something is up. To prove her point, she walks over to her computer and prints a full-page color copy of my picture.

She shoves the 8-by-10 image of "Palenque Spock" at me, but I'm still not prepared to see him. I began to hover close to her home office door for my escape.

Nope. I don't see anyone in that picture. Why won't she stop trying to convince me?

"No, Nadene, it's really just the pattern of those ancient rock walls," I repeat as my body repels any such suggestion.

Nadene laughs. She is wise enough to realize she's wasting her time trying to convince me. After all, I'm responsible for snapping the Palenque photo, so it is my mystery to solve. She bundles me up with all my photos and sends me home.

A few days later, my spouse flips through my Palenque pictures at the kitchen table. She stops at one of the photos.

Glancing at me, "Who's the guy?"

I loudly sigh.

Not this again!

I try to be nonchalant, "What guy? It's just a picture I took of light coming through a window."

She repeats the obvious, "There is a guy right here in the upper left-hand corner."

I believe I've crafted a better response to any intrusive questions about the weird picture.

"It must be some guy in the corner of the room I didn't notice before I took the picture."

I sheepishly dig out the 8 x10 blow-up of the photo Nadene insisted I take home. I hand it over.

My spouse pours over the picture and then declares, "Well, if he is just some random guy, why doesn't he have any legs or feet?"

Seeking a logical explanation, I take a cautious peek at the picture again.

In the upper left-hand corner, an adult male figure faces the camera lens, peering at me. He looks like the original Spock from Star Trek, with an angular face and a tall, slim body. Even his ears look a little pointy. Or is it my imagination?

Try as I might, I can't find any legs or feet in the picture below his full torso. It's beyond doubt the image in the photo is a gift from Palenque. But precisely what is the present? And am I ready to receive it?

I already know there are realities beyond our view. Had Spock beamed in to give me a specific message?

I have no answer, so I put the photo in a drawer. If I don't have a definite response to who or what is in the picture from the Maya initiation room, then I'm not keen on knowing the photo existed.

I was alone in the room with whatever it is in the Palenque picture.

The answer I seek is not long in coming.

Two years later, I attend a Mayan spiritual gathering in Hot Springs, Arkansas, where Mayan Master Miguel is the guest presenter. We are deeply drawn to see Miguel again at the gathering.

I travel with my spouse, plus our friend Nadene, to the quartz crystal sites around Hot Springs a day early so we can dig for crystals prior to the spiritual gathering. We're delighted at the opportunity to add this bucket list adventure. We've dreamed about crystal-digging for years but never organized ourselves to do so.

I also have another agenda.

I'm intent on getting Miguel's response to my "Palenque initiation room" photo, so I am careful to add it to my luggage.

Strange obstacles appear as we begin our road trip to join Master Miguel on a Mayan weekend adventure and dig for crystals.

An unusual hurdle is thrown our way at the beginning of our departure. As the three of us seek to begin the trip in the early morning hours, we notice the driveway is blocked by a heavy tree that fell during an overnight storm. I've lived in our twelve-wooded-acre country home for fifteen years, but I've never experienced a tree blocking our long lane before.

Nothing is stopping us from digging crystals in Arkansas and visiting with Miguel. My spouse realizes her chainsaw is broken, so she has to use a handsaw and drag parts of the large tree to make a path for my red Prius to get out to the county road.

Finally, we're heading to the crystals and to Miguel!

Driving through Missouri, we ride through a literal tornado west of St Louis. Nothing is stopping us from getting to those crystals. We surround our car with white light and keep driving.

At least we'll die happy!

Late at night, we arrive in the Hot Springs area in one piece. The area is world-renowned for the expansive amount of quartz crystal found under the earth.

We choose a popular quartz crystal location to try our luck at digging for treasures the following morning. Laughing like kids in a candy shop, we dig through two-story piles of dirt all around. We haul our precious finds to the vehicle one by one. It only takes about two hours to fill the car with our treasures.

Nadene unearths the prize one. A stunning double-terminated clear crystal gem over three inches long. She painstakingly excavates it while sitting on the ground in a roadway, chiseling it out with a small trowel while dump trucks dodge her.

Yeah, we're pretty crazy about crystals.

We end up harvesting so many beautiful crystals that they weigh down the Prius' bumper. When the

Arkansas sun begins rivaling our experience in the Mexican jungle, we are forced to call it a day.

As I drive on the old, compacted dirt road winding away from our digging adventure, my car's back bumper scrapes in the potholes from our booty of heavy, precious stones.

Enormous fun was had finding the beautiful crystals in different shapes and sizes. But what are we going to do with them all?

We arrive revitalized that evening at the Mayan spiritual gathering. It's held in a local home outside of Hot Springs with several adventurers, like ourselves, who study at Mayan spiritual sites across Mexico and Peru.

After our evening potluck, I approach Master Miguel in the kitchen to show him my initiation room photo. He is gracious as ever with his knowledge and his time. Not wishing to bother him too much with my mystery picture, I briefly describe where I took it and slide the photo to him.

In an instant, Miguel authoritatively identifies the peculiar figure.

"This is Lord Bat. He is the Guardian of Palenque."

What? Miguel knows the figure in my photo!

Miguel wonders aloud about any message meant for him as I brought the photo to him in this place.

"Perhaps Lord Bat wants me to do more Mayan ritual practices while present at Palenque?"

Stunned, my mind explodes with questions.

What am I to do with this information? Does this Lord Bat often make surprise appearances in travelers' photos? Why my camera? Why me?

My questions focusing on my own needs quickly recede. I am open to the idea that perhaps I have something to offer this pop-in guest in my photo.

This figure appearing in my photo is a gift to me. Perhaps I can offer something back?

In a flash, all the magical gems that we lovingly stuffed in my Prius earlier in the day appear in my mind.

Perhaps the beautiful crystals are meant for more than just us.

"Miguel, we have crystals we dug from the earth this morning. You're welcome to choose any to take back for your rituals."

I walk Miguel to my automobile in the front yard, which is heavy with crystals of all different lengths and widths. Opening the hatchback full of the large quartz gems, I encourage Miguel to peruse them.

I begin pulling semi-precious stones out of all the pockets on the side door panels, glove box, cup holders, etc. We'd slipped these gorgeous stones into every nook we could find in the car—even an empty McDonald's coffee cup.

"Miguel, please choose any gems you wish."

Bending at the waist, he examines the multitude of crystalline options before him. After a few minutes, he selects eight smaller stones. Placing them in his bronze hand, Miguel carefully deposited the treasures in his blue jeans pocket to be conveyed back to Mexico.

He foretold, "I'll be merging these crystals into rituals at Palenque. Afterward, I will leave them there for gifts to the Mayan spiritual energies."

I do not know exactly where those precious crystals are in Palenque, but I feel they are home.

I'm so grateful we are a small part of their travels to one of the "active" Mayan feminine spiritual sites on the planet.

I hope Lord Bat enjoys the stunningly unique gems from Hot Springs, which we are delighted to bring into the daylight.

As much as I am delighted to meet the Guardian of Palenque!

See Peggy Patty's
Biography
On Page 199

Putting On Pants And Running Away From Tigers

LORALYN DULEY

What I am about to share, I've never told anyone.

The somewhat convoluted story follows how I stumbled upon my inner voice, which I call HP. HP stands for two things: High Priestess and Higher Power. I like that it's both; it sums up HP's weirdness. The non-linear aspects capture her enigmatic nature. And there's an ironic humor in naming this all-knowing entity inside me after a well-known computer brand.

I grew up Catholic—no timeless mysticism at St. Joseph's Church in Summit, Illinois. Just sit up straight in your brown and yellow plaid skirt, go to church twice a week, don't talk, and (most importantly!) don't have ideas. The conversation goes as follows: Thank you for your interest, young Lora, but we will decide what is best for you. If you do otherwise, there is a slap in the face now and eternal damnation later. Have a blessed day!

Despite my lack of spiritual experiences, fate smiled upon me when I discovered acting classes at a successful theater just down the block from my house. Theatre people are intriguing. I played improv games and participated in guided meditations. I especially loved role-playing as people, animals, and pieces of machinery.

Playing with the possibilities of perception is like a drug to me. I never get enough. Whenever there is a group or a person with a slightly offbeat idea, I am in. Drumming circle? Absolutely. Ecstatic drumming and dancing? Why not. Punk rock? Gabba, gabba, hey! I enjoy listening to anyone who exists just a little (or very much) outside the mainstream because their perspectives offer a refreshing take on life.

I share all this to show you how I came to begin a personal retreat one dark and cold winter weekend. I was a little broke and very lazy, so a high-end spa was out. I took four days off work—pure *me* time. Yippee! With a stack of books and heavenly food, I let everyone believe I was busy with work, travel, or something pressing. I saw it as a chance to brainstorm the next steps in my life and indulge a bit. However, I still can't explain what exactly happened.

I lay in bed reading a book I found in a used bookstore bin, written by Wayne Dyer. The title, "Your Sacred Self: Making the Decision to be Free," fell off a shelf and into my hands. I didn't think it would be wise to argue with fate.

Dyer's book introduces the concept of the compassionate observer—a separate spiritual self who exists alongside (or maybe within, I don't know) our everyday selves. He explains how we can learn to observe our thoughts as if they pass, like clouds in the sky. I am intrigued and determined to reach a deeper understanding of spirituality. I yearned for an exciting experience to connect me to this observer. But mostly, I had questions.

For days, I made attempts to communicate with the observer within me. I would ask, "Anyone there?" and reply, "Nope, just me." Frustrating! The whole premise is just a bunch of hogwash. Or, even more scary, I don't have what it takes. But I persisted, faithfully working through the book's thought exercises: Meditate, read, meditate, read, meditate, nap, journal, journal, read, nap, eat, repeat.

This is depressing. I'm getting nowhere. My eyes lazily follow the words, and then what? OH! Here is something. It suggests if you struggle to connect with your inner voice, recall a time of intense turmoil. Dyer posits that in these moments, the observer within might emerge. Well, no problem there! As luck would have it (sarcasm) I had gone through a horrific and life-altering experience—my husband's passing. Memories of those painful days flooded my mind. *Whoosh*! There I go; I am getting out of my car to choose the cemetery plot. My mom and best friend are holding me up on both sides. I cannot walk on my own. I'm not crying or carrying on—it's just the concept of feet that confuses me.

At the time, I didn't get it, but it is just like he described: I am watching myself in an instant. I connected with something, and it was and wasn't me. I am somehow numb but also interested. As the days and weeks passed, events unfolded from a distance—a series of snapshots. I'm at my desk, I'm teaching a class, I'm talking to family, snap, snap, snap, one scene to the next with nothing in between. HP and I are playing musical consciousness. I would bop in for short scenes, intense pain, oh right, see ya! Like a flashlight just about out of batteries, turn it off for a while, and it might charge up so you can see for a second or two. The name

HP was not something I thought of until later. It is just my shorthand. I see her as a she, but I could be wrong.

Common wisdom dictates that folks should avoid major decisions after a significant loss. Now I get it. The regular "me" is not in control during those times.

It's funny. Well, now it's funny. I try to imagine what it would be like. No wonder those who go through such experiences tend to make questionable decisions. What does a non-physical, non-dying spiritual entity on a field trip to the physical plane know about planning funerals, mortgage payments, and estate sales? Unsurprisingly, I fell a lot, consistently misplaced my keys, and mumbled incoherently—HP got a promotion from stand-in to the lead without prior training or warning.

As the kids on the internet say these days, "IYKYK" (If you know, you know). I would add, "IYDYW" (If you don't, you will) because no one escapes this life unscathed. Two weird things happened simultaneously. As we still don't have mind melds, I have to write this to you in paragraph and sentence structure, but that is not how it hit—it hit all at once as one big thought.

Weird part number 1: Once I remembered HP taking over during the first days of my widowhood, I (Lora) stepped back, and HP took over. I have been trying to contact my higher power for days using Dyer's directions. You know that stupid feeling when you look for your glasses, which are on your head. That. Or when you are talking on your phone, telling your friend you can't find your phone. A rush of connection surges through me as I feel HP's presence and connecting consciousness. How did I not know this sooner?

An unfamiliar sensation took hold, like another consciousness was using my eyes. I became aware of a weird expression on my face. My eyes felt unnaturally and unconsciously wide, and my eyebrows arched high. It reminded me of the anticipation and reality of traveling. When you pour over hotel pictures, building a vision in your mind, and then you finally arrive? Some aspects exceed expectations, others more mundane. Or when you go back to a neighborhood you lived in years ago. You remember the street names, but the landmarks are all different. In this surreal state, my senses seemed to move between wonder, detachment, and confusion.

Weird part number 2: (This is a big one, hold on to your hat!) Unexpectedly, I understood the entire history and future of the world, perceiving that it is all connected by/and made of love. Everything. Beginning, endings, and everything in between. I can't explain it other than to say I just understood it. It was beautiful, but nothing like what I expected. It illustrated what everyone was trying to say to enlighten us, from Jesus to Joel Osteen.

The funniest part is the cliché poem about setting something free if you love it, yadda yadda, realizing it encapsulated life perfectly. What we need comes to us; on every level, it is not for us if it floats away. The Bible, Shakti Gawain's works, Green Eggs and Ham, and tarot cards made mind-blowing perfect sense.

A minute has passed, and I am starting to make connections based on this new information. Thought leaders, authors, and fake, genuine, and aspiring gurus are guiding us toward this profound understanding. I see the everyday me and the other version. HP is my companion, whether I call it my soul, spirit, or inner self. I'm grasping that this inner presence communicates subtly with me through intuitions and instincts, occasionally a burst of insight. But HP often remains detached from the daily grind. When everything becomes too much, when my heart and mind verge on shutting down, this HP within me will step forward to guide and elevate me.

I didn't need anything more; I had everything I would ever require. The realization hit me immediately—a lightning bolt, wonderful, hilarious, and unnerving.

I stood up and walked around my apartment. I had always cherished my quirky, overgrown college-kid aesthetic, but at that moment, I fell in love with every item I owned. Objects sparkled. Not metaphorically, actually. I felt and saw each item link to memory with exploding colors—a sense of perfect place and belonging. I never have to be afraid.

Though not large, my apartment seemed to expand as I walked in circles, noticing something new with each revolution. I felt gratitude for the simplest things—heat, running water, jogging pants. I marveled at the more extraordinary things: electricity, language, and modern medicine. How is this all for me? How is this all mine? Millions of people, years of work, and study. Artists, wood carvers, and drywall installers produced things that made my life possible, big and small. Astounded is not a big enough word, but I can't think of another one.

I am thinking about physicists discussing that we aren't separate entities but all interconnected parts of the universe, and I instinctively grasp it. It resonates with me on a visceral level. Yep. Understood. No further questions.

Now, you may understand why I never told anyone.

As I write this, I scold myself for resorting to clichés. But I don't see any options. I understand why phrases like "mind-expanding," "mind-blowing," and so many more are stupid but commonly used. Everything is made up and connected by love. What? Feeble attempts to convey an experience that defies description—an understanding of connecting with the world through the lens of the high priestess. If I weren't me, I would not believe it. Frankly, I am me, and I am only 81.25% sure.

Consider the big European churches that strike you with awe—masterpieces of painting, sculpture, music, and literature. Great art, in its myriad forms, has a similar purpose. Whether it's Van Gogh's sky, the notes of a Beethoven symphony, or the profound words of a Shakespearean monologue—they are all crafted to draw us out of our routine existence. As you read this, I bet you can think of many examples. The sheer magnificence momentarily disarms our rational minds. All well-meaning attempts to pull us out of our regular life and trigger a sense of overwhelming awe that we may be more inclined to allow our HP to help process this moment.

Then I started to get scared. While still in the thick of the experience, I thought about where all this would lead me. A voice in my head shouted, "Come on," you can't live like this. Love isn't everything. If you continue this path, you'll become some technicolor hippie oddball. You will have to quit your job, then what?" Good questions.

As soon as that thought appeared, the experience began to fade away. I tried to hang on! I wanted just a little more. I was a little sad but also relieved. The connection to all things love and awareness was gone, but I am changed by the knowledge that it exists. Friends said I looked different, that I was calmer.

Years passed. I have not come close to reliving that extraordinary encounter. However, fragments of that experience are within me. I no longer wonder whether the divine is real; I know it is. I experienced it. I am much more likely to be confident in my decision-making. Thank you for your interest, Catholic School, but no one can decide what is best for me. I alone have that information.

What came of this whole wild experience is the most minuscule sense of distance—just a little space between regular me and the world. I laugh and relax more. I get over the realization of false friends a teeny bit faster. They are on their path. Please note I said faster, not fast. I still need time to get over it. I'm nowhere near enlightened.

Now that you know, you will recognize when someone's HP has been summoned to action. I have read that this has happened to spiritual leaders. They forget about eating and living-body maintenance. They have made the full-time switch to HP.

Not as cool as you'd think. In my experience, you and your HP must be partners for all this to work. This living experience thing we are doing here is not for the meek or an autocracy. In this way, I stray philosophically from Dyer. He believes that the spiritual part of ourselves is the only aspect worth knowing. He argues that if we genuinely say to ourselves, for instance, "I am well," we can command our cells to regenerate in a state of ease rather than disease. I can recite "I-am-well" until I'm blue in the face. But if I eat a bunch of peanuts, I will be dealing with cold sores for the foreseeable future.

On the contrary, I believe I and HP are a team. I have the more crucial role. While living here on this plane, I make vital (as in keeping myself alive) decisions. In contrast, HP is spiritual and will continue to exist in some form. We have evolved this way—we needed our usual selves to take care of practical matters, like running away from tigers and putting on pants before we go outside. Me and my amygdala are responsible for fear, aggression, and defensive behavior. I am also responsible for providing myself with the best experiences, seeing the world, doing important work, and sharing my experiences. What we focus on in this physical realm is the stage where we play out our lives. We live in gratefulness; we live in sacredness. If we hold on to hurt—you know the answer.

As technology changes our lives, we fumble through the delicate dance of balancing these two sides of our existence. Maybe our grandmothers had it easier, untouched by the constant noise of the media; they immersed themselves in the Earth's embrace by tending gardens and raising animals. Or not; maybe they had other problems to balance. I'm not sure.

Meet Your HP

I can't guarantee that you will have the same experience. I have yet to encounter someone with a similar struck-by-lightning type experience. Frankly, all these years later, it doesn't matter. What we are going for is just a little distance between being in the world and of the world, watching as the insider and listening to your compassionate observer.

You can come to know your own HP, guide, soul, and inner divinity. You may or may not call your HP HP. It doesn't matter.

They are already reaching out to you, whispering in your ears. A good clue you are talking to the correct voice in your head is that they will never be antagonistic. If you hear a voice berating you about those extra five pounds you want to shed, that's just an echo of some jerk, not your HP.

The trick is to discern the correct in-brain conversation among the demands of the ordinary. Connect with ideas and inspiration from other thought leaders. Let intuition guide you to the people, books, classes, and internet searches. HP does not have language as we understand it. Be on the lookout for a strong interest that seems to come out of nowhere or a feeling like instant lightheartedness, books that seem to fall off the shelf into your hand. That's your HP.

The list of folks who tell similar stories is endless. Kundalini awakenings, religious leaders, ecstatic dancers, and spiritual drummers all have lessons for us. You are currently reading a digital or physical compilation of such guides. I'd be willing to bet at least some of the inspiration you need right now lies within the stories in this book.

Dyer says the presence of your observer is warm and loving, a witness overflowing with boundless affection. They will share ideas and insights without judging if you do not follow their guidance. Instead, they offer quiet support, guiding you gently along your path. I have cultivated a deep trust in my HP—a trust I don't have with anyone else. But to be completely clear, it's not all ponies and rainbows; the words shut the f*ck up have been uttered. By me, of course, not HP; she's delightful.

As I continue to distance myself from unhealthy or unfulfilling activities, I do so with the support of HP, overriding the well-meaning persuasions of my various tribes.

I also screw up—a lot. I am not always a good friend; I have trouble saying I'm sorry and can be greedy and gossipy. And that is just the beginning.

I'd like to end with a wish to you all from HP:

Embrace the purest form of magick—the magick that resides within you. (Apparently, HP spells magic with the k, neato!) It is not the illusion of tricks and spells but the profound awakening of your inner divinity.

So, go forth, my friend, with bravery in your heart, a desire for intelligence, and a sense of wonder that knows no constraints. Embrace your heritage, tap into the power that flows through your veins, and allow the magick within you to weave its spell upon the world. May your journey be one of self-discovery, love, and connection—a journey that unravels the mysteries of the universe and illuminates the path to your destiny.

See? I told you, delightful.

LORALYN DULEY

Loralyn Duley, an author with a unique perspective on life, has established herself as a voice of creative introspection and exploration.

Her blog, "DYA," is a testament to her commitment to living life distinctively, inspired by the quote from Neale Donald Walsch: "Today the earth is populated with billions of people desperately hoping to 'get somewhere,' but having no idea of where they're going." This ethos is embedded in her writing, where she delves into personal growth, self-discovery, and the beauty of seeing the world through a different lens.

Loralyn's literary voyage is marked by her book "(Amazing): Mostly True Stories From a Fake Guru," which is available on Kindle. This work encapsulates her knack for blending humor with insightful musings, presenting readers with a rejuvenating take on navigating life's intricacies. The book has garnered positive reviews for its engaging narrative and thought-provoking content, reflecting Loralyn's skill in connecting with her audience through relatable storytelling.

Additionally, Loralyn has contributed to the educational field with her co-authorship of "Microsoft Office 2010: Productivity Strategies for Today and Tomorrow," a testament to her versatility and expertise in technical writing. This publication, which covers practical applications of Microsoft Office, highlights her ability to streamline complex subjects for a broader audience, another facet of her writing prowess.

Her Goodreads profile reveals another intriguing work, "More (Amazing) Adventures of Mimi Bayczyk," further expanding her repertoire and showcasing her continuous exploration of new themes and ideas in her writing.

Loralyn Duley's writing is not only about the words on the page. It's about the journey and the perspectives she shares throughout. Her work is a guiding light for people seeking a less-traveled path, filled with wit, wisdom, and a tenacious passion for life's eclectic adventures.

You can read more or contact Loralyn Duley at: https://www.linkedin.com/in/loralyn-d-392b3624/

Michael and Me

LAURA SPINNER

I'm cold, Mom." A breathy whispered complaint finally emerged. It had taken an hour and Herculean effort to speak. Whimpering with exhaustion, I tried to talk again. Nothing. *Help.* Tears trickled down my cheeks. Clenched fists tightened. My taut chest constricted my lungs.

"I'll stop, Laura, as soon as I can." Mom's tense voice frightened me.

She's scared. Why? As the station wagon hurtled toward the University of Illinois Research Hospital, billboards flew by and mother's blue smoke wafted back to me in the well of the 1964 seafoam green station wagon. Imprisoned, I lay prone in a homemade bed.

Mom, you're chain-smoking! I caught a glimpse of a gargantuan pack of Winston cigarettes plastered on a giant board, flashing its red and white package as our car passed. *I'm choking; I can't stand the smoke; I can't breathe.*

Preteen attitude popped through the throbbing pain and icy cold consuming my body. *Smoking? It's so gross. Blech, it stinks. Gag me with a spoon, why don't you? No choice. Put up with it.* Overcome by weakness, I couldn't even ask her to stop, though my mind screamed.

Dang her, Dang her, Shit Shit Shit. Smiling in secret triumph, I used her cussword, silently giggling inside as I used them, knowing she couldn't hear. My eleven-year-old anger distracted me from my horrible state. Emotionally, I was all over the place. Anxiety, anger, and frustration took turns ravaging me.

A rattling sound came from my chest as I labored to breathe. Exhaustion cloaked me again, its weight flattening me in the well of the car's backend. We continued to fly past telephone poles, cars, mile marker after mile marker, and exits. Glimpsing sight of them through the smoke-hazed side windows, fear grabbed me by the throat, and I struggled to keep my eyes open.

Ignored, I mustered the energy to plead again. "Will we ever get there? I am *soo coold.*" Fighting back nausea from the stabbing pain, I dug my nails into the palms of my hands.

My surgery site tortured me where the wound chafed and rubbed in the half-cast. The smoke suffocated me. Freezing, I shivered so hard my teeth chattered, threatening to fall out. Sinking deeper into shock, my body continued to shut down.

The rocketing car tossed me about in the backend of the wagon. Mom gunned it, swerved left, and passed a car. *Wham!* My body flung into the side of the car. Bone-crushing pain jolted up and down my left side.

"Stop!" Yelping, my body went rigid. Unending spasms rippled up and down my left side. Impossible to brace myself, Mom's driving threw me around like haybales being tossed from the loft. The car movement battered me about, back and forth, smacking into each side of the car and rocking back to the center. Mom clobbered me each time she passed a car, truck, or motorhome.

The jostling movement of the car and the rhythmic vibrations of the wheels spinning along the highway over smooth and rough terrain caused my ankle to scrape back and forth in the half-cast. Torrents of blood seeped out of the wound in my left ankle with each car jerk.

Streaming blood oozed over the top of the half-cast and spilled onto the floor of the wagon's bed. The sliced artery deep within my ankle flapped open and shut. Unbeknownst to either of us, Mom was killing me with her speeding and the jagged car movements in and out of traffic.

I just want to go to sleep. With bone-rattling shivers, my muffled whimpers increased. Death was imminent, and neither Mom nor I were aware. A glimpse of another billboard shared the words *Stuckey's Exit 80.* Disjointed thoughts streamed through my semi-conscious state.

I want candy. Pecan logs sound good; forget the jam. Hate jelly and jam. Ann, Mary, and I begged to stop every time we passed this exit on our frequent trips to Chicago for my medical appointments. Ann would have *demanded* a stop, pointing out our parents' injustice by deciding not to and sticking up for us kids.

Ann is ten years old, going on eleven in two weeks. I am thirteen months older than her. She is more open with Mom and Dad. She helps us get our way. Mary, age five, is sweet and the baby. Me? I try to please and sometimes get lost by staying quiet or saying yes too often.

I missed Mary's June birthday. Horrified, another thought emerges. *Oh no, I bet I'll miss Ann's eleventh birthday in August!*

Heading back to jail—the hospital—my stomach churned. Drowning in sadness, an ocean of tears poured down my cheeks and rained onto my neck and chest. Grief overtook me.

Kleenex? No Kleenex for me. Hopelessness set in. *I need a blanket.* Crazy, out of control thoughts swirled in my head. *Mom and Dad never stop when I ask. When I get my license, I'll stop wherever I want! Mom's driving like a maniac.*

"Going to sleep, Mom." Flooded with relief, my announcement to let go were my final words in the car.

"Laura, I am trying to make it back to the hospital as quick as I can." Mom's voice cracked as she turned back to me. I heard her wretch. Later, I found out that when she turned, she saw sopping red blankets, and as the pungent, sickening smell of pints of oxygenating blood struck her, she could not hide or stop her impulse to gag and vomit as I bled out in the back of the car.

"Stay awake, Laura!" Mom commanded. We were still over half-an-hour away from the hospital. She couldn't stop the darkness from taking me, no matter how many times she tried to get me to stay with her.

Mom began babbling. I heard her for a while. "What are you going to tell your doctors?" She gagged. "Laura, are you still there? Laura, I will pull over. I can help cover you up."

Help me. What's the matter with you? Stop talking and pull over. A fragile connection to life allowed this thought to pop into my mind. Mom's promise sounded distant. Her voice was hollow and echoey, almost goofy, like the sounds of a voice on the slow speed of a tape recording was floating over the seat. Losing consciousness, a vision of my tape recorder at home appeared in my mind's eye. The flower-power plastic casing held a sticker of *The Monkees* in the corner. Davy Jones's smile appeared amidst Mickey Dolenz's, Peter Tork's, and Michael Nesmith's faces. *I love you, Davy.*

In the darkness, I heard his beautiful voice. "Cheer up, Sleepy Jean. Oh, what can it mean to a daydream believer and a homecoming queen?" Davy's voice sang, repeating the verse over and over to me. I felt safe as Davy sang. I wished Davy were holding my hand. Hanging on to life by a thread and in oblivious innocence, I began to command myself to sleep.

Mom blared the horn to startle me as she responded to my silent withdrawal. "Laura, keep talking to me. Laura, are you there?" Faster and faster, the car rocketed. "Laura, we are almost there. Laura, do not fall asleep. Laura!" Mom yelled, her voice desperate. Her racket made no sense to me.

The floodgates of the artery opened full blast. As I sunk deeper and deeper into the dark, brief nightmarish thoughts registered.

Am I in danger? I am a freak. Will I be in bed for the rest of my life? My foot is so ugly. Just how ugly is it? It's so ugly, people will hate me. No boy will ever like me. It's so dark. I can't see any light. Blind? I am blind! Why won't you tell me why you won't stop, Mom?

My body shook in a ping-pong match between holding onto life and just relaxing into letting go—the dance between primal fear and an effortless, joyous existence that called to me.

Earlier, there had been warning signs—missed warning signs—of this life-threatening journey to come. The critical surgery on my ankle eight weeks ago caused this traumatic ride. Upon removal of an orange-sized tumor from my ankle, the surgeons slit my major artery in the ankle area, which allowed it to flap open and shut, causing this stream of blood to flow. When immobilized in bed in the hospital, the leakage was absorbed into my body, and undetected. But upon transfers and during any movements, the flap opened, gushing blood.

Doctors should have caught this underlying death threat. My hospital stay had prolonged several times as the surgery site wouldn't heal. A four-week stay turned into eight, almost nine, weeks long.

Upon discharge, Mom and I made it halfway home and stopped at Grandma's for a rest. Bleeding out in my second car ride, I relived yesterday as the blood in the car swirled around my legs. I couldn't feel it sticking to my skin and coating my legs and hips during this fatal ride. My dream state took me back to the living room on Grandma's farm.

"Look at the blood. Look at the blood!" My little sister, Ann, rushed to the door as Grandma and Mom returning from Walgreens with a bedpan and walked into Grandma's living room. I'm startled by her shout as she is the quiet, logical one. A pool of blood formed at the hassock's edge on Grandma's living room floor, creating a perfect circle around my footrest.

"Oh, no, Do I have to go back?" My sad and dull voice returned. Once settled in the bedroom I heard Mom on the phone.

"This doesn't look like residual spotting from the surgery, blood is flowing like a river. She needs help," Mom argued.

No way. I hate the hospital.

"If she doesn't stop bleeding, I'm loading her up and you will help her," Mom's strong voice argued.

Those boys are still there. No way, Mom! I can't go.

When I was moved out of surgery, two teenage boys had pulled my blankets up and stared at my crotch. *Did they do anything else? I was so groggy, just out of surgery… I can't tell her. She'd die.* Horrified, I could not sleep.

My heart jumped hearing Mom's voice, "She has been seeping blood for eight hours. I am loading her up now." Neither mom nor I had slept. The moon, high in the sky, shone brightly as she loaded me in the backend of the wagon.

My thoughts raced and tumbled around like clothes in a drier. *No, I want Dad. Will I ever see my sisters? Grandma's chicken tastes so yummy. Hate the hospital food. My friends. Do they even miss me?* I saw Mimi, Wendy, Chris, and Dana. *Stinky, big Blackie, where are you puppy?* Remembering his wet kisses and stinky breath, I had started the trip back to the hospital in hysterics.

These final moments before the car ride played out in my mind, but as I withdrew from life, I placed myself in my yellow bedroom with its flowered wallpaper.

Mom kept talking and talking and talking. I felt my energy ebbing within me like waves receding during low tide, withdrawing from the shore returning to the depths of their great mother sea... The depths of the mother sea.

Nightmares disappeared and peace came. *Sleep. Let go and sleep.* Ragdoll limp, my body thanked me for letting go. I felt that! Pain and fear disappeared. *Free. Safe. Free.* Choosing to let go brought joy and peace. Relief flooded me. I soared in light and love. My soul filled with gratefulness. *So safe here. Stay.* Joy. Deep in reverie, I chose to let go and travel to what I could only call *home*. I welcomed the transition of death and the joy it brought.

A dreamy darkness engulfed me, and turning further inward, I journeyed into a misty deepening away from everyday living. Shifting from life to death, the subtle transition continued as imperceptible as the changes from the brilliance of sunrise into the warmth and light of dawn. Pain ceased. Fear disappeared. *Free. Safe. Free.* Flooding relief led to soaring in light, love, and safety. Completely altered, I became joy.

On this gentle journey, ethereal colors and hues of heavenly colors surrounded and *infused* me. Language doesn't capture the divine beauty and gifts presented. The expansion brought me into becoming all goodness. *Light, I am light. I am sky. I am love.* Hearing, seeing, and feeling nothing in Mom's world, I felt protected, leaving the chaos and pain behind me, in the car. This transformation brought me into an indescribable state of peace and ecstasy.

My essence merged with all that exists. I felt a sense of vast greatness. I reached around the world and melted. I became energy and air. My awareness became all creation, all of the universes, energetically merging with the sun and the songs of birds. I flew with the eagles and became the galaxies and heaven all at once. Becoming love, joy and peace, I completely let go of life and became heaven.

My heart stopped. My last earthly thoughts lingered and disappeared into the sound of a beautiful chord on the most angelic harp. A new consciousness emerged. *I am. I am. I am. I am.* Sensations of sunbursts of joy, loving moonbeams of peace, solid love of the earth, powerful winds, and deep protecting ocean waters rhythmically rocked me as if in the womb. The entirety of all existence honored and welcomed me.

The concept of death did not ever knock on my door. Magnificence, beauty, peace, and freedom were my new world.

My body—sticky and soaking wet, drenched in blood, a vessel that no longer served me—lay discarded, no longer me.

Weeks later, I had to ask Mom what happened afterward. My reality was elsewhere. Mom dealt with her own remnants of trauma by horrifying me with the details. We fought in the living room as she denied my experience in a dismissive, cryptic way. She shared details of my death and resuscitation, my transfer from car to ambulance, and the ride to the hospital.

"This *is* what happened, Laura." Mom was schooled and experienced in medical knowledge and procedures because of my surgeries from birth through age twelve. I had six other major surgeries and many procedures due to a mystifying birth defect. Mom had become an expert as she took on the role of becoming a strong advocate for me. She was always reading medical books. She almost compulsively recorded every detail of my medical life in a little black book. She wrote very detailed notes, like a historian recording for future generations. My medical needs became her purpose.

Regurgitating every single detail she could remember, she buried me in the story of my bloody death, starting with all the blood gushing from the backend of the car when she opened it to my revival and successful arrival at the hospital.

"The police rolled up as I opened the car door. You were dead. They radioed for help, and within a few minutes, medics arrived. You had flatlined. You were defibrillated. They shocked your heart to life." Tears streamed down her face, but without any connection to me sitting on the floor, eyes darkened, her detailed report continued to overwhelm me. "They hung two bags of plasma to keep your heart pumping as you'd lost all your blood in the back of the car, and it splashed onto the ground when I opened the door."

I reacted, grasping for comfort. "Mom, do you remember Officer Michael there holding my hand and helping me?"

"No, you must have hallucinated." Mom countered almost brutally. Her denial of Michael ripped me apart. I could barely speak.

Coming back with a hoarse retort, "I did not hallucinate. I could feel him, and see him, and he talked to me." Dumbfounded by Mom's demeanor and the horrifying details she'd shared, my cheeks flushed hot, and my throat closed. My hot skin prickled and, squeamish, I wanted to run to the bathroom. I wanted to get away from Mom. Her reliving her trauma of the incident sent me reeling. Compelled by something bigger than me, I spoke up again.

"You aren't me. Michael sat with me in the ambulance and in the hospital while you signed me in. I remember being awake through it all, the ambulance trip, the gurney ride into the hospital, and the wait for an emergency room bay to open on the gurney in the hallway in the emergency room during admission. All of it. Michael was with me."

"No, Laura. No one named Michael was there. You must accept you made this up to cope." Being completely dismissed, I swallowed my words. I heaved up off the living room floor and made my way to the stairs to make the climb to my bedroom. I couldn't breathe. As I made it halfway up the stairs and paused on the landing before tackling the final set of steps to the top the answer struck me. I swiveled and caught her eyes. My announcement resonated with conviction. "Then it must have been Michael the angel, Mom." I offered, speaking my truth.

"No," she yelled back. Flattened, I fled. "Laura, there was no policeman, no angel, in the back of the ambulance; just you, me and the EMT guy," she called after me.

My brow furrowed, and my lip jutted out. *You are wrong. Michael, the policeman, held my hand. I remember him!* Knees buckling from her betrayal, I made it up the rest of the stairs and down the hall to my bedroom. Crushed and in a hurricane of grief and intense shock, I retreated and put my chair under the doorknob so any intruders would have to knock to get into my safety zone.

Completely unraveled by the details and shamed, I laid down. Hugging my pillow and burrying into my comforter offered some solace, but I felt as if my world was caving in around me. My mother had been my primary savior for years. *Mom always believes me. I thought she would understand. She called it hallucinations. She called it crazy.* Flushed and breathing fire, I whammed pillows on the floor, throwing my mom's photo on the floor.

Shame flooded me. My best friend and mother had just emotionally slaughtered me. She judged me. *Am I just a stupid kid to her?* The possibility of a beautiful moment with my mother had been dashed and mutilated by her own limitations and trauma. I had trusted the openness she had always offered. She had to have seen Michael, too! *But she didn't?*

Lying in a fetal position, I started to calm. *Am I really just a stupid kid to her?* "No, your mother is proud of you." I spoke out loud. Or someone did. *Maybe Mom needs to see him to believe. I saw him. I'd probably be just like her, saying Angel Michael didn't exist if I hadn't seen him either.*

Forgiveness flooded me. I would have to try again with mother another time. But for now, I resolved to be at peace. I knew in my heart I had been visited by Archangel Michael and she had not.

"Angel Michael thank you, for saving my life. I need you, Michael." Continuing to speak out loud, I resolutely added, "I love you. I know you were there. I am here. You saved me. Thank you. Please come back."

Taking time in my bedroom I allowed myself to return to the ambulance, calling in Michael and my memories. Michael, a policeman, comforted me in the back of the screaming ambulance. As I came into consciousness on the gurney, I was terrified by the prickling needles in my wrists and ankle. Seeing the bags of blood and plasma hanging above me, the intravenous needle shoved into my hand and my imprisonment in the binding straps, I gasped at the confusing monitors and machines.

"Hi. Here, do you remember me helping?" A very handsome young man with a navy blue police hat and uniform with a shiny badge offered a welcoming hello back to the world.

Silenced and mute, I wished I could respond.

"Laura, you are safe. I will ride with you back to the hospital and stay until you are safely checked into your hospital room."

Strapped down and gazing around the ambulance, I saw him sitting across from me on the bench. My mother in the corner of the ambulance, slumped over and rested. (I later learned that she had passed out.) Gratefulness flooded me. *Someone is with me.* Gripped in tension and rigid muscle spasms from the fear, the defibrillator, and the autonomic response to my heart stopping, my rock-hard body began to soften some as I realized Michael sat across from me. *Finally, someone is here to help me. I am not alone anymore.*

"My name is Michael. I am a police officer. You lost a lot of blood, you know, but the guys here have made sure you are getting everything you need. You are okay. You will continue to be okay."

My eyes fluttered. Weak and only minutes from being shocked back to life, my lids wavered open and shut repeatedly. They'd pop open but felt like bricks. Tons of weight pressed me down; it felt like the weight of the entire world sat on my chest. Fading in and out, I felt him nearby. He held my hand and steadied me.

Open, shut, open, shut, open, shut, like a shutter on a camera. Blink. Blink. Blink. It was as if I were falling from the cliff, plummeting into darkness. Try as I might, I couldn't stay awake or relax. I would drop off but then jerk awake in fear, spasms rolling up and down my body.

"Laura, I am still with you."

Fight it. Fight it. My eyes popped open again.

"Laura, I am still with you." I moved my mouth. Nothing. "Laura, you will have more experiences coming up where you may feel in danger or when you are threatened. Remember, you are always safe. I will protect you, and others are around you, protecting you." I did not understand him, but he continued.

"Keep your open heart. You have a lot of work to do—sharing love and helping people. You will be helping others for a very long time. You will be protected, and you are safe. Do not be afraid. You are a gift to this world. The world needs you and your love."

I was in awe of his words. His Presence offered strong, powerful yet sweet and comforting energy. He repeated himself. Hearing it a second time made the message very real. "You will have protection your entire life." My heart strengthened at these very words. "Keep your heart open."

Inside my body, I felt overwhelming warmth and a *deepening*. My heart swelled as I listened. The strength of his words melted my fear. In awe, wonderment filled me *about* me. No adult ever addressed me with such consideration and respect. I connected to some deep inner knowing. I awakened with a sense of pride, accepting his words, this *assignment*.

Yes. Grateful, I tried to reach out to him. I so longed to be held. He squeezed my hands as I strained in the straps. *He recognizes me. Open heart. There's a word for my feelings. He sees me.* Awestruck, I felt humble and so grateful. *Am I important?*

"You will have protection to help you through any rough times. You are a very special girl. You will be kept safe. You are safe. You will have protection then, and you have protection now." His Presence filled the ambulance. The monitors stabilized. Mom's breathing calmed as I watched her chest rise and fall. "Do not be afraid. You will make a difference for many people." He stayed close. "It's safe to sleep." Relief flooded me. I trusted and believed him. The rest of the ride blurred, and finally, I slept.

Once in the hospital, Michael—still with me— patted my shoulder as I waited on the gurney in the hallway while Mom did admissions paperwork. "I will go get you some ice, kiddo," Michael said. "Remember, no matter what happens, you are safe. I'll see you soon." His parting words, "you are safe" carried me through the moment, the rest of the hospital stay, and beyond. Mom walked up to me after finishing the admission. She arrived, and Michael did not return.

But it was real. Michael helped me in isolation and death at age twelve. His Presence secured my life. Peace, Presence, and safety wrapped me in their arms as He spoke.

Even though Mom denied his Presence, Michael has been with me for a lifetime.

The second concrete visit from Archangel Michael happened twelve years later. Having completed a master's degree, I had been hired by a federally funded private not-for-profit mental health outpatient facility in central Illinois. Standing in my office, I noticed a quote in one of the journals on my desk: *"Isolation is insidious work for both the one who needs help and the one helping."* Significant synchronistic events again aligned the rest of the day, and Michael's Presence began to become apparent.

"Michael, are you talking to me?" After reading the quote, my spontaneous remark made me jump. *Quit making things up, Laura.* Mom's words echoed in my mind. Rolling my eyes and muttering, "Oh, for God's sake, get to work, Laura." With plenty to do, even though only the end of my first week as a new hire out of school, I tried to move on to paperwork.

Unable to resist the compulsion, though, my search for Michael and a need to connect took over, cutting away that momentary shame. "Thank you, Michael for helping me get here." It felt natural and soothing to speak those words out loud.

This homecoming caused some of the reality of my office to fade away, and light brightened around me as I spoke to Him. A knowledge that Michael had been by my side since age twelve overtook me within seconds. Looking at my history, I easily confirmed the invisible support that had helped me navigate my life to where I now stood. I had finished a Bachelor's at the University of Illinois with top-notch grades and secured a completely financed (via grants) graduate school placement. After my Master's, I easily landed my first social work position within the same city where my husband-to-be resided. Everything had fallen into place in miraculous ways. The light continued to brighten in my office as I stood fixated, searching for him.

As I looked for Michael, my heart swelled. Motionless, speechless, for God knows how long, the commitment guiding my next steps deepened. Tears trickled as my knees quaked, and trembling, I jumped into action. The shimmering light intensified and filled every corner of my office.

A stack of referrals—many of them no-shows—sat on the corner of my desk, catching my eye. *This position is for an* office-based *therapist. I am not hired to do* home visits.

But I was powerless to resist the urge to do more than accept yet another no-show. I locked in on the top referral on the desk. Grabbing it, I slung my purse over my shoulder in decisive action. A force propelled me to gather and organize and just go visit the mother. "What the heck!" Keys, calendar, jacket, and yelling, "Three no-shows, and you're out? We will see about that." *Ridiculous policy. BS if you ask me. What an easy way to reduce waiting lists.*

Autopilot seemed to take me over. The woman in the file had one final appointment the following week. *She has two no-shows already. One more, and DCFS will be given a record. She'll be labeled as non-compliant in front of the judge at her next court hearing.*

I scanned the referral. "Parent/Child Problems." Department of Children and Family Services had sent the referral to my program. Disgust overtook me. *This referral does not note any abuse or extreme neglect. At best, there is extreme poverty present in this case.* "I thought Mental Health is supposed to be caring." Steam rolled from my ears while I spoke to the tiny plant on my desk.

Standing with the weight of my purse and jacket flopped over my arm, I leaned close to the plant. "What if she doesn't have a quarter for a bus? What if there are eight kids, and she can't manage the bus? What if she has a car with no gas? What if she is saving bus fare for rice? I'd miss my appointment to save money if I had to, wouldn't you?" The little buds on the tiny plant opened and the newly blooming flower birthed my answer. An image of the little girl's face in the file shimmered through the warming sacred light. Jasmine's dirt-smudged face pleaded with me. The mother's pain-filled face begged me. Norma. The image was almost surreal. Her face beckoned, seeming to have just spoken the words, "Help me."

"Go." Loud and clear, I heard the words. Jerking around and looking into the empty hallway for my supervisor, the command reverberated again, "Go." Turning to run to the car, I noticed the tiny plant on my desk. As the brilliance of the Light intensified, the tiny buds birthed and opened into beautiful, intricate blooms. Slamming the door, I galloped down the stairs, a force propelling me to the parking lot.

As the car jumped to life, "Good" rang in my ears, jolting me as much as my early morning alarm clock does. The word was loud and real.

Driving, I played the radio and Stevie Nicks sang, "This little girl is capable of murder if pushed too hard." My body trembled, visible goosebumps appearing as my arm hair stood on edge and Jasmine's image appeared in the windshield, shaking me.

Trust yourself. You are safe. Don't let your mother's fear make you afraid. Michael is talking to you. Go! What you see, hear, and feel is real. My inner twelve-year-old responded to the reassurance and my breathing calmed.

Arriving at the home visit, I was flabbergasted and unprepared for the horrific scene. Fear gripped my heart. The back door hung on one hinge. Unidentifiable rotten mush in the backyard, thick and daunting, threatened me. My nose crinkled and my upper lip curled back, as my throat spasmed. I inhaled noxious fumes from a choking stench. *Is it food? Dead animal? Garbage? God, help me if I slip on it and fall.*

Picking my way up the walk, gray, brownish green-slime with yellowish-brown patches of squishy matter pulled at the soles of my shoes as the toxic gases rose around me.

I wanted to quit.

But Presence guided me to the door. Knocking once, I waited. Knocking a second time, louder, I called, "Ms. Norma, it's Laura from Mental Health. I am here to visit a little bit about next week's appointment."

The urge to run like a bat out of hell swelled, yet a voice steadied me. "She needs help. Stay. You are safe."

I continued to knock; it seemed like an eternity. "Ms. Norma you are safe with me." Echoing Michael's "Laura, you are safe," from the back of the ambulance, I hoped to connect.

A weak voice floated through the door. "Come in." Accepting the invitation, the stench knocked the wind from my lungs, but help appeared as an unseen energy guided me into the home.

I heard, "You will help in great ways here, Laura." *Oh my, God. Help* me.

The kitchen (which must have been public health condemnable) offered moldy dishes with moss-like growth dripping down the stack in the sink. An igloo cooler full of human feces sat in the small closet-like pantry. Trying to hide my eyes from the hideous sight, I then saw a mountain of pots and pans filled with gelatinous substances and quickly pushed through the kitchen area into a living room.

Intimidated and sickened, Presence cloaked me like a hazmat suit and my pounding heart found a calm, reassuring rhythm. I moved forward. "Ms. Norma, how are you? I am here for you." *This mother let me in. How incredible. No way she should trust outsiders. She wants help.*

"Not too good, I'm afraid," Norma replied. My body went rigid as I realized Jasmine spent her time foraging in the garbage bins in the projects for food for them. Scrutinizing the kitchen and dirtied plates and pots and pans made it clear—the two of them were eating and cooking filth.

"Thank you for having me, Ms. Norma."

"I am afraid Jasmine isn't here." I still hadn't reached Ms. Norma, but as we talked, her voice held a sincere apology.

"I am sure she will be here in time; don't worry," I replied, trying to put Ms. Norma at ease. I recognized how silly that sounded. *You idiot, Ms. Norma never knows when Jasmine will be home. Gosh, I wish I could take that back. I should have thanked her for meeting with me.*

"Come sit on the couch," Ms. Norma wheezed. I could see her topknot above the back of her chair. I hadn't quite reached her yet. Leaving the odious kitchen provided relief, yet I faced something much more terrifying than walking through the cooking area. Bugs eked out of seat cushions and cracks in the couch, and in a *whoosh*, as I sat down. Four moving walls of cockroaches, ants, fleas, centipedes, flies, gnats, and all manners of unidentifiable creepy crawlers surrounded Norma and me. I could see that tiny little creatures were the main homeowner here. Little teensy heads, legs, antennae wallpapered the living room and poured over every square inch of furniture. *I am sitting in a teeny critter hotel! Run!*

"No matter what you face, you are safe and protected." Out of nowhere light in the room brightened. Familiar comfort and peace infused every cell of my body. I heard the voice again. *"You are safe."*

"Norma, tell me about Jasmine's life. What has happened in your life? How can I help?" Catching my first full look at Norma, I choked back a sob of compassion. *Did she notice? Norma is suffering. She's a mess. She's been deteriorating for months.* It was chilling. I knew I needed to get medical help for Norma. Norma weighed about four hundred pounds. Her swollen, cracked feet were shoved into flipflops. Involuntarily, I winced at the sight.

"I ain't wanted to let you in, but somethin' 'bout you told me it would be alright." Norma waved her log-like arm and inflated hand toward me, gesturing goodwill. Her ankles were lost in the voluminous mounds of flesh flapping over and wrapping her joints, lost somewhere in the pouring and out of control tissue. Her abdomen overflowed her lap and knees, stretching down the side of her thighs, reaching for the floor. I tried not to focus on the bugs feeding on her ulcerated legs where the cracked skin leaked lymph and blood.

I need to get Norma help as quick as I can. Urgency took over and my throat quivered. Stifling my crying as a deep sadness settled in my heart, I listened. *She needs to be heard. She needs to be seen; her courage must be witnessed.*

"I can't help Jasmine anymore. I can barely move." The next few hours were spent with Norma describing the incredible abuse she'd suffered as a child. Norma's father pimped her from age nine years old until she went into foster care. Horrible memories of being chained to a doghouse in the backyard or the dining room table came spilling forth. Norma shared that she had not received any treatment for her trauma once in foster care and no one had heard these stories.

Jasmine arrived. I jumped as she slammed the door. Out of the corner of my eye, a little foxlike creature in stealth raced up the stairs. Jasmine curled up at the top and hid around the corner. Glancing up, I picked out strands of hair just at the tip-top step. Laying on the floor with her head just behind the wall partition, she was close enough to hear us.

Norma yelled, "She's okay Jasmine. I invited her. She's good people. Ms. Laura will help me." For hours, Jasmine watched me listen to her mother. I asked question after question as Norma seemed eager to share her story.

"Norma, tell me about your health. How did you become immobile." She apologized for the pantry and igloo cooler telling me she couldn't make it up to the bathroom, so she adapted, making a stool downstairs.

"I was abused in foster care. I suffered two hidden abortions when in care. My folks hurt me, and foster parents too. When I ran away, at fourteen, I couch surfed in different homes." She described trauma after trauma and danger from fourteen to eighteen. She faced homelessness, sinister abuse that included beatings and rapes, and living without running water. Years of multiple abuses compounded her physical weight gain. Food sources included trash, cheap sugary foods and sometimes grass. She confessed, "When I can, I overeat to gain weight on purpose to protect myself. Gross girls are less likely picked to screw."

How can Norma even want to survive? With deep reverence, I knew the answer. The light in the room seemed to magically intensify again. My chest swelled and eyes glistened. *Jasmine. Norma loves Jasmine so much.*

You are here to help. The voice encouraged me further. I needed that dose of bravery—the voice gave me the courage to stay seated with her.

I guess my life did this to me." Norma's head dropped forward as she surrendered to the burden of her physical condition and hopelessness. Seeing such intense misery, my heart beat faster. Norma, laboring to speak, offered more information. "When I turned eighteen, I applied for Section Eight. Once in subsidized housing, I supplemented my income by prostituting to survive and make ends meet. I became pregnant with Jasmine. I decided I could have her. I wanted her. Jasmine is my everything." Norma detailed Jasmine's life to age eight. "She is my hero." Norma's pride and love shone.

Jasmine has become the mainstay in their survival. What a miracle she gives her mom. The description of Norma's sinister abuse, her lifetime of degradation and her and Jasmine's extreme poverty, weighed heavy in my mind. It's unbelievable how people are oppressed and tortured like this with no help. *Sinful!* Just at the top of the stairs, I noticed the hair draped on the top step disappear. Jasmine had moved.

Digging fingernails into my palms, I resisted the urge to fly up the steps. *Jasmine, I wish I could scoop you up and hold you in my arms.* Overwhelmed, I felt like giving up. *There are no answers.*

It is time, to help. It is time to help. You are safe. You are meant to help. Hearing the voice helped me.

I gulped and then spoke, "Norma, we need to get you to the hospital tonight. You are in critical condition."

"No way. I can't leave Jasmine," resistance boomed from the chair.

"We can get her into foster care so you can be medically treated. "Oh no, if Jasmine hears you, she will run."

"We will find her, Norma."

"What if what happened to me, happens to her?"

"We must risk a placement, or she won't have you for years to come. Jasmine needs you to do this for her, Norma. I need to call the Department of Children and Family Services to find a place for Jasmine so you can get to the hospital. I need to call 911. I need to call my supervisor. I don't want you to die. Jasmine needs you." Repeating myself, I offered soft encouragement, "Jasmine needs you."

Norma, now cold stone silent, stared at me. Her dark eyes deepened to a black onyx. I held her eyes with an unflinching gaze.

Finally, Norma's chest heaved. "Go."

Did Norma say go? At a deeper level, I knew the response coming from her lips included more than just Norma.

"Thank you, Norma. I'll be right back." Bolting, I ran to the corner phone booth and made call after call. As I finished the last call, a tiny hand slipped in mine. Jasmine's dirt-smudged face and teary eyes looked up into mine. Jasmine, on hyperalert, had listened to every word her mother and I had shared.

Jasmine held a tiny, dirty, well-worn bunny—a little guy who had not been washed in years and held the remnants of hugs, snot, kisses, and tears. "I heard you talking.' Dark, wizened eyes communicated a solemnity so impactful it froze me in time and space.

She leaned into me, looking back and forth between me and the bunny.

"Jasmine, it will be okay. We will get your mom better for you."

"This is Michael." Looking at her bunny, Jasmine shared with deep conviction, "Michael tells me to trust you. He says I will be safe and protected and Mom needs the hospital." Stunned, I could feel Jasmine, Norma, and Michael at a cellular level. Quiet hung between us for several seconds. My body vibrated. Jasmine held my legs, and I held her in a deep hug.

Jasmine continued, the message so big it had to have been guided, "She will be safe." The words were Michael's words. The light surrounded and comforted both of us within the evening dusk. Jasmine allowed me to walk her back home. The ambulance came. Department of Children and Family Services (DCFS) came, and Norma and Jasmine said goodbye to each other. My supervisor called DCFS and complained about how the Department had handled the case as medics should have been involved much earlier, yet the referral had sat and would have been ignored longer.

Norma remained in the hospital for eight weeks. On December fourteenth, Norma came home healthier and mobile, and Jasmine and she were reunited. Their residence had been cleaned and refurbished by DCFS homemakers and several agencies in town. Visitation went well, and Jasmine returned home full-time by the week of Christmas. On December 23rd I received a box full of homemade cookies for Christmas with a thank you note included: "Hi, Laura, thank you for everything, Norma, Jasmine, and Michael."

I cried as the Light in my office brilliantly intensified and cloaked me in sacred warmth and love. We had all been blessed by Michael's help.

****

LAURA SPINNER

Laura Spinner, Licensed Clinical Social Worker, has over forty-five years of psychotherapeutic experience in mental health, education, chemical dependency, child welfare, and private practice settings.

She has built and supervised programs in two mental health centers and one chemical dependency treatment setting. https://www.lauralcsw.com/

During her thirty-one years in the school setting Laura created a successful wraparound program meeting children's and families' needs. Her third specialty license is as a Brain Gym Instructor through Breakthroughs International and her certifications as a Reiki Master Level 4, Shamanic Breathwork Facilitator, and Touch for Health Practitioner Level 4 provides depth to her skills in physical, cognitive, emotional, and spiritual support. Laura also has further training through Epona Quest in facilitating groundwork in equine therapy.

Laura's interest in social work and the healing arts began at age twelve when she realized loving relationship is the true healing property during one of her many major surgeries. She has survived three death experiences.

Laura has a life partner/husband of over forty-eight years, two sons, and one grandchild. A son and her grandchild have also survived major medical incidents. Laura has learned so much from her family and honors them in gratitude.

Her favorite activities include kayaking, swimming, bicycling, camping, horseback riding, nature, family, pets, and friends. She loves and has experience in drama, music, reading, and writing. She's had a houseful of children and animals for the past four decades.

Thank you to all of my professional and personal mentors. Thank you to my spiritual communities for supporting my spiritual growth. Thank you to TL Woodliff and Ruth Southard for believing in me, my writing, and including my story in **Mystic Memoirs.** Thank you to my family Chris, Nick, Camden, Sean, and my mother, father, and sisters (names changed in the chapter) for your love and constant support.

Jogging Ahead

PEGGY PATTY

It feels weird.

Why am I stopping for a surprise visit at Marie's condo for a quick chat? She's my 83-year-old spiritual mentor and dear friend.

I catch myself off guard as I make an odd request to her on that clear January day in 2009.

"Can I take a mid-afternoon nap on your living room loveseat?"

What am I doing? I wasn't even tired when I rang her doorbell.

What's even stranger is the vivid dream on her lumpy couch about embarking into the afterlife!

Such a wonder since I'm just driving into town to pick up some light bulbs. Nothing more.

I'm not afraid of dying. Never have been. Not looking forward to it, but it's not a frightening topic. Talking to dead people holds no interest to me either, so I'm bemused by my ghost-hunting friends. I figure most of us will ascend peacefully somewhere once we aren't walking around in our bodies anymore.

If there are problems to be had with nonliving folks, I'll let someone else check it out. Why borrow trouble?

I have enough on my plate in my present life. However, if I'm available, I'll volunteer to deliver a transcendent message if needed.

Perhaps that is why I'm open to experiencing the unusual dream in the cozy living room of my close spiritual confidante, Marie: A dream highlighting our Reiki friend, Rick.

I've been using Reiki for decades to manage my stress level, especially in my profession as a social justice attorney. As Reiki practitioners, we focus the universal life force energy to promote a balanced flow of healing energy to the mind, body, and emotions.

A relaxing focus I definitely need, given my thirty-year career as a trial lawyer. Throughout my day job, I'm laser-focused on life-saving legal outcomes for low-income domestic violence victims in both the civil and criminal court systems.

Analyzing hundreds of disturbingly violent cases each year, many involving kids, leaves my mind and body exhausted—unrelenting issues of physical violence, mental trauma, and hungry children.

Championing answers to societal ills, often in an ill-equipped legal system, can take a toll on my psyche. However, I find the work uplifting when victims are granted a measure of protection by the courts.

Most folks would describe me as a woman who is seriously grounded in reality.

As an Assistant State's Attorney in a specialized Felony Domestic Violence (DV) Unit, I poured over hundreds of DV police reports. My job is to criminally charge and then prosecute a multitude of felony criminal court cases.

Victims suffer broken bones, choking, deadly threats with guns and knives, and attempted murder. Over 90 % of the DV victims are women enduring the trauma of criminal physical violence and intimidation.

I even prosecuted a local defense attorney who battered his girlfriend. Charges include throwing her against a refrigerator and restraining her by ripping the phone out of the wall so she couldn't call the cops for help.

I charged a Class 4 Felony, given the solid facts in the case, and then the case hit the newspapers. A Judge from another county had to be transferred into the sensitive criminal proceeding since the defendant is a local attorney.

The defendant was found guilty after I concluded the felony prosecution, which expanded the notoriety in the press.

Yes, I can navigate through high-stress situations using provable evidence.

Exploring Reiki and other energy practices gives my left-brain relief from listening to the horrors of interpersonal violence in families and hectic legal pressures.

Reiki also allows me an intuitive outlet where I can relax and not seek a specific goal—just peace and healing for myself and others.

Perfect.

One of the beauties of this hands-on energy modality is its gentle, non-invasive energy healing technique. Used all over the world in some hospitals and hospices, Reiki complements other health treatments.

Even the renowned Cleveland Clinic website advertises the fascinating healing aspects: "Reiki promotes relaxation, stress reduction, and wellness. It supports people receiving traditional treatments such as chemotherapy, radiation, surgery, and kidney dialysis."

In 2015, I was drawn to coordinate local volunteer Reiki practitioners to offer patient sessions at our Cancer Medical Institute. Patients are eager to share how the comforting sessions help relax and soothe them during the debilitating effects of nausea and fatigue.

Some patients visualize calming visions during their thirty-minute sessions on the therapy table, which they spontaneously share with us.

One afternoon, a fifty-year-old woman with short curly hair slowly opened her eyes at the close of her Reiki session with me at the Center.

Her face was calm, but curious.

"During my session, I saw swirling colors, plus a large blue eye. What does it mean?"

I hold my breath. The Medical Center rules are clear. I'm not allowed to answer questions like this.

As Reiki practitioners, we cannot discuss specific energetic responses patients might experience during our sessions in this medical facility. We are just volunteers, not medical professionals.

Sighing, I attempted to give a vague answer, "Everyone can have a different relaxation response."

The patient left satisfied, though I wasn't.

I desired to share a more informed discussion of the benefits of this energy modality with her. However, the only way Reiki volunteers can practice at the medical facility is if we follow *their rules*.

Don't talk about *unseen energy*, like chakras or visions inside a medical facility.

Each year, I look forward to hosting two Reiki retreats in the twelve acres of lush woods surrounding my house.

My home is a perfect retreat location. Rolling hills with old-growth hardwood trees fill the landscape with just a hint of wildflowers peeking out.

Guests park their cars at the top of the hill and enjoy strolling through the wooded scenery surrounding the long lane leading to my country home.

I relish watching a diverse group of attendees carrying their yoga mats, drums, snacks, and desires for a joyful, uplifting day head down the path to an outside circle of chairs overlooking acres of old oak and maple trees.

These Saturday retreats delight local Reiki enthusiasts. We re-energize our personal relationships plus learn new energetic skills. Heartfelt spiritual exchanges reaffirm our inner knowing of the sacredness of life and interweave deep friendships centered on open hearts.

We share synchronicities of meaningful events and conversations with each other as the magic in everyday life is confirmed.

Being active in the Reiki community poised me to befriend other energetically sensitive individuals who grace the world with their healing talents. Individuals who become pivotal in sacred events in my life.

I receive many gifts in my practice of Reiki, which began over thirty years ago.

One beloved gift is a close connection with Marie. She's an immaculately dressed older, gray-haired woman with many surprises. Short in stature, she walks with a pink metal cane adorned with ribbons and small bells. When we met, she was seventy-five years old and she always arrives carrying her Native American drum.

Marie is eager to learn the words to all the energetic songs taught at the retreat. I watch as she closes her eyes while chanting and drumming with others.

Marie's unassuming presence masks her powerful spiritual gifts, plus she's a great storyteller. She has traveled the world, but her wings are now clipped due to health issues, including heart problems.

The morning spiritual gathering begins in my backyard, which opens to a view of a winding creek within the acres of woods. People sit in lawn chairs circling an earth altar created with large crystals and colorful flower adornments highlighting the four directions.

These soul-filled retreats open with our esteemed elder Marie setting the tone of reverence for the sacredness of nature and ourselves by reading mystical passages and visionary poems from writers such as Mary Oliver and Rumi.

We all enjoy gathering with others, like ourselves, who are not shy about sharing open hearts and gifts of the spirit.

At the beginning of one Fall Reiki Retreat, we assemble our chairs in a circle in the beautiful outdoors under blue skies with birds flying overhead. The retreat is about to begin as the last of the latecomers settle into their lawn chairs with their water bottles handy. Others place colored paper with names of loved ones who need to recover from ailments in a basket near the colorful crystals in the center of the altar.

Marie leans close to whisper in hushed tones, "Peggy, I just saw a vision of the Divine Feminine. She's in the form of a young woman. It's probably Mary Magdalene."

My ears perk up. As usual, I'm in awe of her sharing her sacred world with me.

Pausing to absorb her revelation, I whisper back, "Where is she standing?"

"Right in front of us in the middle of the circle."

Never having any words to respond to Marie's visions, all I can muster is a heartfelt, "That's really cool."

It's just another day in the life of hanging with Marie, the Mystic.

I gather myself together to stand and officially open the retreat. Each individual introduces themselves as the morning sun shines through the tall oaks into our circle.

Sinking deep back into my lawn chair, I begin to smile. I'm confident that healing is close at hand for those seeking it that day.

Rick is also an integral part of the retreats. He is one of these genuinely open-hearted individuals you feel is a trustworthy friend. A thoughtful, dark-haired man in his early 40s, Rick makes everyone comfortable when he walks into a room.

A quiet-spoken man of medium build, his comments always reflect his profound intellect. He seems comfortable being centerstage and sharing his thoughts, though he's just as comfortable in the background, allowing others their own opinions.

During the retreats, Rick never shows a need for any unnecessary male ego. In fact, one new Reiki friend called him "Steve" all day at a retreat until Rick's fiancé, Donna, corrected her at the end of the day.

Upon learning his actual name, his new friend is a bit sheepish.

"Rick, why didn't you interrupt me? I referred to you by the wrong name the whole day!"

Unconcerned, Rick shrugged, "It's not important. I didn't want you to be embarrassed."

Rick's life journey leads him to combine two different facets: counseling and law enforcement. He joined the National Guard in his twenties to pay for his Criminal Justice degree in college. Desiring to provide more specialized aid to people in his small central Illinois town, he went into policing and also obtained a Master's Degree in Community Counseling.

As a respected member of law enforcement, Rick exhibits honest concern for the wayward folks who cross his path while on duty as a local police officer.

Looking earnest, Rick shakes his head, "I wish the folks I run into as a cop would listen to my advice. I'm just trying to help them."

Rick is just one of thirty-plus Reiki practitioners who gather at the retreats to send healing Reiki onto the planet, invoke prayers to heal the waters of the world, and learn from one another.

Eager to immerse ourselves in the soothing vibrations of tuning forks and crystal bowls, participants sit in a circle around the mesmerizing sounds I offer to the cosmos.

The offering of kundalini yoga by Tracy always delights us as we lay on our mats, especially when Tracy expertly plays her large gong, whose sounds magically fill the air and our bodies with glorious ripples!

We are all enthusiastic to join in chanting and toning meaningful vibrations as lovely chords reverberate in the air around us.

May the long-time sun shine upon you
All love surrounds you
And the pure light that's within you
Guide your way on.

Drum circles are a favorite retreat activity as many eager attendees join using their own personal drums to feel the energetic vibrations. Sharing insights on chakra energy centers, uses of various crystals, and anyone's latest energetic adventure is always on the agenda. Of course, we also nourish ourselves with healthy food. Plus, some sugary treats!

Drawn to the healing power of the sound vibrations, Rick, Marie, and I immerse ourselves in the vibrations of the crystal bowls and native American drums, along with many retreat participants. We meditate in our chairs as the vibrations soothe our bodies and our minds.

I don't know Rick well, but when he offers his perspective at the Reiki gatherings in my home, I feel his wisdom and the genuine kindness of his heart.

There's a deep purpose in the ease of our connection, although I didn't know it yet.

I'm honored when Rick's fiancé, Donna requests that I attune her to Reiki. We enjoy a peaceful afternoon in my large living room with the beamed ceiling overlooking acres of woods.

As a Reiki Master Teacher, I still have the powerful buffalo drum that I used during the energetic attunement process that day.

Months pass where Rick's path and mine don't cross since he lives an hour away.

On occasion, he attends the Healing Crystal Bowls Meditation I host each month in the sanctuary of a local church for the last fifteen years. The Crystal Bowls are tuned to the main chakra energy centers in the body.

To facilitate this Vibrational Meditation, I sit on a cushion surrounded by these beautiful large white orbs that exude magical harmonious vibrations when lightly played with a mallet.

Attendees may bring mats to relax on the floor or choose to sit in chairs and enjoy the soothing sounds.

During my "Crystallize Your Intentions with Crystal Bowls" gathering on New Year's Day 2009, I noticed Rick and Donna sitting near the front. Looking serene, they both smile while relaxing into the soothing vibrational sounds of seven chakra crystal bowls. After the vibrations fade in the room, a few individuals quietly talked among themselves.

Rick sighed.

"Sometimes it gets discouraging. I wish folks would just listen while I'm giving them advice. When I pull these young kids over because they are driving dangerously, I'm really trying to help them."

Rick seemed disheartened, which was odd.

"Sometimes all I can do is surround them in white light, as they go on their way."

His usual groundedness and good humor seem tarnished by his daily grind. My heart goes out to him since it sounds like his job is getting to him.

"I've been feeling very physically tired lately."

As I leave the gathering, I feel a little concerned for such a usually optimistic guy.

Marie was also there. For the last six years, she has regularly attended my Crystal Bowls Meditation with her car filled with close friends.

A few days after, on January 6th, I drive into town to buy some light bulbs. I drop in at Marie's condo—with its large stone fireplace—to reminisce about our lives, while relaxing in each other's company.

Marie is no stranger to spiritual energies and I love listening to her recall adventures of her travels around the world. She observes what others might not. She'll casually tell me wild stories of her energetic spiritual encounters, leaving me in awe.

It is no concern if someone believes her or not. However, she is very selective about whom she trusts with her stories.

Some people tell fantastic stories that later turn out to be fiction. But my experience with Marie tells me her tales are true.

Marie's lineage is Blackfoot from her great-grandfather, who is linked to the Rosebud Reservation. She also has a Jewish grandfather. She hid both these lineages, allowing her to rise in the social circles her husband aspired to be in.

Her ancestral lineage was whitewashed on official paperwork so her spouse could join the male-only Country Club in the 1960s. Only a specific type of Caucasian lineage was allowed to enter. Club rules prohibit their members or wives from having any Jewish or Native American ancestry, so Marie's ancestors' names and other identifying information were altered.

Her most captivating tales involve her challenging the Catholic Church head-on. I've never desired any direct experience with the Catholic Church, given the

Church's destructive history against females on many fronts.

But I sit spellbound when Marie shares her experiences as a Catholic woman directly challenging the overwhelming male power of the Catholic Church.

I still marvel at her strength, integrity, and focus.

Marie is proud she upheld the humanity of the authentic female experience in Catholicism. She is closely aligned with many Catholic nuns, so she has no doubts about the power of the divine female presence underpinning the Church.

Her life experiences brought her to a point of *knowing*, of understanding her own, divine power.

Marie has various friends across the U.S. who openly advocate for females to become Priests. She personally knows the editors of underground liberal Catholic newsletters. Sitting in the living room of this gray-haired woman in her eighties, I scrutinize these banned Catholic newsletters and marvel.

"Marie, how do these Catholic women dare write their opinions in full view in direct opposition to such a powerful religious institution?"

A confident smile slowly spread across her face.

"Well, Priests and other strict Catholics do ban parishioners from reading these supposedly heretical newsletters. But how are they going to enforce that dogma? The leaders just try to scare people."

How strong are these women to challenge the religious tenets of male hierarchy in the most powerful Church in the world? What are the personal traits of such women that prevent them from being consumed by the fire ignited around them?

The Truth became apparent to me.

Marie had already experienced the fire.

She knows *Who* and *What* she is.

She is an aspect of the Female Divine. Perhaps we all are, but Marie knows how to embody it.

Marie is a hero to me, and just being in her presence has enriched many lives. I ask why she thought she experienced so many energetic encounters throughout her life? Was she thinking or doing something unique when she became aware of unseen forces around her?

A quiet look comes to her countenance. She pauses, "I simply make myself available to Spirit."

Her firm conviction is an inspiration to me.

Now, I'm not prone to flights of fancy. I'm a serious person who has done serious work.

When I was the Legal Institute Director of the Illinois Coalition Against Domestic Violence, I loved traveling around the state, providing technical assistance to shelters, and helping train civil and criminal court personnel. Each time, I'd leave the two-day DV Conferences hoping we'd made enough impact to humanize the court system a bit more for victims.

DV criminal cases are notoriously difficult to prosecute successfully. My home office wall boasts a plaque the State's Attorney awarded me for my dedication to prosecution in the DV Felony Unit. My jury trial statistic is a 75% success rate, which is quite high in the legal field.

I'm grounded in reality…the good and the bad.

As we begin our usual chat, Marie relaxes in her leather recliner in front of the huge stone fireplace, sipping tea in a cup she brought back from Greece.

Her living room looks ordinary to the untrained eye. However, upon closer inspection, sacred objects are spread throughout. A small medicine wheel, eagle feather, metal singing bowl, and her native American drum all could be viewed in their places of honor. A graceful ceramic sculpture of Mary Magdalene rests among her best china. A well-worn Christian Bible lay within reach on her walnut side table.

Marie's dishwasher isn't working well, so we discuss options. While sitting on her couch, I suddenly feel exhausted mid-sentence as we discuss dish detergents.

Waves of weariness wash over me and I'm barely able to keep my eyes open. I begin shaking my head in confusion.

What is happening? I feel tiredness overwhelming my body. My mind is becoming fuzzy. All I want to do is go to sleep!

"Marie, I feel exhausted right now. I don't understand why."

Marie just shrugs at my unusual request, "Go ahead and lie down to rest."

I hesitate.

It's pretty rude of me to visit her and then say I really want to use your living room couch for a nap right in front of you!

She picks up her book unbothered, "I'll finish reading."

I have no idea how I can go into immediate sleep laying on the uncomfortable lime green loveseat. But I crunched my five feet and six-inch body on her four feet couch, and drop off fast asleep.

A very vivid dream begins unfolding.

In my dream, Rick and I are jogging together down a path. The bright blue sky is lovely, and the air is crisp.

Rick turns toward me to smile. "I'm going to go on ahead up here. I will see you later!"

Rick then jogs ahead out of my sight. I continue moving forward as the dream ends.

I find myself waking up on Marie's green loveseat. My whole dream couldn't have been longer than a minute, though about 10 minutes had passed.

Upon sitting up, I can remember every detail of the dream. The last frame of the picture features only his light t-shirt and distinctive smiling face, leaving my view.

As my mouth began to open to share my unusual dream with Marie while scrunched up on her little sofa, I stopped myself.

Intuitively, I received clear direction.

Give Marie a break! Don't bother her with the details of every little dream I have.

I sit on the couch for a couple of minutes to be sure I'm fully awake before thanking Marie for allowing me to crash in her living room. I leave without sharing my dream and drive directly home.

Two hours later, I open a group email on my computer from Trish, a Reiki friend. She's a close family friend of Rick.

I'm motionless in front of my computer as my mind begins absorbing the meaning of the words on the screen. I keep reading Trish's email over and over again.

She wrote, "I've learned the shocking news that Rick died a few hours ago."

The realization floods in as I feel time stop.

Sacred silence draws me in.

The message I read is distressing and humbling. Slowly, my muscles begin to relax, and my mind becomes clear, as I melt into the moment.

Trish's mystifying email shares the sorrowful news that Rick passed that afternoon while jogging down a street in his small Illinois town. On the bright sunny day, he had decided to run outside and his heart simply gave out.

My senses are heightened as I share Rick's poignant message from my dream to his fiancé and other Reiki friends. We speak on the phone as well as in person.

As I relay Rick's comforting communication to his friends, I sense them become quiet as they take in the profound meaning.

We remain in silence for a few minutes as the expansiveness of his loving gift to us soaks into our consciousness in waves.

Miraculously, Rick also appeared to a close friend that same January afternoon, as he did to me. His friend, Janice, was walking across her living room alone. Suddenly, she saw Rick standing in front of her, smiling and laughing. Just as quickly, he disappeared from her sight. Shortly after, Janice picked up her ringing phone and learned Rick passed within the hour.

In divine timing, each of us had our metaphysical experience with Rick's spirit around the same time that afternoon.

Our uplifting, sacred messages from Rick are sorely needed among his grieving family and friends. His passing in the prime of his life has ripples of poignant repercussions in the community.

Later, we hear Rick had a genetic heart condition, as his brother died of heart issues around the same age.

Marie gives me a solemn smile the following day when I describe the prophetic dream from Rick that I experienced while asleep on her couch. She has no ego when it comes to these matters.

Marie rarely showed surprise about spiritual experiences unseen by the regular eye. As a deeply spiritual woman, it was routine for her.

Speaking quietly from a timeless space, I wonder aloud, "Marie, I didn't know my dream's meaning until I opened up Trish's email at home yesterday. Everyone is in shock and mourning right now. I hope his message helps his loved ones."

Marie nods her head in agreement. "Yes, it will take time to absorb what has happened. His message can be very deeply healing."

We continue to sit in silence on her lime green loveseat in the same spot where I received the dream gift from Rick the previous day.

To attempt to try to talk about the profound meaning of his message is beyond me, so I take comfort in Marie's presence.

Rick's calm smile is what I recall as we jog side by side in my dream.

He appears without a care in the world.

"I'm going on ahead. I will see you later!"

Then he leaves my view.

Why did I receive the spiritual knowledge of Rick's passing as I did?

Perhaps sacred energies were looking to manifest a spiritual message that afternoon, and I became "available" in Marie's evocative presence to receive his loving message of comfort.

Perhaps I'm open to experiencing undeniable evidence of love without boundaries.

Regardless, I'm honored to convey Rick's strong desire to leave some words of solace to his loved ones.

I don't question the authenticity of my experience. It's unmistakable.

Indeed, his message is a timeless Blessed Truth.

I'm going ahead. See you later!

I cherish the tremendous gift Rick gave me as he was shifting energies that day.

Thanks, Rick.

Forever grateful to you.

Catch up to you later!

See Peggy Patty's Biography On Page 199

She Couldn't Have Known

Regina DuRocher Keefe

What if it doesn't work on me?" This is what I asked myself before I experienced my first past-life regression. "What if I'm lying there and nothing happens?"

I began questioning myself the same way I would ask whether I had cleaned maple syrup off the counter well enough. Doubt spread ever so slowly across my confidence. We all know this kind of sticky doubt—it encases everything it touches with a deep, amber shine and subtly fills your nostrils with its sickly, sweet scent.

Even after I've cleaned it from every surface it touched, when I drag my fingers across the counter, I'm still not sure if it's in my head or if syrup was left behind.

That's how I felt about magic for a long time.

Deep down, I knew it existed. I'd even had experiences I could only describe with that word. However, the logical side of my brain kept trying to find explanations for the moments I considered magical.

Connections that stretched across a decade seemed to be guiding me down a path that opened the door to the world of magic. This is what brought me to learn about past-life regression.

The past-life regression would be done through hypnosis. I had never been hypnotized before and didn't know what to expect of the process or the results. Would I have memories from another life I once lived, or would it be my imagination running wild?

I found myself driving seventy miles an hour down the interstate in Central Illinois shortly after lunch to meet Ruth, my friend and local hypnotherapist, at her office. The grey March air crept through the vents, making my clammy hands and feet stiff. The heated steering wheel brought little relief to my tingling fingertips.

I adjusted my hands, releasing my tight grip on the wheel. I kept trying to wiggle my toes to warm them up, but every time I stretched them, it seemed as if the walls of my socks seized the opportunity to tighten against my skin.

I felt trapped somewhere between thrill and a passive-aggressive eye roll, just like my foot felt trapped in a cold, sweaty sock.

Images and ideas of what I might see floated through my mind. Discovering past lives seemed like a sort of choose-your-own adventure game. Maybe it would be a life set in the times of Gods and Greek mythology. Perhaps I would find myself in a desert under the refreshing shadow of a pyramid protecting me from the formidable heat of the sun.

Determined not to lead myself down these already contrived paths, I shoved the few images that popped into my head back out. I wanted this experience to truly show me something I didn't expect so I would know it was real. This would give me the confidence to eclipse my doubts, no longer allowing them to obscure my every experience.

Excited yet nervous, I told a few of my friends I scheduled an appointment for a past-life hypnosis session. They listened even though I sounded like a giddy schoolgirl and showed genuine interest in their responses, but I couldn't help but assume they felt a bit skeptical. If I couldn't even bury my doubts, I found it highly unlikely they hadn't raised their eyebrows a bit as well.

"How exactly does it work?" Beth sat across the wooden table from me. Her friendly smile allowed me to carry on.

"Well, I'm not 100% sure, but Ruth says she will guide me in a meditation where I will enter experiences from my past lives."

"That seems really interesting. What made you want to do this?"

"I've been curious ever since a lady read my palm and told me I had more lifelines than she typically saw on someone. And I've always been curious about magic and this kind of stuff."

"Do you think it will work?"

"I hope so. I think a glimpse into a past life feels like the proof I need, a glimpse into *my* magical story, not someone else's. If it comes from me, then it can't be a trick."

"I am very excited for you and can't wait to hear how it goes."

So why *did* I have this ball of nerves as heavy and cold as an anchor in the pit of my stomach as I drove there? Why did I feel like this experiment was the make-or-break moment? It felt as if this was judgment day. If this didn't work, doubt would finally prevail and show me magic wasn't real.

This all seemed a little wild. Unbelievable, some might even call it. No, really, unbelievable is what my inner self bellowed against the walls of my skull.

This is made up. It's fake. This nonsense is all just a bunch of woo you're falling for, Regina.

I did believe, despite all the uncertainty. Even if society tried to tell me repeatedly that none of this exists…magic isn't real…people are just good at manipulating others and telling lies, I believed in magic.

My senior year, Mrs. Quick handed me back my paper on The Turn of the Screw. She had a puzzled look on her face. As I looked at the marks on the paper, the results were good, with minor grammatical errors and a few notes here and there, but I got a B.

"You know Henry James wasn't talking about real ghosts, right?"

"Yes, he was," I replied.

"Regina, it was a metaphor. Ghosts aren't real; that's make-believe."

"Well, I know what lessons Henry James wanted us to take away from the book. I covered them in the paper, but I believe he was talking about actual ghosts."

"Hmmm," slipped through her pursed lips, laced with doubt.

Once again, society was telling me magic didn't exist. I remember the way my stomach knotted and how nervous I'd felt responding to her disbelief. I felt a similar knot in my stomach as I passed the dull, brown corn fields on both sides of the interstate. We both started the day empty, but soon, everything would be churned and the seeds would be planted.

Forty minutes later, I stepped out of my car and into the crisp air. If nervousness could make a sound, it would be the noise that comes from those ankle bracelets with the little bells around them. With every step I took toward the door to Ruth's building, my nerves clinked and rang uncontrollably.

The room I entered first was a warm yellow color and it felt as if it stopped the cold air from following me inside. Immediately, I felt the heat return to my skin as Ruth wrapped her arms around me in a tight, welcoming hug. We are both only about 5 feet tall, so we fit together perfectly, and my nerves calmed with one exhale as we embraced.

The door to her office was a few feet away and I stared at her light purple hair as I followed her to it. She held her arm out, encouraging me to enter, and I heard the door shut with a quiet click as I walked deeper into the room.

The office was dark and peaceful. Books and papers rested on shelves, and my eyes darted from one trinket to another throughout the room. There were two chairs with a small table in between them, where a stained-glass dome gave off a glowing light as the bulb below it radiated through. Along the back wall was a thin massage table, not as wide as a twin bed but big enough for an adult to stretch out on for a hypnosis session.

I lay there on the thin mattress, feeling my ribs expand and release with every deep breath I took. Her slow, steady voice guided me into the meditation. As my chest began to rise and fall, my body relaxed into the table like an invisible weighted blanket was pushing me down into it. My thoughts shifted back and forth, the only thing still moving inside of my now still body.

Is this working? This isn't working. Stop thinking, Regina. Did I make that up myself? Am I actually seeing this? Is this just me seeing anything because I'm supposed to see something? Stop thinking, Regina. Stop worrying. This will work. See where this takes you next. Focus on her voice.

First, Ruth's voice told me to pick my favorite place, anywhere in the world, whether or not I had been there before. Instantly, I was in my living room. My legs were across my husband's lap and his hand created a spot of warmth where it rested on my leg.

I looked around the room and saw the three people most important to me in this life. The smell of warm chocolate chip cookies and buttery popcorn filled my nostrils. Laughter filled the room, our daughters' eyes crinkled with their smiles and they both held their stomachs from laughing so hard. Yes, this was my happiest place.

I go to the door, slide it open on the track with ease, and walk outside. My skin felt warm as I stood under the tall trees, sunlight piercing through the canopy in rays here and there along a path stretching out in front of me. I heard a slight pat-pat-pat sound whenever my bare feet connected with the next cool stone.

As I walked down a very manicured path, where dark green ferns uncurled and stepping stones wove their way back and forth between mature tree trunks, nature began to take control. Ruth said there would be a second path; this is where the foliage began to grow wilder, like arms of grass stretching up to meet the sun.

Ahead was a cave, just off the path, supposedly. However, I couldn't see it. There was a dark, fuzzy, grey area where the cave should have been. *Shit. This isn't working. There's no cave… imagine a cave, Regina.*

Ruth was telling me to enter the mouth of the cavern. I could feel the panic starting to bounce around under my skin like tiny bolts of lightning. I wanted to see it. But I also didn't want to force the image because that would only solidify my doubt that this was all make-believe. So, I took a leap of faith and stepped inside whatever was supposed to be in front of me before Ruth's words could leave me in the dust behind.

And just like that, grey stone walls appeared with a slight curve like the walls inside a castle's turret, and a staircase beckoned me to follow it downward. I ran my fingers across the cool stone walls as I descended the spiral stairwell into the unknown. Each time my foot connected with a new step, it would light up beneath me. Bright pink, white, blue, and green burst from each stair like neon colors in an arcade.

With each step, I also felt my assurance grow. I could have explained away being in my living room with my family because, of course, that's my happiest, favorite place to be. I could have explained away the path outside my door because it looked like one I had saved on Pinterest years ago and hoped someday to recreate it in my yard.

People could say Ruth's directions put images into my head and made me see those things. But Ruth told me to see the entrance of a cave…and I did not. Ruth told me to keep going inside. But instead, I went down a set of steps inside a castle.

No, I couldn't explain away what I was seeing and feeling. A castle with neon lights in the steps wasn't something I'd ever seen in a movie. No, these weren't made-up images planted in my head. This was where I was walking right now.

Things were still a bit hazy when I reached the bottom of the steps. I couldn't make out the details but knew I was in a room where architecture mixed with natural stone walls. It was as if the marble pillars and arches were growing right out of the rocks with no separation between the two. The edges blurred together like the room wasn't finished yet.

"This is your soul, your core, your temple. You will return to this center in between each past life you experience. This is a safe place because it is you at your purest self. What does your temple look like? What does it smell like? What colors do you see?"

As I aimlessly walked through my temple's core, things slowly began to come into focus. The marble walls became smooth red stone with brown, grey, white, and gold designs running through them.

Above me, a red, domed ceiling with beautiful and elaborate motifs caught my attention. Rectangular, wide windows circled the dome's base, letting filtered sunlight spill through as if its peak was just breaking through the earth's surface above.

Rows and rows of shelves reached up toward the top, more floors than I could count. The shelves were full of books and scrolls waiting to be opened. Beautiful mahogany cabinets with glass fronts held the most precious artifacts that I knew I had selected to be there.

Each treasured item was safe behind the glass with a metal plaque describing why it was important to me.

Crystals, bones, pieces of wood, and glass gave a twinkle of magic throughout the room.

The shelves and cabinets were not in perfect rows, but they didn't feel random either. Each one was in the right place and I no longer walked aimlessly between them. I walked to the edge of the room and saw corridors circling my temple's center, not just on the ground floor but along the upper levels.

"Choose a corridor," Ruth suggested.

I began to walk down a sterile white hall full of endless sterile white doors. They all looked the same. *Should one of them stand out to me?*

"When you are ready, choose a door."

Instinctively, I felt my mind invite worry inside because I hadn't picked a door yet, but I wiped the sweat from my brow and kept walking. Just then, I discovered the emerald-green door made of worn, wooden slats. Cautiously, I stepped through into this new, unknown life, yet it somehow felt familiar.

As I explored my surroundings through my own eyes, from within my own body, I could hear the morning chatter of the people bustling around me. Hard-working people, by the looks of it, but accustomed to being friendly with those who worked around them.

The salty smell in the air told me I would find a body of water just around the corner and I felt the sun's warmth spread down from the top of my head to my rosy cheeks on the otherwise brisk morning.

In either direction, a cobblestone road led to shops and tents set up to sell their goods for the day. I stood alone. I kept looking for someone, wondering if I would recognize a family member coming around the corner, but no one ever came. *Why did I not have a family here?* Sadness wasn't present; I seemed satisfied.

A feeling of peace fell over me like a blanket, and although I could have stayed longer, I knew the time had come to explore another life.

The meditation took me back to my center, and I found myself surrounded by the endless number of hallways. Doors beyond my ability to count continued down the halls, each holding another place to explore. Before Ruth could even suggest I travel down a corridor in search of another door, there it was.

I could see nothing else. Everything around me had disappeared into a void.

The most beautiful, deep navy-blue door with gold trim and lines to distinguish each section stood before me. An ornate, golden knob with intricately etched details glistened as it waited for me to turn it. There was no choice to be made. I did not find this door. This door found me.

I entered my second past life and an overwhelming feeling of dread and discomfort crashed into me.

Phantom fingers curled around my windpipe, tightening their hold. I could feel nothing else but the burning in my throat as I struggled to find my breath. Escaping from this grip of dread, I rushed down the endless hallway saying these words, but no sound emerged.

Keep going. Don't stop. Don't get caught. This is important. Keep going. Don't stop. Don't get caught. This is important.

The mantra repeated in my head as I hurried down the hall fast enough to feel the air rushing past the sides of my face, sending chills down my neck. With every beat my heart made against my tightening chest, a deep, echoing thump rang in my ears.

The walls squeezed closer around me, trapping me, the weight on my breast crushing my lungs. I knew I needed to be here, but the tension in my body told me that I was most certainly not *supposed* to be here.

Ruth's voice traveled down the corridor with me and was the only comfort I could feel, reminding me to look around and take note of what I saw, heard, or felt. The floors were made of beautifully polished marble. Though I never touched them, I could feel the cool temperature from the smooth stone below my feet. On my left, plain doors flashed past me rhythmically as I progressed down the eternal hallway.

To my right lay a marble ledge with windows reaching up to a ceiling so high it seemed to stretch away from me. I felt warmth creep up my glowing cheeks as the sun beamed against my skin through their glass panes.

The building itself seemed very official. It looked old but well-maintained. The hands that built it had undoubtedly impeccable craftsmanship. Both the building and my being here felt equally important, though for what purpose, I did not know.

I never saw another person. As in the other life, I found myself in my body, looking out through my own eyes. I wanted to see something else. A person. Another room. A turn in the hallway led me somewhere else. Anywhere else. However, nothing ever changed. I still found myself alone, walking as fast and as far as I could for what seemed like an eternity but making no progress.

Dread chased me down this never-ending hallway. I put one foot in front of the other because I knew I had to. I couldn't outrun it. Anxiety had me by the throat and it would not release its grip, the same way an executioner would not release his hold on the axe.

I could not have escaped this life fast enough. I was getting nowhere. Nothing was changing. I would never reach my destination.

"When you're ready to leave this life, you can exit the door," Ruth's friendly voice interrupted my panic.

Yes. Get out, my mind screamed in response.

She slowly brought me out of the meditation, prompting me to wiggle my fingers and toes, and finally, to open my eyes. I sat up slowly, a bit light-headed still but gaining awareness of my surroundings.

"Could I ask you a couple of questions about your experience," Ruth said.

"Of course, I don't mind."

"Did something happen to you when you walked through the second door? As soon as you entered, my chest got tight and I had to fight the urge to cough and clear my throat because I felt so choked up."

How could she have known that? She couldn't have known.

I shared my experience after entering the second door with Ruth. I saw her put her hand to her throat as if she could still feel the burning in it, as I retold my story.

"I was concerned about what may be happening," she admitted.

"There are times when people can experience traumatic accidents, or injuries, sometimes even their deaths," she continued. "I wondered if you had been injured in the throat or neck as soon as you went in. I wanted to give you time to explore but was worried about letting it go on for too long, either."

"I am glad you didn't let me stay there any longer than you did. I was ready to get out the moment I walked in."

Over the next few months, I jumped in head-first, taking another class with Ruth and learning about this new metaphysical world I wanted to explore. The classes were online, and we participated in a group mediation every other week. During the first few meditations, I still had my doubts over whether or not what I was seeing was real or if I was just being tricked into seeing what they wanted me to see.

Maybe she was saying a lot of words that started with the letter P so that we would see the color purple, or perhaps other subtle cues were hidden in Ruth's words so we would all imagine being in the same place.

However, we didn't *all* see the same places every time…but some of us did. Hearing someone explain their experience before I shared my own, hearing them describe precisely what I saw, sent chills up my arms.

They couldn't have known that.

"I was holding Regina's hand to my left and Bev's to my right," Michelle told the group as we went around one by one, discussing what we saw. Staring in disbelief at the notes I took when I came out of the meditation were three circles with "Me," "Michelle," and "Bev" written above each one, representing where each of us was standing, with the words "holding hands."

She couldn't have known that.

Then there was the time someone recounted a being they had seen. I saw it, too. There was no physical body or vessel; he was just this energy appearing like a galaxy swirling, full of constellations and stardust made of beautiful blues, whites, and purples. I say *he* because whatever the being was, it felt masculine to me.

They couldn't have known that I saw him too.

Repeatedly, others reported events that I witnessed in our meditations before I ever revealed any of my quickly jotted notes. Surely, this was proof that what I was experiencing was real. I wrote it down before they spoke!

They couldn't have known.

At this point, excitement spilled out of me like an overflowing bathtub. Whatever move I made to calm the waves just made the water crash harder against the porcelain sides and splash higher outside of its boundaries. Small doubts still lingered, but the slippery walls gave no handholds. There were too many things I couldn't explain from my meditations and exploring my past lives.

My elation could not be washed away. Memories of Mrs. Quick, the cynical look some people gave as I shared my experiences, and others telling me that magic didn't exist were hard to shake. I knew it was real, and yet, I still had questions.

I needed to know more.

The first time I heard the name Bree Roberts, I was standing barefoot, feeling the wood grain beneath my feet at the Jax Yoga Freaky Flow Halloween event. I look forward to this night every 365 days. This night each year, I can connect my body and mind, practice yoga with the most inclusive group of people I know, have my tarot cards read, and drink a glass...okay, maybe a bottle of wine.

Someone mentioned having a past-life hypnosis session with Bree. It was fun to exchange similar experiences with another individual. I needed to reach out to Bree. I needed to know more, and she could help me facilitate that.

We set up a Zoom call to discuss what I hoped to get out of a past-life regression, if I had any particular childhood traumas I wanted to focus on and attempt to heal, and what I felt comfortable exploring. We chose a date we were both available and a week later, I was back in the car, heart racing, hands gripping the steering wheel on my way to another session in Springfield, Illinois.

Warm sunshine splashed across every surface on this day, unlike the dreary, cold day I visited Ruth. Spring was emerging and new green life was sprouting from the ground. Sweet, chipper whistles from restless birds created the perfect soundtrack for the day.

Bree's home welcomed me into it the moment I stepped across the threshold. Fresh pink, purple, and orange flowers filled the table, and original artwork full of vibrant colors and patterns hung on the walls. Everything in the space matched her exuberant personality and I felt the eagerness bouncing inside me, just like her light brown curls bounced as she moved around the room.

A soft futon couch with textured pillows made me feel at home the moment I sat down. Bree invited me to get comfortable and I laid back, resting my head on the plush pillow. Before we began, she explained that she would ask me questions and, if I felt comfortable, she encouraged me to respond aloud.

She opened her laptop and instrumental music began to drift around us and mix with her rich voice. She began the meditation by taking me back to a childhood memory to establish a safe place.

"I want you to imagine yourself as a child. It can be any memory. How old are you?"

"I'm eight or nine. It's my birthday."

"How do you feel?"

"Carefree. Happy. Everyone is smiling."

I found myself in the green backyard of my childhood home. There, between two large maple trees, sat my family members, the light reflecting off their glasses, while causing others to squint in the bright September sun. We found relief in the cool shade while my cousins and I played on the wooden swing, air rushing past our flushed cheeks.

My Grandpa Bond sat in an aluminum lawn chair at a tan card table. His white hair was combed over, nice and slick, not a strand out of place. His short-sleeved, blue button-up shirt with a pocket on the chest was freshly ironed, the collar still crisp. His khaki dress slacks held a stiff crease down them, always looking his best, even for a backyard birthday party.

I was surprised to have chosen this moment as my memory. It was nothing significant. It was not the happiest day of my childhood. But at that moment on that day, I was stress-free and comfortable. Anxiety and I had not yet been formally introduced. I had the confidence of a child who hadn't begun to doubt herself yet. It reminded me of my daughter's confidence.

Once, when our daughter Lydia was about four years old, we went to a friend's wedding. The beautiful, warm day was perfect for an outside celebration at a local state park. The trees were full and green, the birds flew wildly in the sky above us, and the sun warmed the tops of our heads.

I didn't know many in attendance, just a few of their friends and family. Lydia immediately hit it off with their daughter, Carmen, who was only a couple of years older than her. Midway through the day, the groom's Grandmother walked up to me.

"You won't believe what your daughter just said to me."

"I'm so sorry…" I began, but she quickly cut me off.

"No, no, it's nothing bad. She tugged on my sleeve, and I leaned down to hear her, and she said, 'I saw you riding on a fire truck.' And then she just ran off. It surprised me because that was once my job as a nurse when I was about 18 years old. We would ride on the back of the trucks when there were chemical fires to help treat the burn victims."

"Oh, her great-grandpa was a firefighter. She's been telling people about him recently, so Carmen must have told her you had ridden on fire trucks, too."

"No, that's the thing; Carmen doesn't know I ever did that. I've never talked to her about it before. I'm not even sure her Dad knows.

"Your daughter couldn't have known that."

I instantly felt the skin on my arms prickle and the chills rolled up my spine. There was no explaining what Lydia said. She couldn't have known that. She couldn't have known that woman had ever ridden on a fire truck unless Grandpa told her. There were other times she told us about talking to *Grandpa Bond*. However, he died before she was born. She'd never had the chance to meet him.

Relatives tried to dismiss it, saying she'd heard the other cousins mention him. Except she always referred to him as Grandpa Bond, which was how we'd referred to him as children. Now, the cousins called him by a different name, Poppy Dale. If she were copying her cousins, she would have called him Poppy Dale, right? No, there were too many times she said things that she couldn't have known.

We tried to clarify some of the encounters by asking her questions. She always answered with the same confidence I felt in that childhood memory. There was no doubt in her voice and there were no other explanations. Lydia had either spoken to my Grandpa Bond, or perhaps she had ridden on a fire truck alongside that woman in another life.

"Now that you've experienced your childhood memory, are you ready to enter your previous life?" Bree's voice brought my focus back from drifting through my charming recollection.

"Yes."

The image of my childhood backyard shifted into a meadow with a row of trees circling it. Tall yellow and tan fronds tickled the palms of my hands as I walked ahead, feeling the grass brushing my legs. The light breeze made the blades wave gently back and forth and seemed to nudge me forward to the tree line.

The wet earth of the forest floor gave way under the weight of my feet. My head began to spin as I looked up at trees so tall their tops were not visible. Mist hung in the air, making everything damp and grey.

An invisible compass guided each step as I entered a village filled with dark brown, almost black, simple wooden houses. Visions from this life came into view and then blurred out of focus as if I were looking through a child's viewfinder.

With every pull of the lever, I felt my emotions shift as if I were experiencing each moment over again. Finally, one image became still, and I felt the heavy weight of guilt rest upon my back, like Atlas holding the weight of the whole world.

Standing shoulder to shoulder with other villagers, I shuffled alongside them into a large wooden building. I didn't choose where to sit; rather, I just settled where the flow of people took me. Everyone was still and quiet. Occasionally, I heard a wooden bench creak as someone shifted their weight.

"Can you tell how old you are? Can you see what you are wearing? What do you see around you?"

"I'm younger, not a child, but not an adult, either—maybe sixteen or seventeen. I'm wearing a thick, long-sleeved, black dress. The fabric is scratchy and uncomfortable, just like I feel. A man stands before us, leading some kind of meeting."

"Tell me what is happening around you. How does the man make you feel?"

"I don't want him to notice me. Everyone in the room is anxious and nervous. I don't want to be here."

Looking around, I feel no connection to those near me. I can tell the *others* are somewhere out of sight in the room, not my family by blood, but a group of people I somehow belong with. The people in front of me shift and create a space between them. I finally see her.

A woman. My friend. She looks so confident. Her hands are folded gently in her lap, her shoulders are relaxed and her light brown hair is swept around, flowing over one shoulder. The corners of her lips curve upwards; not a smile but a content expression rests upon her face. She knows she is right. She also knows it won't matter and has accepted her fate.

"Is it some kind of witch trial," Bree asked.

"No. We aren't witches. We use the earth and help people that live here. It's just how we do things."

"Why is the woman being questioned?"

"She tried to help someone, but it didn't work. They still died. They blame her, but she didn't do anything wrong."

I felt like I should say something to her, but in that quiet room, I couldn't find any words. *I'll just make it worse. I've already messed up enough. What else could I have done?*

A decision has been made. Everyone has condemned the woman. She is banished from the village. Suddenly, everyone except me has turned their back on her like a physical representation of their feelings. Slowly, I turn too, and just as I flow in, I follow behind the other villagers and step outside.

As the woman leaves the village for the last time, she turns toward me. Looking into her deep blue eyes, I thought to myself, *I should have helped. I should have spoken up.*

As clearly as if she'd spoken the words aloud, she said to me, *you did exactly how much and no less than you were meant to do.*

A laugh escaped her and rang in my ears. Again, I heard her voice only in my mind say, *it's fine. It's not your fault. You know what to do.*

But I have no idea what that means. I want to ask her to explain. What am I supposed to do? But she begins to fade.

The image in front of me dimmed. I pushed through the mist that now obscured everything around me. Rays of sunshine began to break through the haze and a small, white-planked house came into view. I felt my body grow tired with age as I surveyed my surroundings. A lush garden stretched across the yard. Dirt paths separated beds of colorful flowers and green herbs. Everywhere I looked, there was a new plant, a different flower, and fresh growth coming out of the dirt.

My now grey hair was fixed back out of my face, and the light reflected off the top of my head as if the soft strands were made of silver. I looked down at my hard-working hands, wrinkled with age, tanned by the sun, gathering asters.

The sound of Bree's voice caused me to look up at the front of my house.

"We are nearing the moment of your death in this life. Can you tell me how your life has been up until now?"

With a long sigh, I released my breath and spoke.

"I've lived alone. I've gone about my life. I never had a family of my own, but I still found ways to help others in the community. I led a fulfilled life, a good one, though I've struggled to find a balance between enjoying it and constantly feeling regret for turning my back on the other part of myself.

"What part of yourself did you turn away from?"

"Away from my magic. But it had to be that way."

"Where are you now?"

I gaze around my small cottage. I've lived here many years. Pillows against my back prop me up in my simple, wooden bed and I can feel the lightweight quilt resting across me. Everything seems so bright and white, almost unreal for an unextraordinary cottage on the edge of a forest whose resident is constantly tending to her garden and dirtying her hands.

"It is almost time," Bree assured me.

People came to visit, but I always sent them away after a few pleasantries were exchanged. I was ready and happy to die. I was alone in my cottage at the very end.

Suddenly, they were all there. The *others* I gave up years ago, even the woman from that dreadful day, filled the room. Their spirits came to greet me and remind me of our connection. I was not alone when I died. They all gathered around me. They waited many years for me to join them in the next life.

"How are you feeling about your death?"

"I feel a release. I still hold the guilt and regret, but they are no longer negative. They are just part of me. I feel accepted."

"Sometimes people can see their soul—or their aura—after they have passed over. Often, it's a color. Do you see your aura or a color?"

"I don't see just one color...I am the color of the sun, shining through tall green

grass, mixed with light brown earth all at once. It's all moving and blending in a circle."

"I've never had someone describe their aura to me that way."

Hearing the surprise in her voice gave me some strange form of comfort. I was so worried the logical side of my brain would find ways to discredit my experience that being told I wasn't giving Bree the same kind of answers others usually gave made me feel it was even more authentic.

Bree asked if there was anyone else I wanted to talk to before we returned to the present. It could be an ancestor, it could be a guide, it could be an angel; if there was anyone special I needed to ask anything of, now was the time.

Grandpa Bond was there before I could think about it. Again, in his freshly pressed collared shirt, at the little card table. I felt a smile spread across my face. It felt good to see him after he'd been gone for so many years. My smile turned into a little smirk, though, as I thought, *You're not Grandpa.*

Suddenly it *wasn't* Grandpa anymore; it was the being I saw during other meditations. He visited me many times over the last several months. The familiarity of him stood out to me the most. I knew this being. He knew me.

I asked him without words, but just by thinking the question in my mind, *why did you look like my Grandpa?* I felt him laugh and say, *I thought you might like that because of the memory you had earlier.*

Why am I always alone in the past lives I visit?

You had to be; the timing wasn't right. To accomplish the things that you needed to do, you had to be by yourself. But you've never truly been alone. I've visited you before, from time to time. I am always watching. And there are others.

Others?

Suddenly, I could feel another group of beings out of sight. I could tell they were different than me but like him.

They are interested in you. They watch you, too.

Several thoughts crossed my mind as I began to feel my body shake as if my atoms were all moving in a wave. *Keep going. You can be happy. No expectations. No anything. Just be. If something goes wrong, it'll be okay. It is okay. We're never that far away. We'll wait for you.*

It was as if I was hearing the others' thoughts simultaneously.

The waves in my body stopped as quickly as they started, and I felt my awareness land back on Bree's futon. Her soothing voice encouraged me to wiggle my fingers and toes, open my eyes when ready, and to sit up at my own pace.

After I felt more awake, I slowly sat up. Since I was speaking to Bree during the session, she already knew what I saw and felt. We thanked each other for sharing such a unique experience. She started to turn off the music on her laptop that played during the meditation.

She exclaimed to me, "You are not going to believe this. Remember how you described your aura to me, not as a color, but all the colors all at once. Look at this."

She turned the screen toward me, where the video providing the music we'd been hearing during the session still played. There was an image of tall green grass stretching around a circle, gently waving back and forth, reaching toward the sphere's center. The colors were like sunshine bouncing off the green blades—you could see the light brown color of dirt where they grew from the earth below them.

In front of me was the visual representation of what I felt and saw my aura to be. I was shocked. I couldn't have known that image would be playing on her screen. And she couldn't have known how I would describe my aura. She told me she randomly picked the video she used for the day, and the image must have changed while the music played because it looked completely different when she started it.

The logical side of my brain could have picked apart the meditation. Perhaps it was my hands tingling as they fell asleep instead of the tall grass tickling my palms as I walked through the meadow. I could have declared the woman being questioned was my version of a witch trial because that's the most common theme we see depicted in the movies.

However, there was no way to dispute that the way I described my aura was the same as we later found on her screen. I couldn't have known. The only explanation was magic.

These experiences felt like the proof I needed. My analytical brain would have preferred a written, verifiable record of my past lives and maybe a scientific graph giving my experiences validity, but the spiritual side of my brain didn't need any of that.

For years, I believed in magic. But far too often felt the need to be skeptical or consider other explanations. Why did I think I needed more proof all this time? I know magic is real. Sometimes there is no other explanation for an occurrence. Sometimes the only answer is *magic*.

There are too many times the phrase *she couldn't have known that* has applied to me. Like the time I read Michelle's tarot cards.

"The cards are saying you already know what to do and that you just need to take the leap and put in the work."

Their eyes widened and Michelle uttered in amazement first to me, then her friend, "That's literally what I just told him on the car ride over here. She couldn't have known that."

With the encouragement of Ruth and some of my friends, I permitted myself to believe. I embraced the fact that I can't provide evidence for some experiences because I no longer need it. I know people will still have suspicions.

Rather than carry around their uncertainty, I created my own space and business to help myself and others explore the art of tarot, other magical topics, and different mediums of art with Earthy Girl Arts.

Where I once felt isolated in my magical curiosities and unsure of myself, I now know I have gifts to share with others. If someone doesn't believe me, so be it. For those ready to embrace magic in their lives, I'm here to help them on their journey, like so many others have helped me.

I have become the woman I saw in the village during my past-life regression. I am now the one with the untroubled look on my face. I know magic *is* real. I know it won't matter; some others won't believe it, and I accept that.

There will always be someone trying to discredit unexplainable moments. Relatives will keep saying a child must have overheard someone else utter a phrase or suggest they've seen it in a movie. Inevitably, anything dealing with magic will be chalked up to books about boys named Harry or someone having a vivid imagination.

Despite that, magic will continue to occur. Maybe if we spent less time looking for explanations and paid more attention to what is happening around us every day, we'd all see a little more magic. Open your eyes. The fact that you're reading this chapter in this book today is magical, and it may just be the nudge you needed.

****

REGINA DUROCHER KEEFE

Regina DuRocher Keefe is new author contributing here and in The Chaos of Covid. Writing this piece allowed for growth and permission to accept what she cannot explain, awarding her freedom she's searched for many years to find. Her education revolves around art, yet surprisingly she finds herself with an 18-year career in finance.

Regina is an artist working with pen & ink, watercolor and ceramics. She enjoys the art of intuitive tarot reading and offers opportunities through her Earthy Girl Arts pages on Facebook and Instagram for others to explore these areas with her. We live in a world full of magic and she hopes to help others experience that.

Regina is forever grateful for the love and support from her husband, Scott of 19 years, who thinks she is a witch but doesn't really know what that means. They share two spirited daughters; Lydia and Cora. She admires their sense of adventure, strong opinions and independence. Balancing marriage, motherhood, work and her own interests is Regina's greatest challenge. She believes everything that happens to us along our path makes an impact and knows we can not bypass the journey.

Regina thinks finding your authentic voice is one of the most valuable things you can do in life. She holds firmly the belief that everyone could benefit from therapy. She knows having uncomfortable conversations are important and admitting our mistakes is how we change the world. The mother of two pit-bulls, she encourages everyone to look past stereotypes and adopt a rescue. She thinks adding cello to any song makes it better, powerful works of art in any medium should spark emotion, and she still believes in Santa. If you can't prove to her it doesn't exist, then she will always believe it is possible.

THE END